TRAC 2009

TRAC 2009

Proceedings of the Nineteenth Annual

THEORETICAL ROMAN ARCHAEOLOGY CONFERENCE

which took place at

The University of Michigan
3–5 April 2009

The University of Southampton
17–18 April 2009

edited by

Alison Moore, Geoff Taylor, Emily Harris, Peter Girdwood
and Lucy Shipley

Oxbow Books
Oxford and Oakville

Published by
Oxbow Books, Oxford, UK

ISBN 978-1-84217-972-7

This book is available direct from

Oxbow Books, Oxford, UK
(Phone: 01865-214249; Fax 01865-794449)

and

The David Brown Book Company
PO Box 511, Oakville, CT 06779, USA
(Phone: 860-945-9329; Fax 860-945-9468)

or from our website

www.oxbowbooks.com

A CIP record for this book is available from the British Library

Library of Congress Cataloging-in-Publication Data

Theoretical Roman Archaeology Conference (19th : 2009 : University of Michigan)
TRAC 2009 : proceedings of the nineteenth annual Theoretical Roman Archaeology Conference which took place at the University of Michigan 3-5 April 2009 [and] the University of Southampton 17-18 April 2009 / edited by Alison Moore ... [et al.].
p. cm.
Selected conference papers.
Includes bibliographical references.
ISBN 978-1-84217-972-7
1. Archaeology--Rome--Philosophy--Congresses. 2. Civilization, Western--Roman influences--Congresses. 3. Romans--Europe--Congresses. 4. Europe--Antiquities, Roman--Congresses. I. Moore, Alison. II. Theoretical Roman Archaeology Conference (19th : 2009 : University of Southampton) III. Title.
DG12.5.T44 2009
937--dc22
2010006200

Printed in Great Britain by
Short Run Press, Exeter

Contents

Preface

The nineteenth annual Theoretical Roman Archaeology Conference was held in two locations. The first, run in conjunction with the Roman Archaeology Conference, was hosted by the University of Michigan, Ann Arbor, on 3rd–5th April 2009. The second conference, held in the United Kingdom for those who could not attend in the United States, was hosted by the Archaeology Department of the University of Southampton on 17th–18th April 2009. Papers were delivered in both thematic and general sessions; of the seventeen papers presented in the USA and eighteen in the UK, twelve appear in this volume, representing a cross-section of the themes and topics represented at both TRAC conferences.

The volume opens with a critique of Romanization from a feminist perspective by **Louise Revell**, who argues that marginalized areas of research, such as gender and family structures, need to be brought into the mainstream. She uses published studies to demonstrate how this can provide a deeper and more nuanced understanding of cultural change.

The next two papers are concerned with the physical construction of the Roman Empire, exploring approaches to understanding how vital resources were developed, maintained, accessed and utilised. **Ronald Visser**'s paper draws on a number of sources to consider what knowledge of silvicultural systems existed in the Roman period and the evidence for their use in managing forests in the Lower Rhine area. Addressing the Roman exploitation of stone as a resource, **Bradley Sekedat**'s paper highlights the importance of the interplay between agent and location to development of an idea of place associated with the quarries of Roman Anatolia.

A theme of both TRAC conferences was the implementation and use of new technologies to further develop our understanding of the Roman world – here concerned with the context of material culture, artefact distribution and the environment. **Gareth Beale** and **Graeme Earl**'s paper, seeks to undermine many of the assumptions made about the permanent, unchanging nature of classical marble statuary. To this effect they make particular reference to the use of digital simulations of classical statuary and an applied understanding of sculptural polychromy. Utilising GPS technology, **Annick Lepot** maps the distribution of cooking ware vessels in northern Gaul, identifying regional variations in pottery fabrics and styles and tracing the impact of Roman production technologies and typologies on pre-Roman pottery forms. In comparison to Beale and Earl, and Lepot's emphasis on the use of computer technology, **Ivo van der Graaf, Robert Vander Poppen** and **Thijs Nales**' paper is concerned with new applications for well established field techniques. Through a discussion of a field study of the Mugello Valley, they advocate the advantages of coring as a survey methodology, allowing for the discovery of potential occupation sites that may otherwise have been overlooked.

Three papers then focus on the use of space, considering both urban contexts and the impact of Rome on the wider landscape. **Cecelia Feldman Weiss** uses performativity theory to illustrate the active role of water in creating an idea of 'place' in the city of Ephesus, exploring the interactions and relationships created between this fluid resource and the population that depended upon it. **Simon Wood** traces the development of *horti* in Rome from Republican kitchen-gardens to public pleasure gardens under the emperors, reaching their peak in Nero's *Domus Aurea* which continued to influence the development of green space in Rome. **Rick Bonnie** looks at the possibility of cadastres (centuriation) having been imposed in the north-western provinces, deconstructing previous arguments against their existence and providing strong evidence of a cadastre in Belgium.

Identity has been a particular theme of TRAC conferences, both past and present. Utilising funerary evidence, **Alison Moore** explores whether the elderly could be seen as a distinct grouping in southern Britain; her life course analysis shows that differences in identity are visible both between genders and between rural and urban sites. **Rafael Scopacasa** also uses funerary evidence to examine the relationship between grave goods and gender in pre-Roman Samnium, identifying that communities acknowledged different forms of gender relations, particularly in regard to communal drinking practices.

Finally, **Keith Fitzpatrick-Matthews** addresses issues relating to the evidence for sub-Roman activity at Baldock, emphasising the important role which 'small towns' have to play in developing a clearer picture of both everyday life, and wider issues of cultural change, in post-Roman Britain.

The Theoretical Roman Archaeology Conference continues to attract dynamic scholars from across Europe to present and discuss their work, providing an environment that allows new and challenging approaches which can provide new avenues for future research. Holding TRAC 2009 in both the USA and Europe this year has further widened participation and, as TRAC continues to develop and expand, it is hoped that Roman scholars from even more countries will be able to participate.

This volume was edited by members of the Southampton TRAC organising committee, Alison Moore, Geoff Taylor, Emily Harris, Peter Girdwood and Lucy Shipley. A great many thanks are due to all the students and faculty at the University of Michigan, particularly Lisa M. Anderson and Katherine Marino who organised the American TRAC conference. Particular thanks are also due to Dr Louise Revell, who organised the UK conference at short notice.

We would like to thank all those from the University of Southampton whose efforts allowed the UK conference to be held, particularly Sue Niblock, School of Humanities, for facilitating the conference, Dr Jon Adams in Archaeology for support and refreshments and all the student helpers who ensured the conference ran smoothly. Our thanks go to those who chaired sessions at both conferences, including Professor Simon Keay, Professor Tim Champion and Dr Louise Revell. We would also like to thank Nicola Terrenato and John Humphrey, organisers of RAC Michigan, and Ronald Visser, who edited last year's TRAC volume, for his advice and support. Special thanks to Val Lamb at Oxbow Books for her advice in regard to the editing process, and her continued commitment to the publication of the TRAC proceedings, as well as to Helen Richmond for providing the artwork for the cover. We are grateful to the anonymous reviewers for their prompt and helpful comments on the papers; their input within the editorial process remains invaluable. Finally, we would like to thank the many people who presented at both TRAC conferences and those who submitted their papers for publication in these conference proceedings.

Alison Moore, Geoff Taylor, Emily Harris, Peter Girdwood and Lucy Shipley

Romanization: A Feminist Critique

Louise Revell

Introduction

The question of gender studies within Roman archaeology has been integrally bound up with TRAC since its inception. It was one of the stated aims of Eleanor Scott in founding TRAC to challenge the androcentrism of contemporary approaches to the Roman provinces (Scott 1993). In the first conferences all looked good, and there was a flurry of papers deconstructing present approaches (Scott 1995; 1997) and looking for the evidence for the lives of women within the Roman provinces (van Driel-Murray 1995), or challenging assumptions about the gendered meaning of material culture (Allason-Jones 1995). Later conferences saw a reduction in the numbers of papers on gender, leading to Patty Baker's paper in the proceedings from Canterbury lamenting the fact that things were still no better (Baker 2003). In 2009, accounts of the Roman provinces are still marked by an unquestioned androcentrism; there are few practitioners who would dispute that the feminist critique is important, but this has not led to them integrating such approaches into their own reconstructions of the Roman past. This is in contrast with Ancient History and Classical Art History, which has generated a wide-ranging literature on the subject.

Nevertheless, it is not my aim in this paper to reiterate the call for more research into gender and other marginalised groups in the Roman provinces. The situation is starting to change; for example, in the last ten years there has been a growth in the question of the life-course within the Roman provinces (Gowland 2001). However, one danger is that this is becoming a ghetto area, studied by women and distinguished from the mainstream topics of cultural change, settlement and economics. Instead, I want to argue that gender studies have a part to play in our examination of these questions. At the moment, we generally either depopulate them, or repopulate them with an under theorised adult male (the simulacrum of the majority of researchers) (Scott 1998; Swift 2007). By keeping the question of people distinct, we hamper our understanding of the "big" questions. Without incorporating questions such as gender, age and family structures, we cannot hope to understand these topics fully. In this paper, I want to take the central topic of Romanization (or cultural change, depending upon your theoretical allegiance) and demonstrate how a feminist approach provides a new perspective on an old chestnut.

A feminist archaeology?

During the nineteenth century, male-driven views of scientific history and the political context of the emerging nation-states led to historians and archaeologists concentrating on ideas of political organization, imperialism and historical narrative. Questions such as gender and childhood were considered marginal to 'proper' research. These limited agendas continued throughout much of the twentieth century, and, although from the 1970s onwards new theoretical ideas have challenged them, research into women, children and the family is still to some extent considered as a distinct sub-discipline. Gender is a question which has largely been ignored within Roman archaeology, particularly the archaeology of the western provinces. This is in spite of the post-Foucauldian concentration on gender in Ancient History, and the growth of post-processual agendas within Roman archaeology. Structuration theory and the question of identity have provided new avenues for the study of imperialism and cultural change (for example, Barrett 1997; Gardner 2002; Revell 2009; Woolf 1998), but ethnic identity is still often assumed to mean adult male identity (Revell 2000 attempts to break down this homogenisation).

The idea that our reconstruction of the past has been carried out through male dominated agendas has been explicitly raised by a number of feminist archaeologists, anthropologists and historians. In their seminal article on the subject, Conkey and Spector explicitly sought to challenge androcentric agendas in Archaeology, based upon the growth of feminist approaches within Anthropology (Conkey and Spector 1984). They identified three distinct stages in the development of feminist theories:

1. Critiques of male bias
2. Studies of women's lives
3. Studies of the relationship between genders and the factors which structure them

These stages can be applied to the study of the Roman provinces. The primary stage of critiquing the androcentric epistemology can be seen in the work of Eleanor Scott (1995), who outlined ways in which women were marginalised from accounts of Roman archaeology. This has been continued by others such as Lindsey Allason-Jones and J.D. Hill (Allason-Jones 2001; Hill 2001). We are now at the stage where it is accepted that studies of the marginalised are a valid part of Roman archaeology and this has led to work within the second area: the studies of women's lives. For Roman Britain, we could cite Allason-Jones' *Women in Roman Britain* (Allason-Jones 1989; similarly Pelletier 1984). However, there is the danger that this is becoming a marginalised part of Roman archaeology. Shelby Brown has argued that following Sarah Pomeroy's (1975) groundbreaking study of women in antiquity, '[c]onsideration of women and supposed women's issues was often directed into a subfield called Women in Antiquity, which left the normal field of study as male' (Brown 1997: 25). We are in danger of developing a similar subfield entitled "Women in the Roman Provinces".

I would argue that we are at the stage where we need to integrate studies of gender into the dominant narratives of Roman Archaeology. One area where this can be accomplished is in the question of cultural change. Conkey and Spector (1984) identified this as one part of a feminist Archaeology, and work on other periods has demonstrated that we cannot assume continuity of gender roles across periods of cultural change. This was explicitly raised by Joan Kelly in her article *Did women have a Renaissance?* (Kelly 1984). She argued that, whereas the Renaissance is generally viewed as a time of positive social and cultural change, for women this was a time when the power and authority which they could wield during the Medieval period was removed, due to a new division between personal and public life and new ideas of the relationships between men and women. Kelly's work can be set alongside that of feminist archaeologists who have similarly questioned the role of women in cultural change. An early study was that by Hastorf (1991) of pre-Hispanic Andean communities. She argued that, as the area came under Inca control, there was a reduction in women's access to the production and consumption of certain foodstuffs, pointing to a reduction in their social authority. This raises the question of the impact of incorporation into the Roman empire on the gender relations of the provinces, and the possibility of an active role for women within this process.

Although there has been a renewed interest in the question of cultural change in the last twenty years, a review of the key works on this topic sees a distinct lack of consideration of gender. Millett's model of Romanization is based upon changes within quite specific social structures (Millett 1990a; 1990b), framed within the processual epistemology focussed on rank and status (Millett 2003/04: 169). Ironically, there is an implicit discussion of changing gender relations within Millett's work: he argues that the incorporation of the conquered elites into the administration of the empire led to their position being defined around their status as a magistrate rather than a warrior. At the same time as ideologies of rank were changing, so ideologies of masculinity were similarly being altered, with new forms of material culture being adopted to express this (Revell 1999). However, this consequence of Millett's argument has not been explicitly articulated either in his own work, or in the various responses to it. This idea that Romanization led to a redefinition of masculinity can also be seen in Woolf's *Becoming Roman*, which looked at the formation of a specifically regional cultural identity in the Gallic provinces: 'men literally came down from the hills, shaved off their beards and learned to bathe themselves' (Woolf 1998: ix). Woolf's gender specificity leaves the question of what the women were doing: were they left behind in the hill-forts, or did they similarly come down to the new Roman towns, learn elaborate new hairstyles, as suggested by the increase in hairpins, and take on new economic roles.

In an alternative approach, Mattingly's work on discrepant identities has sought to break down the idea of a homogenised response to Roman imperialism. This may seem more promising, but it sees the cultural changes as based upon economic exploitation, producing a tripartite division into urban, rural and military communities (Mattingly 2004; 2006). Although women and gender relations are more visible in his arguments, women are largely considered in relation to men, whether in terms of unbalanced populations within urban cemeteries (Mattingly 2006: 323–4, 344–5) or assumptions about male soldiers' need for female prostitutes (Mattingly 2006: 175–6). Ironically, the question of the impact of sexual interaction between Roman soldiers and native women is also briefly considered by Millett (1990a: 60), who argues that it could have led to women playing an active role in the acculturation of the rest of society, a possibility not subsequently pursued. Similarly, Nicola Terrenato has also argued for a more nuanced picture, with the co-incidence of change and conservatism in different elements of society within Roman Etruria (Terrenato 1998). This model allows for gender relations to play a different role within the process of cultural change, although it is not raised by Terrenato himself.

Whilst much of this review has focussed on the north-western provinces, and in particular Britain, this reflects archaeological studies of imperialism and cultural change elsewhere in the empire. If the current paradigms of cultural change are unsatisfactory, how do we write an alternative narrative? Whilst we do need new synthetic research which directly addresses the question of gender relations, it is also possible to reread some of the existing studies to raise certain issues which would have impacted on the way gender relations were structured. In the remainder of this paper, I want to take a series of published studies, and use these to both rethink what impact Roman conquest and the process of cultural change might have had upon family structures, but also to demonstrate that a feminist approach has more to offer Roman archaeology than the subfield of "Women in the Roman Provinces".

Regional variability in gender identities

One of the current questions in the study of cultural change is that of regionality and regional variability. The idea of localised responses to Roman imperialism has been explored predominantly through artefact types, architectural styles, and settlement patterns. We can see the same regional variability in structures of age and gender, as expressed through (and in part constructed through) family roles. This has been most clearly demonstrated by Richard Saller and Brent Shaw for the Latin west (Saller 1987; Shaw 1987). In a series of inter-related studies, they looked at the question of age at marriage and who was named as the commemorator of the deceased, both of which have a bearing on the organisation of the family unit. Their solution to the low number of epitaphs from which it is possible to calculate age at marriage was to argue that the deceased was commemorated primarily by their parents until marriage, and then by their spouse. By calculating the average age at which the spouse took over from the parents as the most frequent commemorator, it is possible to estimate the average age at marriage.

Most of the variations shown in their results are quite subtle. For example, in both Northern and Southern Italy, age at marriage for women seems to be in their early twenties. However, for men, average age at marriage seems to have been their early thirties in Northern Italy, and their late thirties in Southern Italy. The differences are clearest in the case of Spain, where husbands do not become the dominant commemorators until women are in their late 20s and early 30s, and conversely for men the transition is even later, in their early 40s. In this case, I am doubtful whether this relates directly to age at marriage. Instead, it suggests that the change in primary commemorator did not occur at the same time as marriage, pointing to different notions of how parental and spousal families interacted with each other and the way in which parental authority and power was conceptualised. These differences are further reinforced in the patterns of who was named as the commemorator, which point to the relationship between the deceased and the person responsible for his/her memorial inscription. Any variation in the primary commemorator may relate to differences in the structure of the family unit, and in particular, the strength of the nuclear family. Again, there is a notable difference between the Iberian peninsula and the other western provinces. In Iberia, women are far more visible as the named commemorator: there are almost as many wives commemorating their husbands as vice versa, and far more mothers than fathers commemorating their children (Saller and Shaw 1984; also Edmondson 2005).

In both of these aspects of the process of commemoration, we can see regional variability in gender roles and family structures. This is not an isolated case-study, and there is mounting evidence that this variability can be seen in other aspects of the material culture (Revell in press). Mary Boatwright has argued for a difference between Pannonia and Rome in how interaction between children and parents is depicted pictorially (Boatwright 2005). In Rome, there is very little interaction represented, whereas in Pannonia there is much more, with images of the nursing mothers a distinctive Pannonian trait. Others have used the structure of the house to argue for regional differences in the family structures (Guijarro 1997; Smith 1997). This suggests that we cannot assume the adoption of the legal and social structure of the Roman *familia* within the provinces, and that the gender roles within the family reconstructed from textual sources at Rome were not necessarily replicated outside of the city.

Continuity in a changing environment

So, if we have this regional variability in family structures and gender roles within the family, how do we account for it? Is this due to conservatism, or are there changes but on a particular, localised trajectory? The evidence suggests that there is no simple, single answer. In some places we can see possible continuity, and this is demonstrated in the analysis of the epitaphs from Tarquinia and Etruria (Revell 2005). Amongst the information given about the deceased within the epitaph may be the age at death. It has long been recognised that the pattern of age statements does not follow expected patterns of mortality, which suggests that their inclusion can be used to reconstruct ideologies of gender and age. The epitaphs from *regiones* 4–6 in central Italy show a marked emphasis on the commemoration of children and young adults, with over 80% of age-statements corresponding to those aged 30 and under (Fig. 1). This profile reflects an ideology of gender where the transition to adulthood was marked by taking up the roles of wife and mother for women, usually in the late teens, and magistrate and husband for men at age of 25. Death is seen as more poignant when the deceased has not yet made this transition. Age-statements for those whose deaths occurred in childhood and the years through to the early twenties are included because they point to this unfulfilled promise of the deceased. This echoes the forms of life-course which we see in the Roman textual sources (Harlow and Laurence 2002), and suggests that, in these areas, we are seeing a change in family and age structures to align with those at Rome itself.

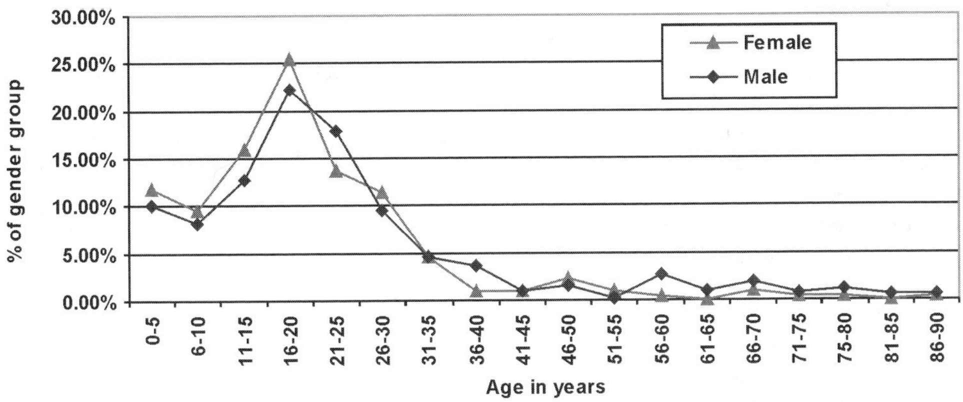

Figure 1: Distribution of age-statements on tombstones from regiones 4, 5 and 6 (n=634; males=414, females=220).

In contrast, when we look at the evidence from Tarquinia we see a different pattern of commemoration which reflects a different ideology of age (Fig. 2). There is less concentration on childhood, and a more pronounced concentration on those in their 40s to 70s. The percentage of epitaphs commemorating those aged 30 years and under is much lower, at just over 30%, and we see a much higher proportion of age-statements referring to those in their 60s and above. This follows the pattern of the Etruscan-language inscriptions from South Etruria, which date to the fourth century B.C. (Nielsen 1989). Here there is a dual emphasis on those dying in early adulthood and old age. Nielsen has argued that this shows a respect for the older generations and grandparents in particular. Whether this is the case or not, it demonstrates a certain level of continuity in age structures from the Etruscan to the Roman period in this area.

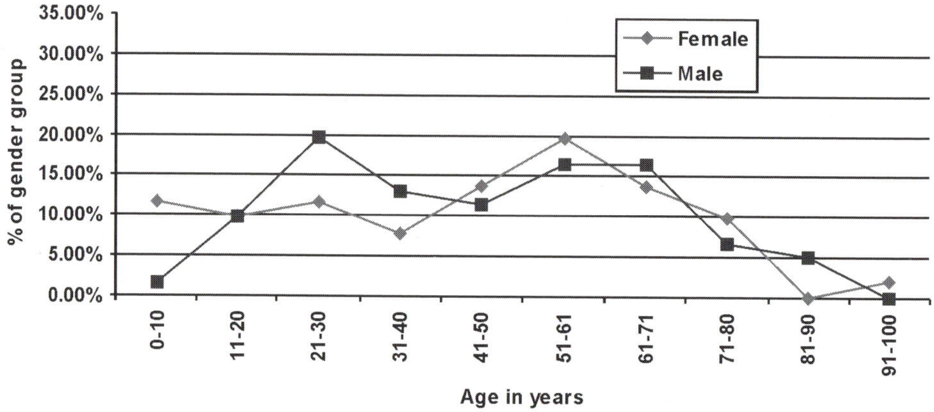

Figure 2: Distribution of age-statements on tombstones from Tarquinia (n=112; males=61, females=51).

Studies of other forms of material culture have also argued for continuity of family structures. J.T. Smith (1997) has argued that, in Britain and north-western Europe, villa layout points to a continuation of the extended family. Many of the villas in these areas have a feature of duality, such as reduplicated rooms and entrances, which alongside their size point to occupation by more than one nuclear family. He argues that prior to conquest, land was owned by kinship-groups, although not all member family units were necessarily of the same status. This organization continued after conquest, and is reflected in the design of villas, which can be divided into individual sections for each family. One part was often larger than the others suggesting that one family was considered senior to the others. Other studies have also argued for some continuity in Egypt, North Africa and Lusitania (Alston 2005; Corbier 2005; Edmondson 2005 respectively).

Potential disruption from Roman imperialism

In these case-studies, we can see family structures and gender relations continuing through the process of wider cultural changes. However, in other areas we see potential disruption to family relations caused by the demands of incorporation into the Roman empire. This is true when we look at the case of the military. To return to the Saller and Shaw study, there is a different pattern of civilian and military commemoration (Saller and Shaw 1984), with marked differences in the patterns of commemoration between the military and civilian zones in Britain and Germany (Table 1). Within the civilian population, there are high levels of commemoration by the nuclear family, whereas, amongst the military population, the majority of named commemorators are drawn from outside of the family. However, in the case of the African provinces, the differences are less pronounced. This contrasts with the African provinces, where commemoration by the nuclear family is more frequent for soldiers. Even amongst the *milites* of Lambaesis, 77% of the deceased are commemorated by their nuclear family.

Table 1. Commemoration by nuclear family, as a percentage of total relationships mentioned on epitaphs by region and social group; figures taken from Saller and Shaw 1984: appendix.

Province	Civilian (%)	Military (%)
Britain	80	40
Germania Inferior	86	34
Germania Superior	89	34
Africa Caesarea	89	63
Lambaesis	91	81

Nevertheless, this does not mean that the military populations were men-only zones. The archaeological evidence from Hadrian's Wall points to a mixed community, with material culture indicating the presence of women and children in and around the forts. The sizes of the leather shoes found at Vindolanda and a number of German forts points to the presence of women and children (van Driel-Murray 1995), and epigraphic evidence shows that in some cases these were not only wives and children, but also unmarried sisters and widowed mothers, who were presumably the legal dependents of the soldiers (Allason-Jones 1989: 62–3). This suggests that the soldiers were forming family units with women and children based in the forts themselves and their environs, but that, for whatever reason, the strength and social pull of these relationships were less strong than the soldiers' relationships with their fellow soldiers. We can posit two alternative interpretations for this. Firstly that within the army unit as a community, the military ties were more important than familial ones. Because the soldiers were recruited from outside the immediate area, liaisons may have been formed with local women, and as these unions were not recognised in Roman law during the first and second centuries A.D. (Phang 2002), the women and children may have been left behind on their retirement. Alternatively, as the designated commemorator was to a certain extent a legal relationship and as many of the soldiers were non-citizen auxiliaries, their families' lack of standing in Roman law may have made them seem less suitable as a commemorator.

There is another side to the possible disruption caused by army recruitment, and that is the impact on family structure amongst those left behind. Any numerical figure given to the levels of recruitment from these areas must at best be an estimate, but calculations by Willems suggest that, in Batavia, each household may have contributed at least one man to military service (Willems 1984). The impact this had on family relationships is difficult to reconstruct, but it may have had the effect of giving women a more prominent role in the family. Carol van Driel-Murray has argued for family-based agricultural production, which ethnographic parallels suggest may have been run by women (van Driel-Murray 2002). This level of recruitment is not confined to Batavia, but can also be seen in north-western Iberia. It has been estimated that at least 15,180 men were recruited as auxiliary soldiers, and there is also evidence for recruitment from the local towns into the legions and the Praetorian Cohorts (Millett 2001). In contrast to Batavia, there is a strong likelihood that these men never returned home once discharged. This raises the question of precisely what impact the departure of this quantity of young men had on family relations and, in particular, the impact on the role of women within the society. Perhaps, as suggested for Batavia, this gave women a more prominent role within the family or alternatively, as there would have been more women of marriageable age than men, this decreased their importance and status. Although we cannot answer these questions, the demands of Roman military recruitment had the potential to disrupt gender and family relationships and to produce a different form of social transformation to those in areas with lower levels of military recruitment.

Re-reading Romanization

The aim of this paper has been to demonstrate how the integration of questions of gender can inform our wider reading of traditional questions of Roman archaeology. When we look at the question of gender identities and family structures, we can see many of the same issues central to current discussions of Romanization. We can see the way in which new forms of material culture, such as Latin epitaphs and house structures, were used in a dynamic and deliberate way. We can also see the way in which there were different, or discrepant, responses to the imperial context at a regional level. However, we can take this further. We concentrate on political participation and military service as ways in which the people of the provinces were incorporated into the empire. With these came new ways of defining masculinity as soldier or the active citizen through changing social structures. There was only a limited political role for women through priesthoods or benefaction, and this was only applicable to women of elite families (Hemelrijk 2004). Ideologies of female-ness and age may have remained substantially unchanged, although new ways learnt of expressing them. The alternative scenario is that ideologies of gender (for both men and women) may have changed due to the demands of a new imperial context, but that the changes were more complex than the wholesale adoption of the *familia* as defined by law and custom in Rome. By looking at whether or not there were changes in how gender and family relations were structured, Romanization takes on an added dimension. It serves to put the social structures where there was more substantial change into greater focus, and so allows a more nuanced understanding of the related phenomena of Roman imperialism and Romanization.

However, a feminist perspective has the power to add much more to Roman archaeology. The implications of this argument also have a more fundamental impact on how we frame research questions within Roman archaeology more widely. Other topics such as landscape, settlement, religion and the economy can be similarly reinterpreted using the question of how they were the product of, and at the same time created, different forms of identities. This requires new methodologies for interpreting the evidence in order to go beyond the uncritical reconstruction of people from the textual sources. It also calls upon us to do more than place the marginalised identities (women, children, slaves etc.) back into the archaeological evidence, and to problematize the normative model of the adult male. In this way, we can move beyond the sub-field of 'Women in the Roman Provinces' and truly begin to write a social archaeology of the Roman empire.

Archaeology, School of Humanities, University of Southampton

Bibliography

Allason-Jones, L. 1989. *Women in Roman Britain.* London: British Museum Press.

Allason-Jones, L. 1995. 'Sexing' small finds. In P. Rush (ed.) *Theoretical Roman Archaeology: Second Conference Proceedings*. Aldershot: Avebury: 22–32.
Allason-Jones, L. 2001. Material culture and identity. In S. James and M. Millet (eds.) *Britons and Romans: Advancing an Archaeological Agenda*. York: Council for British Archaeology Research Report 125. 19–25
Alston, R. 2005. Searching for the Romano-Egyptian family. In M. George (ed.) *The Roman Family in the Empire: Rome, Italy and Beyond*. Oxford: Oxford University Press: 129–157.
Baker, P. 2003. A brief comment on the TRAC session dedicated to the interdisciplinary approaches to the study of Roman women. In (G. Carr, E. Swift and J. Weekes (eds.) *TRAC 2002: Proceedings of the Twelfth Annual Theoretical Roman Archaeology Conference, Canterbury 2002*. Oxford: Oxbow Books: 140–146.
Barrett, J.C. 1997. Theorising Roman archaeology. In K. Meadows, C. Lemke and J. Heron (eds.) *TRAC 98: Proceedings of the Sixth Annual Theoretical Roman Archaeology Conference, Sheffield 1996*. Oxford: Oxbow Books: 1–7.
Boatwright, M.T. 2005. Children and parents on the tombstones of Pannonia. In M. George (ed.) *The Roman Family in the Empire: Rome, Italy and Beyond*. Oxford: Oxford University Press: 287–318.
Brown, S. 1997. "Ways of seeing" women in antiquity: An introduction to feminism in classical archaeology and ancient art history. In A.O. Koloski-Ostrow and C.L. Lyons (eds.) *Naked Truths: Women, Sexuality and Gender in Classical Art and Archaeology*. London: Routledge: 12–42.
Conkey, M.W. and Spector, J.D. 1984. Archaeology and the study of gender. *Advances in Archaeological Method and Theory* 7: 1–38.
Corbier, M. 2005. Family and kinship in Roman Africa. In M. George (ed.) *The Roman Family in the Empire: Rome, Italy and Beyond*. Oxford: Oxford University Press: 255–285.
Edmondson, J. 2005. Family relations in Roman Lusitania: social change in a Roman province. In M. George (ed.) *The Roman Family in the Empire: Rome, Italy and Beyond*. Oxford: Oxford University Press: 183–229.
Gardner, A. 2002. Social identity and the duality of structure in late Roman-period Britain. *Journal of Social Archaeology* 2(3): 323–351.
Gowland, R. 2001. Playing dead: implications of mortuary evidence for the social construction of childhood in Roman Britain. In G. Davies, A. Gardner and K. Lockyer (eds.) *TRAC 2000: Proceedings of the Tenth Annual Theoretical Roman Archaeology Conference, London 2000*. Oxford: Oxbow Books: 152–168.
Guijarro, S. 1997. The family in first century Galilee. In H. Moxnes (eds.) *Constructing Early Christian Families: Family as Social Reality and Metaphor*. London: Routledge: 42–65.
Harlow, M. and Laurence, R. 2002. *Growing Up and Growing Old in Ancient Rome*, London: Routledge.
Hastorf, C.A. 1991. Gender, space and food in prehistory. In J.M. Gero and M.W. Conkey (eds.) *Engendering Archaeology: Women and Prehistory*. Oxford: Blackwells: 132–159.
Hemelrijk, E.A. 2004. City patronesses in the Roman empire. *Historia*, 53(2): 209–245.
Hill, J.D. 2001. Romanisation, gender and class: recent approaches to identity in Britain and their possible consequences. In S. James and M. Millett (eds.) *Britons and Romans: Advancing an Archaeological Agenda*. York: Council for British Archaeology Research Report 125. 12–18.
Kelly, J. 1984. Did women have a renaissance? In J. Kelly (ed.) *Women, History and Theory: The Essays of Joan Kelly*. Chicago: University of Chicago Press: 19–50.
Mattingly, D. 2004. Becoming Roman: expressing identity in a provincial setting. *Journal of Roman Archaeology* 17: 5–25.
Mattingly, D. 2006. *Britain: An Imperial Possession*. London: Allen Lane.
Millett, M. 1990a. *The Romanization of Britain: An Essay in Archaeological Interpretation*. Cambridge: Cambridge University Press.
Millett, M. 1990b. Romanization: historical issues and archaeological interpretations. In T.F.C. Blagg and M. Millett (eds.) *The Early Roman Empire in the West*. Oxford: Oxbow Books: 35–41.
Millett, M. 2001. Roman interaction in north-western Iberia. *Oxford Journal of Archaeology*, 20(2): 157–170.

Millett, M. 2003/04. The Romanization of Britain: changing perspectives. *Kodai: Journal of Ancient History* 13–14: 169–173.

Nielsen, M. 1989. Women and family in a changing society: a quantitative approach to late Etruscan burials. *Analecta Romana Instituti Danici* 17–18: 53–98.

Pelletier, A. 1984. *La Femme dans la Société Gallo-Romaine:* Paris: Picard.

Phang, S.A. 2002. The families of Roman soldiers (first and second centuries A.D.): culture, law and practice. *Journal of Family History* 27: 352–373.

Pomeroy, S.B. 1975. *Goddesses, Whores, Wives and Slaves.* New York: Schocken Books.

Revell, L. 1999. Constructing Romanitas: Roman public architecture and the archaeology of practice, In P. Baker, C. Forcey, S. Jundi and R. Witcher (eds.) *TRAC 98: Proceedings of the Eighth Annual Theoretical Roman Archaeology Conference, Leicester 1998.* Oxford: Oxbow Books: 52–8.

Revell, L. 2000. The creation of multiple identities in Roman Italica. In G. Fincham. G. Harrison, R. Holland and L. Revell (eds.) *TRAC 99: Proceedings of the Ninth Annual Theoretical Roman Archaeology Conference, Durham 1999.* Oxford: Oxbow Books: 1–7.

Revell, L. 2005. The Roman life-course: a view from the inscriptions. *European Journal of Archaeology* 8(1): 43–63.

Revell, L. 2009. *Roman Imperialism and Local Identities.* Cambridge: Cambridge University Press.

Revell, L. in press. Geography and environment. In M. Harlow and R. Laurence (eds.) *The History of Children and the Family Volume 1: Antiquity (500 B.C.E. – 800 C.E.).* Oxford: Berg.

Saller, R.P. 1987. Men's age at marriage and its consequences in the Roman family. *Classical Philology* 82: 21–34.

Saller, R.P. and Shaw, B.D. 1984. Tombstones and Roman family relations in the Principate: civilians, soldiers and slaves. *Journal of Roman Studies* 74: 124–56.

Scott, E 1993. Introduction: TRAC (Theoretical Roman Archaeology Conference) 1991. In E. Scott (ed.) *Theoretical Roman Archaeology: First Conference Proceedings.* Aldershot: Avebury: 1–4.

Scott, E. 1995. Women and gender relations in the Roman empire. In P. Rush (ed.) in *Theoretical Roman Archaeology: Second Conference Proceedings.* Aldershot: Avebury: 174–89.

Scott, E. 1997. Introduction: on the incompleteness of archaeological narratives. In J. Moore and E. Scott (eds.) *Invisible People and Processes: Writing Gender and Childhood in European Archaeology.* Leicester: Leicester University Press: 1–12.

Scott, E. 1998. Tales from a Romanist: a personal view of archaeology and 'equal opportunities'. In C. Forcey, J. Hawthorne and R. Witcher (eds.) *TRAC 97: Proceedings of the Eighth Annual Theoretical Roman Archaeology Conference, Nottingham 1997.* Oxford: Oxbow Books: 138–147.

Shaw, B.D. 1987. The age of Roman girls at marriage: some reconsiderations. *Journal of Roman Studies* 77: 30–46.

Smith, J.T. 1997. *Roman Villas: A Study in Social Structure.* London: Routledge.

Swift, E. 2007. Small objects, small questions? Perceptions of finds research in the academic community. In R. Hingley and S. Willis (eds.) *Roman Finds: Context and Theory.* Oxford: Oxbow Books: 18–28.

Terrenato, N. 1998. *Tam firmum municipium*: The Romanization of Volaterrae and its cultural implications. *Journal of Roman Studies* 88: 94–114.

van Driel-Murray, C. 1995. Gender in question. In P. Rush (ed.) *Theoretical Roman Archaeology: Second Conference Proceedings.* Aldershot: Avebury: 3–21.

van Driel-Murray, C. 2002. Ethnic soldiers: the experience of the Lower Rhine tribes. In T. Grünewald & T. Seibel (eds.) *Kontinuität und Diskontinuität. Germania inferior um Geginn und am Ende der römischen Herrschaft. Beiträge des deutsch-niederländischen Kolloquiums in der Katholieke Universiteit Nijmegen (27. bis 30.06.2001).* Berlin: Walter de Gruyter: 200–217.

Willems, W.H.J. 1984. Romans and Batavians: a regional study in the Dutch East River Area II. *Berichten van de Rijksdienst voor het Oudheidkundig Bodemonderzoek* 34: 39–331.

Woolf, G. 1998. Becoming Roman: The Origins of Provincial Civilization in Gaul. Cambridge: Cambridge University Press.

Growing and Felling? Theory and Evidence Related to the Application of Silvicultural Systems in the Roman Period

Ronald M. Visser

> *'de omnibus agris optimoque loco iugera agri centum* [...] *septimo silva caedua, octavo arbustum, nono glandaria silva'* (For the best kind of farms, I [Cato] would say that [...] in the seventh place comes a coppice wood, in the eighth an orchard and in the ninth a *silva glandari*) (Cato *a.c.* 1.7, transl. by author)
>
> *'Ut enim mulieres habent ad partum dies certos, sic arbores ac fruges'* (Just like women give birth after a certain number of days, so do trees carry fruit) (Varro *r.r.* I.XLIV.4, transl. by author)

Introduction

When discussing buildings or building activity in previous TRAC volumes, people have dealt with subjects such as monumentality (Aitchison 1999), ideology (Kerr 2002), the role of buildings when navigating in towns (Malmberg 2009), the (functional) classification of domestic space (Anderson 2005) or the unifying aspects of a legionary camp (Driessen 2005). Most of these papers were focussed on stone buildings, whereas timber has been the most important building material from the Neolithic onwards. It is also interesting to note that only a few theoretical papers have dealt with the basics, such as supply of resources (although a special TRAC volume dealing with food supply has recently been published (Stalibrass and Thomas 2008)). The famous and thorough study Meiggs (1982) wrote on timber and wood in the Mediterranean area mainly dealt with the use of this material, but also described some aspects of supply. However, he hardly ever mentioned the production of wood or the management of woodlands. This also holds true for Hanson (1978) in his well written paper on the Roman military timber supply in the north of England.

In this paper I will try to bridge this gap and summarize evidence for the production of wood and timber in the Roman period. This is not an all inclusive study of Roman forestry, but must be seen as a starting point. For my PhD on the Roman timber supply in the Lower Rhine area I will write more extensively on this subject (Visser in prep.). The main research question for the paper presented here is, then, what historical and dendrochronological evidence exists for the application of modern silvicultural systems during the Roman period? I am consciously using the word modern here, since the systems explained later in the text are those applied in modern forestry and not necessarily the systems applied and discerned as such during the Roman period. These modern systems are used as a theoretical framework to enhance our understanding of an important part of the Roman economy.

By looking for the application of modern systems in the ancient economy I do not *a priori* assume that the economy or the economic rationale (Mickwitz 1937) was modern. Several recent overviews of the Roman economy (e.g. Greene 2000; Woolf 2001) have shown that the Roman economy was not as primitive as suggested by Finley (1973), nor as modern as Rostovtzeff (1957) thought it was. I share the current and more balanced view of the ancient economy, in which we should understand the Roman economy as different, but not necessarily lacking modern aspects. This view enables us to consider whether rationalism applied in production systems, here in silvicultural systems.

Knowledge needed for forestry

Before looking into the evidence relating to ancient forestry, we first need to understand what a silvicultural system is. According to Matthews (1989: 3) it embodies three ideas:

> '1) The method of regeneration of the individual crops constituting the forest;
> 2) the form of crop produced; and
> 3) the orderly arrangement of the crops over the whole forest with special reference to silvicultural and protective considerations and efficient harvesting of produce.'

The last item, in particular, points out that specific knowledge is needed when a silvicultural system is applied. This knowledge is related to the processes and circumstances that influence the growth of trees. Several factors can affect the growth of plants in general and trees specifically, such as soil, climate, competition, slope, ground water level, etc. If knowledge of these factors did exist during the Roman period, we can proceed further in aiming to find out whether silvicultural systems were applied then. The knowledge needed for the application of silvicultural systems can be divided into three groups, namely knowledge related to reproduction, production and harvesting the produce. In the discussion of this knowledge below I have not distinguished between that which is needed for silviculture and that for arboriculture (production of tree crops), since techniques applied in arboriculture can also be applied in silviculture, while there is no difference in the knowledge. However, it should be noted that the processes can differ.

The first type of knowledge needed embodies the reproduction of trees. Trees can be propagated in two ways: sexual and asexual. Pliny (*n.h.* XVI.134) mentions a third method of propagation, namely spontaneous growth of trees, but this is biologically impossible. Sexual propagation embodies the growth of trees 'from the memory of a single seed' (Kainulainen 2009). Varro (*r.r;* I.IV.1) mentions that the casting of seed is the first step in all production. Many other Roman and Greek authors also mention the growth of trees from seed (e.g. Columella *r.r.* III.I.1; Pliny *n.h.* XVI.134; Theophrastus II.I.3, II.VI.1, VII.I.1–2; Varro *r.r.* I.XXIII.6, I.XL.1, I.XLI.6). Propagation from seed is widely mentioned in ancient sources and from this it can safely be concluded that trees were seeded in the Roman period. Asexual propagation is also known as vegetative reproduction. This can be achieved in several ways, the most common being the use of cuttings, layering and suckering. Reproduction of trees or shrubs by cuttings is widely mentioned in ancient sources (e.g. Cato *a.c.* VI.3, XXIII; Columella *r.r.* several places in book III & IV, e.g. IV.IV.2 (mallet cutting of vine) or IV.XXXIII.2 (chestnut); Pliny *n.h.* XVII.58; Varro *r.r.* I.XXXIX.3; Virgil *Georgica* II.23–25, 64–68), and is sometimes even seen as the preferred method of propagation (Varro *r.r.* I.XLI.6). Suckering, or basal shoots, is among others mentioned by Columella (*r.r.* IV.XXXIII.4), Pliny the Elder (*n.h.* XVI.134) and Virgil (*Georgica* II.17). Propagation of trees by layering was also practised in the ancient world (Cato *a.c.* LI; Columella *d.a*, VII; Pliny *n.h.* XVII.58).

After knowledge on propagation, it is necessary to know how to enhance production when applying any silvicultural system. Columella (*r.r.* III.I.1) acknowledges that trees should be managed and that it is a very important part of farming. It was also known that some species grew faster than others (Varro *r.r.* I.XLI.4). In relation to management and tree growth, the words of Cato (*a.g.* LXI) on the growth of olives are very important: '*Quid est agrum bene colere? bene arare. Quid secundum? arare. Quid tertium? Stercorare.*' In other words, the most important things when growing plants are, according to Cato, manuring, manuring and ploughing. The latter is also mentioned by Virgil (G. II.397–400) in relation to a vineyard, which often included trees to support the branches of the vine. Manuring or fertilizing trees was probably common practice, since it is mentioned by several other ancient authors (e.g. Cato *a.g.* V.8, VIII.1, XXIX, XXXIII; Columella *r.r.* I.VI.22, II.II.13, II.V, III.XI.9; Pliny *n.h.* XVII.50–53; Virgil G. II.347). Thinning, pruning and the orderly placement of trees in a stand are also very important for enhancing production in modern plantations. Examples regarding the orderly placement of trees can be found in writings of Varro (*r.r.* I.XXIII.6), who mentions that young trees should be placed in rows. Theophrastus (II.V.1,5–6) and Pliny (n.h. XVII.59) both describe the preferred planting distance between trees. Thinning was also widely practised in the ancient world and is mentioned by Cato (*a.g.* CXXXIX), in relation to thinning of a grove, and Virgil (*G.* II.400–401), who describes how a vineyard is thinned. Columella (r.r. IV.XXXIII.2–3) gives us a description of the orderly placement of chestnut trees, the thinning process and the care taken while growing them.

Special measures to enhance production, or at least protect the current production, were taken by Hadrian around A.D. 138. Over a hundred inscriptions have been found in Lebanon covering a large area, the most common text being '*IMP.HAD.AUG.ARBORUM GENERA IV CETERA PRIVATA D(E)F(INITIO) S(ILVARUM)*'. This can be freely translated as: In the woods of the emperor Hadrianus four species have been demarcated; the rest can be used by private people (Honigmann 1926: 5–7; Meiggs 1982: 85–87). Thus the emperor had clearly taken protective measures to prevent illegal felling in his woods in Lebanon. Unfortunately, it is not known which species he wanted to protect, nor are the reasons for protection mentioned.

The third type of knowledge needed for the application of silvicultural systems is related to harvesting the crop and its effects on the remaining trees and the landscape. Although authors such as Vitruvius (II.9.1.) and Cato (*a.g.* XXXI.2) seem to agree that felling should be done during the autumn or winter, not many sources describe what should happen with the land after felling trees. Virgil (*G.* II.207) is the only author who speaks directly of the felling of a forest, and tells us that the land now finally yields crop after many years of no gain. He also states that the land should be ploughed after felling the trees. Since the ancients clearly knew that manuring the land enhanced production, it seems likely that this was also done after woodland was cleared.

Silvicultural systems in the Roman period

Clear cutting

The clear cutting system is the most basic silvicultural system (Fig. 1). When this system is applied a large area of a woodland is felled completely. After the felling of all the trees, the cleared area is left to regenerate by itself or new seedlings are planted in. In the ideal situation some sections would be cleared each year, as was the case in some pine-forests in Germany during the eighteenth century. However, it was soon realized there that trees did not grow as regularly as expected, and during the early nineteenth century trees were felled less frequently (Matthews 1989: 65–66). Protective measures are often taken, such as retaining the outer trees to protect the young trees from strong winds or removing other competing plants (more examples can be found in (Matthews 1989: 66–76)).

Since this system is described as 'the simplest of all high forest systems' (Matthews 1989: 87), it is likely that such a system was applied in the ancient world. Several sources describe the clear felling of an area, such as Caesar (*Bello Civili* 2.15.1) describing all the trees in the area around Massillia being felled during the war efforts. The felling of a complete woodland could also be punishment after an enemy was conquered (Nenninger 2001: 111*ff.*), but the reverse could also happen. After the Romans had defeated Phillip V of Macedonia in 198 B.C., he was forced to replant the forests (*silvae*) and sacred groves (*luci*) he had cleared during his war efforts (Livius 32.34.10). Although these textual sources seem to indicate clear felling, the question remains whether this is evidence for the application of a silvicultural system or just systematic destruction.

Figure 1: Modern clear cutting in the Sauerland (Germany). A felled patch is seen on the left side of the slope, in the middle older clear cutting is recognizable and on the right the woodland is nearly fully regenerated after clear cutting longer ago (photo by author).

It is important to look at other sources than just the written ones to find out whether the clear cutting system could have been applied in the Roman period. At the end of the first century a road was built along the *limes* in the Lower Rhine area. In the Netherlands, this road has been excavated at Valkenburg (Zuid-Holland). The wood that was used for the road came from trees that probably grew in the nearby coastal peat area, since the material shows strong correlation with the timbers used for an indigenous settlement at Nieuwenhoorn and the wood used in an early Roman fort at Velsen. However, when this road was rebuilt at the same location twenty five years later, wood with a different provenance was used (Visser and Jansma 2009). This seems to suggest that, when the road was first built, all the available trees were felled, so that no trees of the right size could be found in the same area twenty five years later. Clear felling had clearly taken place here, but it can not be said whether this was part of a silvicultural system or if it was just military clear cutting without any considerations for future use of the area. However, the latter would be strange for an area that was meant to be part of the Roman empire for a longer period, as implied by the reorganization of the region into the provinces Germania Inferior and Germania Superior around A.D. 85 (Carroll 2001: 41). Furthermore, the elevation of the civilian settlement near Xanten to Colonia Ulpia Traiana (Rüger 1968: 85–87), and Nijmegen to Ulpia Noviamagus Batavodurum (van Enckevort *et al.* 2000: 92) around A.D. 100, also shows that this area was seen as a permanent part of the

Imperium Romanum. If the Roman state or local government considered the area as a stable part of the empire, one would expect the executives of this policy, the army, to take more responsibility than to simply clear the landscape without replanting some trees. However, it might be the case that the commanders or soldiers building these roads were not concerned with these issues or could not see the long term effects of their actions (see Groenman-van Waateringe 1983; van der Leeuw and de Vries 2003 for a discussion on unintentional effects of Roman occupation and colonization).

Clear cutting obviously took place during the Roman period, but it remains unclear whether any silvicultural considerations were taken into account. The examples mentioned here are mostly related to military practices and seem to point toward systematic clear felling, but no hard evidence can be presented for systematic replanting after these (military) clearings.

Selection

If the selection system is applied, a selection is made of trees that will be felled within a forest. Felling and regeneration are not confined to certain areas in the forest, but are distributed throughout the stand. The application of this system results in a forest with trees of different ages, and sizes, geographically widely spread throughout the forest. After felling natural regeneration springs up in the gaps that are created in the forest. In the most primitive form all trees of a certain diameter or size are felled, but in a real selection system, the mixture of species, age-classes, sizes and regeneration of the forest should all be considered when felling a selection. The major advantages of this system are that saplings and younger trees are constantly protected by older trees and that the forested area is better protected from erosion than when, for example, the clear-cutting system is applied (Matthews 1989: 163–169).

An indication of the application of the selection system in the Roman period can be derived from the existence of the *saltuarii*. The distribution of inscriptions of these found in the Roman empire (Fig. 2) shows that they were present in several provinces. *Saltuarii* worked on the imperial domains, which were known under the term *saltus* (Sprater 1929: 62). These men were either slaves or freedmen and were led by a *villicus* (Meiggs 1982: 330), whose function was to guard the borders of the estate and to protect the crops on the estate (Rostowzew 1904: 299). As well as these functions, their role as foresters has also been mentioned (Sprater 1950). The different functions of this group of people is also reflected in the distribution on the map in Fig. 2, since evidence for *saltuarii* is not restricted to densely wooded areas.

Their function as foresters is nevertheless underlined by the depiction of a *saltuarius* on a grave stone that has been found in the Heidelsburg at Waldfischbach (Germany). On this stone, Titus Publicus Tertius is depicted with his wife, and he is carrying an axe that represents, according to Roller (1986: 61), a *securis* (Fig. 3). The same kind of axe has also been found during excavations at the same location (Sprater 1950: 425). Roller (1986: 61–63) has shown that a *securis* shows strong resemblance to the so-called *Loogaxt*, an axe that was used from the early Middle Ages until the eighteenth century to mark trees that should be felled. This *Loogaxt* not only had a functional use, but was also a status symbol. The use as a marking axe seems quite possible for the *securis* and, if this was the case, it might be an indication of the application of the selection system during the Roman period. The use of the *securis* as a symbol of status is suggested by its use on the grave stone of Titus Publicus Tertius and his wife. Since it is the only object he holds, and he or his relatives obviously wanted him to be depicted with it, the *securis* must clearly have had a strong meaning for him or his heirs.

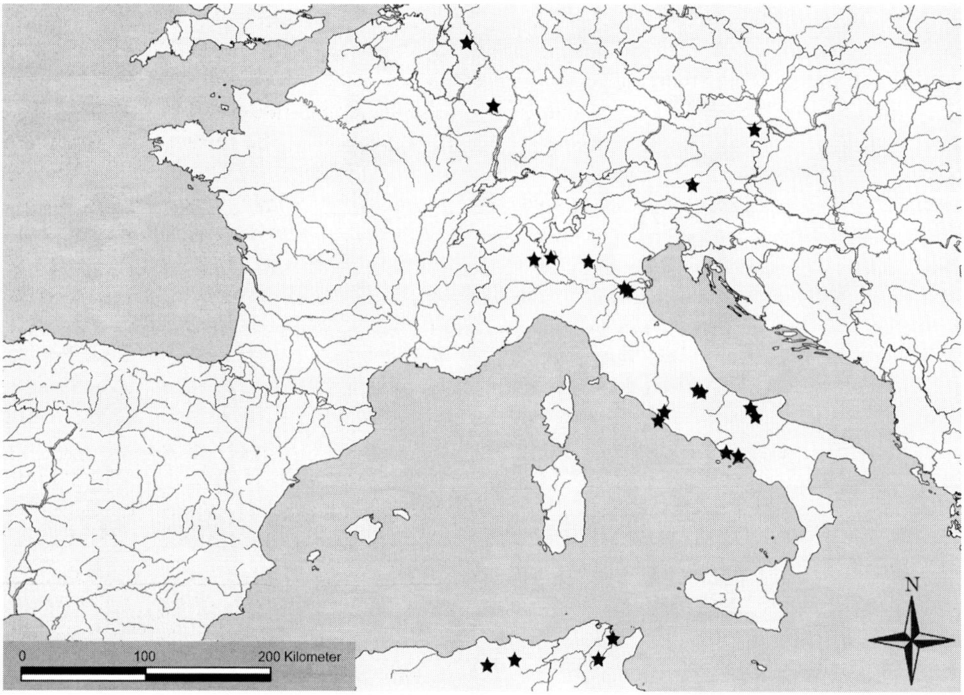

Figure 2: The distribution of the twenty four inscriptions of the saltuarii (map by author).

Figure 3: The relief from Waldfischbach showing a saltuarius (Sprater 1929: 64) (left). The excavated securis from the same location is shown on the upper right, with a Loogaxt below (drawings by author).

Selection of trees within a forest can also be derived from dendrochronological material. During the late Roman period, water wells in a native settlement near Gennep (Heidinga and Offenberg 1992) and a Roman bridge at Cuijk (Goudswaard *et al.* 2001) were built in the eastern River area in the Netherlands. The bridge was constructed between 347–349, renovated in 368 and between 388–398 it underwent the last large scale restoration, whilst the wells were constructed in the late fourth or early fifth century. The correlation between the dendrochronological material from these two sites is remarkable, pointing to the fact that the trees used there during different periods probably grew in the same forest (see also Jansma 1995: 65). It is interesting to note that, after the first felling of trees to build the bridge around 347–349, enough older trees must have been left standing to enable a second felling in 368. The trees used in 368 were older than twenty years and were already growing in 347, so it can be deduced that in 347 some selection took place. The same is true for the trees used in 388–398; some were even a hundred years old by this time. Several trees used for the wells were over a century old and were therefore growing while the bridge was built around 347–349, when it was renovated twenty years later and also when it was restored at the end of the fourth century. This shows that selection took place in the woods of the Lower Rhine area during the fourth century A.D. However, we must be cautious, since selection of trees in a forest could just be a selection based on the demand for wood with specific dimensions and not a selection which has been made after (careful) silvicultural considerations. Furthermore, the selection here could also have been possible because more woodland was available, so that the builders of the bridge had more to choose from. The population declined strongly during the second half of the third century (van Enckevort 2001). This led to less pressure on the landscape and probably expansion of the woodland (see Groenman-van Waateringe 1983: 147–148 for some pollen evidence). However, an argument in favour of selection is the relatively short distance between Cuijk and Gennep, which suggests that both the builders of the bridge and the wells were using the same woodland.

Coppicing

The coppice system is based on the regenerative properties of several tree species (Fig. 4). When most broad-leafed species, up to a certain age, are felled near the ground, they will form new shoots. These new shoots can be felled when they have reached the preferred size (either diameter or length). The mean maximum age at which the first felling should take place is around forty years, but with chestnut the first cut to create shoots can even be done after the tree has been growing normally for over a hundred years. The coppicing system can be combined with the selection system, in which case it is called a coppice selection system. Coppicing is particularly suitable for production of fire wood or of smaller constructional timbers. Larger timbers can be produced by leaving some trees to grow longer, when we speak of coppice with standards (Matthews 1989, 190–193, 213–224). Pollarding is related to coppicing, the only difference being that the trees are not cut at ground level but between two to five meters above ground (Rackham 1977: 65).

Evidence for coppicing in the Roman period can be found in several ancient sources. The term that was used for coppice woodland was *silva caedua* according to Meiggs (1982: 263). Makkonen (1967: 40) defines this term more broadly, when he states that a *silva caedua* 'comprised all utility forests, whose main function was to supply wood'. Nenninger (2001: 45–47), however, mentions a juridical text that states that a *silva caedua* is a forest where trees are felled, but in such a way that the stems sprout again. Hence, the term *silva caedua* is used for coppiced woodland. Independently from this debate on the ancient Latin terms for these woodlands, it is undeniable that coppicing took place during the Roman period, since several sources describe it. A very clear description of a five year coppice cycle comes from Columella (r.r. IV. XXXIII.1):

> 'Its nut, too, when planted in prepared ground, quickly springs up; and when cut down, after five years, it renews itself in the manner of the willow, and when made into a stake it lasts usually to the next cutting'

Columella (IV.XXI.2–3) also mentions the practice of pollarding, and Pliny (XVI.141–142) writes on the basics of coppicing, describing how a cypress will grow again from the roots after it is felled.

Figure 4: A coppiced oak stand at the Laarzenberg near Rhenen in the Netherlands (photo by author).

Archaeological evidence for coppicing dates back to the Neolithic. Based on the shape of the wood and its rapid early growth, Rackham (1977) concludes that coppiced hazel was used in the construction of several Neolithic trackways in Somerset. In contrast with the later medieval practice of clear felling the coppice stools, the Neolithic coppiced wood shows that coppicing was combined with selection on the basis of size. During the Roman period the application of coppice can also be proved archaeologically. It will suffice here to mention examples from two regions in the Roman West; Picardy and Flanders.

In the Picardy region, in north western France, many pieces of wood have been researched dendrochronologically and archaeologically by Bernard (2003). He has concluded that areas of approximately fifty square kilometres around the larger Roman settlements were used to supply them with wood and timber. His dendrochronological and morphological research on the shape, size and age of the wood points towards standardization after the end of the first century A.D. According to Bernard, this was the result of a forty year coppice cycle. Wood used for two wells in the late Roman settlement of Oudenburg (Belgium) was analysed dendrochronologically by Haneca *et al.* (2005). They compared the growth patterns, and more specifically the growth rate, of this archaeological wood with the growth rate of (natural and managed) high forests and coppiced stands. Based on this comparison the conclusion was drawn that this wood from the Roman period came from a coppiced woodland. Although the results of this study are very promising, I feel that we must be careful when concluding a linear relation between one modern coppice stand and archaeological material. However, when these results are combined with the written evidence mentioned earlier, the use of coppiced wood seems very probable at Oudenburg (and other locations) during the Roman period.

Based on historical sources it can be concluded that the theory behind coppicing was known and that it was probably applied. This is corroborated by the archaeological evidence, which shows that coppicing was practised in the Roman period.

Agro-forestry

This widespread practice is a combination of growing timber trees, fruit trees and/or shrubs in combination with agricultural crops and/or animals. When combined with crops, the trees protect the plants from strong winds and the branches or stems can be used to build fences or used as poles to grow, for example, beans. Coppicing the woodland is especially suitable for producing small timbers for these purposes. Woodlands can also be used as pasture. In this case the animals remove the undergrowth and their dung fertilizes the soil. If trees are coppiced or pollarded, the leaves can be used as fodder for the animals. Pastoral use of woodlands can be combined with clear-cutting. If the young trees are sufficiently protected, the livestock can eat away the competing weeds or shrubs giving the young trees more light (Matthews 1989: 240–243).

The Latin term for the combination of agriculture and forestry is *silva glandaria*. The term was originally used for woods with oak (*glans* = acorn) but, according to Meiggs (1982: 263), it can also be used for beech-forest. The nuts from the trees were used to feed the pigs. This conclusion of Meiggs is clearly based on the passage from Pliny (*n.h.* XVI.15–34), where he describes how these nuts are fed to pigs and that these animals especially like the nuts from the beech. A *silva glandaria* was seen as a very good investment in Gallia during the Roman period, and pigs that were fattened in them supplied a large part of the meat consumption in the (western) Roman empire (Meiggs 1982: 263; Nenninger 2001: 46–47).

Another combination of forestry and agriculture is described by Varro (*r.r.* I.XV), when he mentions the planting of trees on a farm. Here he points out that trees on a farm are important to make the boundaries of the estate more secure and prevent any quarrels with neighbours. Furthermore, the young branches of the elm trees can be used to make baskets, the larger ones to build fences, the foliage used as fodder for sheep and cattle and, finally, that the wood can be used as fuel. The use of leaves of elm as well as oak and poplar as fodder is also mentioned by Cato (*a.g.* V.8).

Conclusion

In this paper I have shown that the knowledge that is needed for the application of silvicultural systems existed during the Roman period. In a short survey of the historical sources and some dendrochronological publications and material, evidence has been presented for four silvicultural systems. For the clear cutting system, no irrefutable evidence could be found for its application in the Roman period, but some evidence of clear felling has been mentioned. It remains unclear whether measures were taken to ensure regeneration of the woodland after clear cutting. In relation to the selection system, the existence of the *saltuarii* is seen as an indication for the application of this system. Furthermore, the choice of certain trees to build a bridge in the fourth century seems to indicate selection, although selection for use does not necessarily imply the application of the selection system. Coppicing is certainly the system for which the most evidence has been found; both the historical sources and several dendrochronological studies point to the application of this system. Based on historical sources it can be argued that agro-forestry was applied during the Roman period.

Cultural Heritage Agency Amersfoort / Archaeological Centre VU University Amsterdam

Acknowledgements

Special thanks to Jos Bazelmans, Anja Fischer, Esther Jansma, Yardeni Vorst and the anonymous reviewers for their helpful comments and suggestions. Access to the Dutch dendrochronological material was kindly granted by Esther Jansma of Stichting RING. My research project is part of a larger research programme, *Arts and Crafts in Roman Shipbuilding*, and is generously funded by the Netherlands Organisation for Scientific Research (NWO) (see http://www.onderzoekinformatie.nl/en/oi/nod/onderzoek/OND1325276/). Finally, I would also like to thank the editors and the organizers of TRAC 2009 for their valuable comments, for organizing TRAC 2009 and making this publication possible.

Bibliography

Ancient sources

Caesar (translated by A.G. Peskett 1914). *Commentarii de bello civili*, Cambridge, Mass.: Harvard University Press.

Columella (translated by E.S. Forstner and E.H. Heffner 1955). *De arboribus*. Cambridge, Mass.: Harvard University Press.

Columella (translated by H.B. Ash, 1941). *De Re Rustica, Libri I–IV*. Cambridge, Mass.: Harvard University Press.

Columella (translated by E.S. Forstner and E.H. Heffner 1954). *De Re Rustica, Libri V*–IX. Cambridge, Mass.: Harvard University Press.

Columella (translated by E.S. Forstner and E.H. Heffner 1955), *De Re Rustica, Libri X–XII*. Cambridge, Mass.: Harvard University Press.

Cato (translated by H.B. Ash/W.D. Hooper 1934). *De agri cultura*. Cambridge, Mass.: Harvard University Press.

Titus Livius (translated by E.T. Sage 1935). *Ab Urbe condita*. Cambridge, Mass.: Harvard University Press.

Pliny Maior (translated by J. Van Gelder, M. Nieuwenhuis and T. Peters, 2004). *Naturalis Historia*. Amsterdam: Athenaeum/Polak & Van Gennep.

Theophrastus (translated by A.F. Hort 1916). *Historia Plantarum*. Cambridge, Mass.: Harvard University Press.

Varro (translated by H.B. Ash and W.D. Hooper 1934). *Rerum Rusticarum*, Cambridge, Mass.: Harvard University Press.

Virgil (translated by H.R. Fairclough and G.P Gould 1916). *Georgica*. Cambridge, Mass.: Harvard University Press.

Vitruvius (translated by F. Granger 1931). *De Architectura*. Cambridge, Mass.: Harvard University Press.

Modern sources

Aitchison, K. 1999. Monumental architecture & becoming Roman in the first centuries BC and AD. In P. Baker, C. Forcey, S. Jundi and J. Witcher (eds.) *TRAC 1998: Proceedings of the Eighth Annual Theoretical Roman Archaeology Conference Leicester 1998.* Oxford: Oxbow Books: 24–33.

Anderson, M. 2005. Houses, GIS and the microtopology of Pompeian domestic space. In J. Bruhn, B. Croxford and D. Grigoropoulos (eds.) *TRAC 2004: Proceedings of the Fourteenth Annual Theoretical Roman Archaeology Conference Durham 2004.* Oxford: Oxbow Books: 144–156.

Bernard, V. 2003. Stratégie d'approvisionnement en bois en Gaulle du nord-ouest (du Ier siècle après J.-C). *Revue archeologique de Picardie* 2003: 77–86.

Carroll, M. 2001. *Romans, Celts and Germans: The German Provinces of Rome.* Stroud: Tempus Publishing.

Driessen, M. 2005. Unifying aspects of Roman forts. In J. Bruhn, B. Croxford and D. Grigoropoulos (eds.) *TRAC 2004: Proceedings of the Fourteenth Annual Theoretical Roman Archaeology Conference Durham 2004.* Oxford: Oxbow Books: 157–162.

Enckevort, H. van. 2001. Bemerkungen zum Besiedlungssystem in den südöstlichen Niederlanden während der späten vorrömischen Eisenzeit und der römischen Kaiserzeit. In T. Grünewald and H.J. Schalles (eds.) *Germania Inferior. Besiedlung, Gesellschaft und Wirtschaft an der Grenze der römisch-germanischen Welt.* Reallexikon der germanischen Altertumskunde Ergänzungsband 28. Berlin: Walter de Gruyter: 336–396.

Enckevort, H. van, Haalebos, J.K. and Thijssen, J. 2000. *Nijmegen : legerplaats en stad in het achterland van de Romeinse limes*. Archeologische Berichten Nijmegen 3. Abcoude: Uniepers.

Finley, M. 1973. *The Ancient Economy.* London: University of California Press.

Goudswaard, B., Kroes, R.A.C. and van der Beek, H.S.M. 2001. The Late Roman Bridge at Cuijk, *Berichten van de Rijksdienst voor het Oudheidkundig Bodemonderzoek* 44: 439–560.

Greene, K. 2000. Technological Innovation and Economic Progress in the Ancient World: M.I. Finley Re-Considered. *The Economic History Review* 53(1): 29–59.

Groenman-van Waateringe, W. 1983. The disastrous effect of the Roman occupation. In R. Brandt and J. Slofstra (eds.) *Roman and native in the Low Countries : spheres of interaction.* BAR International series 184. Oxford: Archaeopress.

Haneca, K., van Acker, J. and Beeckman, H. 2005. Growth trends reveal the forest structure during Roman and Medieval times in Western Europe: a comparison between archaeological and actual oak ring series (Quercus robur and Quercus petraea). *Annals of Forest Science* 62: 797–805.

Hanson, W.S. 1978. The Organisation of Roman Military Timber-Supply. *Britannia* 9: 293–305.

Heidinga, H.A. and Offenberg, G.A.M. 1992. *Op zoek naar de vijfde eeuw – de Franken tussen Rijn en Maas.* Amsterdam: De Bataafsche Leeuw.

Honigmann, E. 1926. Libanos, *Paulys Realencyclopädie der classischen Altertumswissenschaft.* Stuttgart: Alfred Druckenmüller Verlag: 1–13.

Jansma, E. 1995. *RemembeRINGs; The development and application of local and regional tree-ring chronologies of oak for the purposes of archaeological and historical research in the Netherlands.* Nederlandse Archeologische Rapporten 19. Amersfoort: Rijksdienst voor het Oudheidkundig Bodemonderzoek.

Kainulainen, P. 2009. From the Heaven of my Heart. In Amorphis (ed.) *Skyforger.* Helsinki: King Foo Entertainment Ltd: 3.

Kerr, L. 2002. A topography of death: the buildings of emperor Maxentius on the Via Appia , Rome. In M. Carruthers, C. van Driel-Murray, A. Gardner, J. Lucas, L. Revell and E. Swift (eds.) *TRAC 2001: Proceedings of the Eleventh Annual Theoretical Roman Archaeology Conference Glasgow 2001.* Oxford: Oxbow Books: 24–33.

Leeuw, S. van der and Vries, B. de 2003. Empire: the Romans and the Mediterranean. In B. de Vries and J. Goudsblom (eds.) *Mappae Mundi. Humans and their Habitats in a Long-Term Socio-Ecological Perspective Myths, Maps and Models*. Amsterdam: Amsterdam University Press: 209–256.

Makkonen, O. 1967. *Ancient forestry. An historical study. Part I. Facts and information on trees.* Acta Forestalia Fennica 82. Helsinki: Akateeminen Kirjakauppa.

Malmberg, S. 2009. Finding your way in the Subura. In M. Driessen, S. Heeren, J. Hendriks, F. Kemmers and R. Visser (eds.) *TRAC 2008: Proceedings of the Eighteenth Annual Theoretical Roman Archaeology Conference, Amsterdam 2008.* Oxford: Oxbow Books: 39–51.

Matthews, J.D. 1989. *Silvicultural Systems*. Oxford: Clarendon Press (Oxford Science Publications).

Meiggs, R. 1982. *Trees and Timber in the Ancient Mediterranean World.* Oxford: Oxford University Press.

Mickwitz, G. 1937. Economic Rationalism in Graeco-Roman Agriculture. *The English Historical Review* 52(208): 577–589.

Nenninger, M. 2001. *Die Römer und der Wald. Untersuchungen zum Umgang mit einem Naturraum am Beispiel der römischen Nordwestprovinzen*. Geographica Historica 16. Stuttgart: Franz Steiner Verlag.

Rackham, O. 1977. Neolithic woodland management in the Somerset Levels: Garvin's, Walton Heath, and Rowland's tracks. *Somerset Levels Papers* 3: 65–71.

Roller, O. 1986. Zu den Axtdarstellungen auf den Förstergrabsteinen von der Heidelsburg bei Waldfischbach. *Mitteilungen des historischen Vereins der Pfalz* 84: 59–72.

Rostovtzeff, M.I. 1957. *The Social and Economic History of the Roman Empire.* Oxford: Clarendon Press.

Rostowzew, M. 1904. Die Domänenpolizei in dem römischen Kaiserreiche. *Philologus* 64: 297–307.

Rüger, C. 1968. *Germania Inferior: Untersuchungen zur Territorial- und Verwaltungsgeschichte Niedergermaniens in der Prinzipatszeit*. Bonner Jahrbücher; Beiheft 30. Köln: Böhlau Verlag.

Sprater, F. 1929. *Die Pfalz unter den Römern. Zugleich Führer durch die römische Abteilung des historischen Museums der Pfalz*, Speyer am Rhein: Pfälzische Gesellschaft zur Förderung der Wissenschaften.

Sprater, F. 1950. Deutschlands Ältestes Forstamt. *Forstwissenschaftliches Zentralblatt* 69(7): 421–426.

Stalibrass, S. and Thomas, R. (eds.). 2008. *Feeding the Roman Army.* Oxford: Oxbow Books.

Visser, R.M. In prep. *Roman trees, woods and timbers. Dendrochronological and archaeological research on the Roman wood and timber economy in the Lower Rhine area.* PhD thesis. Amsterdam: Amsterdam VU University.

Visser, R.M. and Jansma, E. 2009. Dendrochronologische analyse van het hout van de limesweg te Leidsche Rijn. In J. S. van der Kamp (ed.) *Werk aan de weg. LR 31 Zandweg: Archeologisch onderzoek aan een verspoelde sectie van de limesweg.* Basisrapportage Archeologie 21. Utrecht: Cultuurhistorie Gemeente Utrecht: 77–87.

Woolf, G. 2001. Regional productions in early Roman Gaul. In D.J. Mattingly and J. Salmon (eds.) *Economies Beyond Agriculture in the Classical World.* Leicester-Nottingham Studies in Ancient Society 9. London and New York: Routledge: 49–65.

No Place Like Stone? Assessing Social and Material Networks of Place at Quarries in Roman Anatolia

Bradley M. Sekedat

Introduction

This paper originated from a moment of haphazard discovery, a chance encounter. While visiting a site called Fasıllar in the province of Konya in south central Turkey, the aspect of the site I was initially aware of – a massive basalt rock carving dating to the Late Bronze Age lying flat on its back – became part of much broader network of social and material interactions at the site. Walking across the site, I encountered Bronze Age carvings next to Classical carvings, such as the Lucianus monument, with a life-size horse standing to the right of an open and inscribed niche, and unfinished Roman sarcophagi next to cut marks in the abundant rock outcrops that appearance would date to multiple periods in the past. Conceptually, the site, for me, began as a monumental Hittite location, but quickly took on many more attributes. Fasıllar was quarried extensively in antiquity, bringing practices from different periods in time together in the material of the site itself (Waelkens 1990). Even more significantly for this paper, Fasıllar and other Anatolian quarries offer evidence of the ways in which quarries bring together different practices. The unfinished sarcophagi that dot the plateau above the northern slope of Fasıllar suggest that material cut here was *moved*, and apparently over great distances, even though the specific destination of the stone is not always knowable. Because of this, it is difficult to assign to Fasıllar any sense of an overarching authority under which the stonecutters operated. Quarries are not just resources for other places; they are not separate entities within a landscape, but are, rather, an integrated part of a broad network within landscapes. Quarries expand well beyond their immediate scopes, as the evidence of unfinished Roman sarcophagi, which were transported widely, suggests.

In light of these encounters at one quarry site in central Anatolia, I will use this paper to explore the ways that quarries expose numerous social and material networks. Such an undertaking entails a discussion on the state of quarry studies, evaluating what they emphasize, how quarries are generally studied, and where there are areas for expansion and improvement. Using case studies of three quarries that operated on different scales in central Anatolia, this paper suggests that a more complete understanding of quarries can be gained by considering them within the context of theories of place and materiality, inserting into the equation notions of what happens at quarries, how the social and material networks that arise at them influence what goes on at a broader level, and how these networks necessitate a reconsideration of the role of quarries in the development and maintenance of large-scale institutions such as the Roman Empire. Ultimately, this paper suggests that quarry studies should integrate the existing emphasis on function, technique and economy at quarries with notions of place.

The State of Quarry Studies

For most of the Mediterranean world, scholars who study quarries have privileged certain factors that are readily associated with them. This falls primarily upon, though is not necessarily limited to, functional approaches that consider quarries as resources that are exploited for specific purposes. In the case of the Roman Empire, this generally revolves around the notion of quarries as resources for construction projects and sculptural programs that enter into frameworks of elite display, imperial benefaction and cultural value. To this end, scholars focus their efforts on studies that source building materials, with the aim of developing a picture of circum-Mediterranean trade patterns in stone. Questions include the degree to which stone resources were controlled by Roman authorities, the scale of extraction at known sources, and the levels of economic dependence between urban centres and quarries. How widely were materials travelling and who controlled that trade? In this model, issues such as the value of stone and its subsequent extraction follow as a secondary condition to ideologically driven efforts to procure such materials. In this vein, Roman social values precede the practices that actually go into the quarrying of stone, so that the choice of stone, and efforts to control stone sources, were determined by such pre-existing social structures. The work at quarries is thus understood as functional, in that it served other geographical needs, which were themselves perceived to be of greater importance than the practices that went into material procurement, or at least that shaped the structures of material procurement. This hierarchy of thought and practice is noticeable with even a cursory look at what is emphasized in the publications on quarries.

Of note is that most of the literature on quarries focuses on the large-scale and imperially controlled sources, though it is not uniformly limited to this. Studies of this type in Anatolia include the quarries at Docimium, Haut-Tembris, Ezine, Teos and Marmara; although work has been done on many others, these often do not appear in publications. Quarries that were not imperial owned, yet which have received significant attention due in large part to their role in the construction of major urban centres, include the quarries outside of cities such as Aphrodisias (Rockwell 1992; Ponti 1992). Binding these studies together is the strong emphasis that scholars place on understanding how broader patterns of administration relate to extraction at these sites. Thus, much of the scholarship on these quarries focuses on evidence for the hierarchy and standardization of stonecutting practices, and on evidence that pertains to the quarry's administration, such as that offered by inscriptions (see especially Fant 1989a). Efforts are also made to link the stones found in urban structures with these practices of extraction, which highlights the functional role that quarries play in construction projects located elsewhere, such as Fant's study of the Teos marble quarries (Fant 1988). Here, literary references to the amount of Teos marble used in imperial construction are used to support the apparently small size of the quarries themselves, which Fant (1989b: 212–213, 217) used to argue for minimal interaction between the city of Teos and the quarries in its immediate vicinity. In other words, the question is framed in the following sequence: how do the desires of those in charge of constructing the city play out in practices at the quarry, and what evidence do we have for this? Fant (1993), who wrote extensively about the quarries at Docimium, placed this sequence of investigation into the broader context of Roman economic practices writ large, and particularly those that were driven by imperial demand. The standardization of practices was taken to stand in for broad patterns of economic activity and control. The effect is that quarries are reduced to resources that are subservient to other social mechanisms whose roots are inevitably located at a distance. The specifics of the quarry lose ground to broad social and economic patterns.

Good examples of this are the studies done by Waelkens (1985; 1990) and Fant (1989a) at the Docimium quarries in Phrygia. Waelkens, who Fant draws upon, delivered a picture of the quarries that neatly aligned with the view of site-specific practices within broad social and economic frameworks. While both authors note that Docimium was likely used as a quarry during the pre-Roman period, their interest in the quarries there largely revolved around documenting the scale of extraction, the tools used in the extraction process, and why technologies and policies changed over time. In this vein, Waelkens (1990: 63) noted that 500,000 cubic metres of stone were removed from the various extraction *bracchia* (branches or arms of the quarry) during the Roman imperial period. Furthermore, there was a marked change in the scale of production at the site over time. Waelkens (1990) discussed the significant transformation of quarry practices that occurred once Docimium was brought under some form of direct imperial authority during the Augustan period, and proceeded to note changes in the scale, location and tools of extraction along a documented chronological and historical trajectory. Much of this information was gathered through intensive investigation of the site for changes in cut marks and in the size of the blocks cut. These lines of evidence indicated changes in the modes of resource procurement to both Waelkens and Fant. Different marks, for instance, showed that different tools and techniques were in place at various points in time, with the evidence literally etched into the extant stone. What is particularly interesting, at least for this paper, is the overarching explanation that Waelkens and Fant used to interpret the causes of these changes: these two scholars both pointed to different forms of evidence to link these quarrying practices to changes in demand produced by the flourishing economic conditions of the principate and imperial periods at Docimium. Waelkens (1985), in particular, was able to develop a picture of Docimium's multiple quarries, and their associated workshops, as being elaborately controlled from a centralized point.

Waelkens (1990) noted that, in addition to evidence for changes in tool use, the size of the blocks that were cut indicated changes in demand from imperial centres, notably Rome, where numerous monuments used the *pavonazzetto* marble for architectural adornment, especially in the late first and early second centuries A.D. He situated this change within the sporadic impulses that characterized imperial needs. During periods of large-scale building campaigns, certain quarries were exploited more intensively than others, depending on the needs of the state. As architectural styles and influences changed, so too did the shape and size of cut stones, which also had an impact on the stone extraction process. Indeed, it was possible in some instances to recognize different chronological phases of quarrying (Fant 1989a). The demands of the state are also shown by Waelkens (1990) as a reason for technological change: as demand for more marble from Docimium grew, workers had to modify the means of extraction. This resulted in a shift from smaller, lighter pickaxes to a heavier pickaxe that could more readily cut the stone. In these accounts, the quarries at Docimium simply respond to outside needs. My point of contention is not with the efforts to tie specific extraction phases to historical and economic trends. Rather, the issue becomes significant when we stop there. Explaining the quarry in terms of broader developments diminishes our ability to explain the significance of the quarry as a place in its own terms, with actions occurring that are not dependent on state level demands.

Fant (1989a), who commented on Waelkens's earlier work on Docimium, took a similar position on the hierarchy of activities that occurred there, but reached this conclusion by following the inscribed record rather than the evidence for stonecutting. Fant provided an extensive list of recorded examples of stone inscribing that occurred during the extraction process, summarized within three general categories for all of the markings he found during 4 two-week seasons of surveying the Docimium quarries. Briefly, the markings recorded several important aspects of the quarrying process, including the 'slave' who cut the stone, the *bracchium* (region) within the quarry in which the stone was cut, levels of administration at the quarry, and the consular date. Fant was able to discern a change in what was recorded on the cut blocks over time, which enabled him to postulate that the quarry underwent a process of standardization and monopolization. In the imperial context articulated through the inscriptions, Fant (1993: 146, 155) argued, the workers, their techniques, and their modes of recording became highly regulated and subject to the whim of an imperial monopoly.

Quarries near urban centres such as Aphrodisias, though smaller in scale, are discussed similarly in the scholarship on ancient stonecutting. In this case, however, the discussion turns more explicitly to how quarries are defined and perceived. As with much of the original work done for the Docimium quarries, the quarries in the immediate proximity of Aphrodisias are described in terms of their geological condition, orientation and material characteristics, although more complete publication of the recent quarry survey at Aphrodisias could add to this (Ponti 1992; Rockwell 1992). There has been some discussion of the proximity of these quarries to the urban centre, but the interplay between these locations has not been discussed. Instead, the quarry is situated in the literature as something distinct, something isolated and something self contained. The surveyors at Aphrodisias, in discussing where discard piles are placed, locate this feature as something outside of the quarry. This speaks to a general consensus that quarries are to be considered for their functional attributes. Under this definition, a quarry is merely a stone resource.

Potential Ways Forward

As in other areas of archaeology, such as pedestrian survey of ploughsoil assemblages, this definition raises the question of how to define boundaries. In the case of quarries, challenges to the functional definition are easily raised, particularly when one accounts for the broad array of practices related to the initial step of stonecutting. Multiple stages of operation are attested for the quarries at Marmara and Docimium, for instance, where some of the finishing steps were done very near to the locations where the stone was initially cut. As Waelkens (1990; Waelkens *et al.* 1988) pointed out, tools and their production are related to quarrying. So too are the markings and changes brought to a quarry as the result of long-term or intermittent use over many years. Every act of stone extraction physically alters the terrain of the quarry. But the association of networks that is being developed here can be extended to things such as discard piles, areas of primary cutting and secondary cutting, finishing workshops, the pathways on which quarried stones were carried, and the locations at which the cut materials arrived. Therefore, a quarry is not so easily defined when one begins to trace the depth of interrelationships at work in any given situation.

Also of significance here is the awareness that not all Anatolian quarries in the Roman period were subject to the same levels of oversight and control as the grand imperial quarries. It is critical not to lose sight of the variety of quarrying that occurred in Anatolia and other regions. As above, Waelkens (1985) and Fant (1989a) both mentioned the existence of a town near Docimium. Fant (1989a: 4) suggested that the quarry workers probably lived in the town, commuting daily to the site for work. In this instance, it is possible to expand a network of quarrying-related practices to the towns as well, since activity within the town was, in certain ways, related to activity at the quarries. For example, roads were built or paths created that led to and from towns. Workshops were sometimes located within the towns close to, but away from, the actual source of the material. In small-scale, more opportunistically situated, quarries, such as that of Fasıllar mentioned at the beginning of the paper, the practices related to quarrying took the material well beyond the confines of the source, implicating the quarrying of particular blocks in numerous non-functional associations. Local populations were involved in extraction, carrying some of their social networks between the settlements and the quarries.

Furthermore, quarries, because they are places of social and material interaction, often exhibit construction for the temporary populations that live at them. Sanctuaries and temples, for instance, were constructed at quarries in Egypt (Rothenberg 1988). This intersection of stone source, materials from related industries, and social interaction blurs the line between the quarry (as a strictly defined and bounded thing) and the extended networks within which stone circulates. The point is not that all of these points in the network were quarries, but that all of them were involved in the process of quarrying on some level, in terms of labour, community formation, tool manufacture, distribution, consumption, etc. In this sense, exactly what a quarry was depended on the kinds of associations that developed in synchronicity with it.

This, then, brings me to the crux of this paper. Having outlined some general observations about quarry studies in Anatolia, it appears that there are several ways to enhance and expand quarry studies. The position advocated here is that an understanding of the networks that quarries comprise, including the development and running of something as large as imperial Rome, brings quarries into fruitful discussions of 'place' and reinserts a sense of quarries as significant for reasons beyond their functional roles. What follows expands upon what is meant by this.

Edward Casey (2001: 406), a prominent theorist on the issue of 'place', argues that:

> '[A]ny effort to assess the relationship between self and place should point not just to reciprocal influence (that much any ecologically sensitive account would maintain) but, more radically, to constitutive co-ingredience: each is essential to the being of the other.'

Casey is, in essence, arguing that actions in a location are predetermined by neither the human agent nor the location itself. Rather, the form, meaning and essence of a location is derived from the mutual actions of agents and terrain. This provides an exciting metaphor for work on quarries precisely because quarries are, in all of their forms and varieties, changing aspects of the landscape by means of a complicated and co-constitutive mechanism of human/material relationships.

This is best seen when we consider the long-term use of quarries. Again, in the case of Docimium, Aphrodisias and Fasıllar, there is abundant evidence of long-term, if intermittent, extraction. For Docimium in particular, the cut marks on the rock and the evidence for tunnelling in different *bracchia* of the quarry, sometimes returning to long abandoned positions after many years, were explained as the product of changing social and economic values that arose due to an imperial monopoly. A place-based perspective, however, can add to these apparent links between small-scale practices and large-scale processes in significant ways. All of the quarries discussed in this paper have long histories of extraction. Extraction changes the physical or material composition of the site. Therefore, rather than simply thinking about new economic motivations as the impulse for changing actions at quarries, a stronger sense of what a quarry is would incorporate the impact that changes to the landscape in the past had on the nature of later quarry interactions. In this sense, quarries are multi-temporal in that they comprise the actions, in many cases, of the very long-term: the traces of actions from multiple pasts are simultaneously present, each having equal impact on present interactions with the landscape. The material of the quarry, therefore, does not lend itself neatly to a chronological or historical arrangement based on the archaeologist's interaction with the site.

Furthermore, quarries lend themselves to issues of place through the notion of movement. Materials for stonecutting and extraction converge at quarries, and the products or outcomes of cutting practices are often distributed. Quarries and quarrying quite literally inhere in motion and movement, a notion that blends quite nicely with the approach to 'place' that Tim Ingold (1993; 2007) advocates. Notably, Ingold notes that any given points A and B (like quarry A and city B, for example) are reached through movement between them and within them. Moreover, they bring together the movement of a multiplicity of materials and people as they intersect in particular locations, or places. Thus places comprise movement. Quarries speak of this flow very effectively, suggesting that a productive way to think about them is to regard them as intricately connected regionally through the movement of people and materials, instead of isolating them from their surroundings, which necessitates a regional approach. For the Teos quarries, Fant (1989b: 213) argues that the extraction process was so thoroughly driven by Roman imperial needs that the scale of operations remained small and the quarries were effectively isolated from neighbouring communities. This may hold true from an economic perspective, in the sense that the communities around the city of Teos were not entirely dependent on quarrying for their livelihood, but it does not account for the quarry as place. It reduces quarries to specific kinds of site interactions rather than questioning the kinds of movement that coalesce around them. It effectively reduces their significance as locations.

Recent studies that incorporate network analysis provide useful insights into the high degree of connectivity between people and locations, many of which pertain directly to the movement of industrial goods. Ruffini's (2008; Graham and Ruffini 2007) work on Byzantine Egypt, for example, showed that hierarchical models for social interaction need to be reconfigured. In summary, the scale of human interaction across socio-economic boundaries was shown through network analysis of papyri to be unexpectedly high. Similarly, Graham (Graham and Ruffini 2007) performed social network analysis on Italian brick stamps, revealing some of the complexity inherent in the trade and movement of industrially produced goods. Studies like these indicate a variability and extent to social networks that force us to think beyond straightforward organizational control of something like brick stamp production and, by extension, quarries. Looking at combinations of *material* networks may prove a fruitful way of expanding such analyses. Thus, with respect to quarries, we may be able to think about the human networks involved – who worked at the quarries, who purchased stone and who was involved in the movement of stone – but we may also begin to think about what other materials were required for stonecutting and transport, what the geographic origins of other architectural and decorative elements were at the point of destination, and how all of this, the human and material, comes together. The quarry, it is argued, does not exist prior to these networks; rather, multiple kinds of quarries emerge from the different combinations of networks.

Building from the notion that quarrying in the Roman Empire took a variety of forms enables a final commentary on one of the issues outlined at the beginning of the paper – instead of considering quarry practices as dependent on the Roman Empire, quarries participated in the kinds of networks that define what the Roman Empire was. The opportunistic use of limestone outcrops all over Anatolia during the Roman period, for instance, suggests that one overarching model of stone interaction does not apply across the board. Instead, the Empire and the social and economic principles that characterized it developed out of a complex interaction between locations and actions. The imperial models that comprise Rome were possible because of interactions on the local level. Rather than Rome dictating new forms and new structures that affected stonecutting, work with stone and the varieties of stone that exist in a place as geologically rich as Anatolia should be regarded as having helped to constitute the structures of the Empire. The long-term trends that are present at many quarries go a long way towards revealing this. The structures and practices were seldom entirely new, but related to the long-term history of a location, and the durability of the traces of past action. From a place-based view, the fact that quarries inherently involve continuous reshaping of the physical terrain, with which subsequent communities must interact, suggests that Roman stonecutting dealt intimately with local knowledge, craft specialization that had developed over great lengths of time, and networks of local communities. An imperial endeavour at Docimium, for instance, was not free of other structures, but related to them in a multitude of ways.

Conclusion

By way of conclusion, I would like to point out that this paper has been, in many ways, a position piece. The position taken has derived from an examination of how quarry studies have developed in general and from looking at how this can be bolstered, or undertaken, differently. A place-based approach, as discussed here, does not imply that it is unimportant to understand broad social, historical, political and economic processes with regard to specific quarries and the processes that went on at them. Rather, it is suggested here that such studies can work to reinsert a stronger role for quarries in the production of these large-scale processes if some of our attention is turned to the vast networks of interaction that occurred at and around them. Quarries then become much richer places, with deep histories and complexities that transcend economics through the diversity of their material qualities. Looking at quarries as integral to social formation, rather than as secondary to pre-existing social structures, provides a new avenue for research in this important aspect of Roman, and indeed all periods of, Anatolia.

Joukowsky Institute for Archaeology and the Ancient World, Brown University

Bibliography

Casey, E.S. 2001. Body, self, and landscape: a geophilosophical inquiry into the place-world. In P.C. Adams, S. Hoelscher and K.E. Till (eds.) *Textures of Place: Exploring Humanist Geographies*. Minneapolis: University of Minnesota Press: 403–425.

Fant, J.C. 1988. The Roman emperors in the marble business: capitalists, middlemen or philanthropists? In N. Herz and M. Waelkens (eds.) *Classical Marble: Geochemistry, Technology, Trade*. Boston: Kluwer Academic Publishers: 147–158.

Fant, J.C. 1989a. *Cavum Antrum Phrygiae: The Organization and Operations of the Roman Imperial Marble Quarries in Phrygia*. British Archaeological Reports International Series 482. Oxford: British Archaeological Reports.

Fant, J.C. 1989b. *Poikiloi Lithoi:* the anomalous economics of the Roman imperial marble quarry at Teos. In S. Walker and A. Cameron (eds.) *The Greek Renaissance in the Roman Empire: Papers from the Tenth British Museum Classical Colloquium*. University of London Institute of Classical Studies Bulletin Supplement 55. London: Institute of Classical Studies: 206–217.

Fant, J.C. 1993. Ideology, gift, and trade: a distribution model for the Roman imperial marbles. In W.V. Harris (ed.) *The Inscribed Economy: Production and Distribution in the Roman Empire in the Light of Instrumentum Domesticum*. Journal of Roman Archaeology Supplementary Series 6. Ann Arbor: Journal of Roman Archaeology: 145–170.

Graham, S. and Ruffini, G.R. 2007. Network analysis and Greco-Roman prosopography. In K.S.B. Keats-Rohan (ed.) *Prosopography Approaches and Applications: A Handbook*. Oxford: Unit for Prosopographical Research, Lineacre College: 325–336.

Ingold, T. 1993. The temporality of landscapes. *World Archaeology* 25(2): 152–174.

Ingold, T. 2007. *Lines: A Brief History*. London/New York: Routledge.

Ponti, G. 1992. Ancient quarrying at Aphrodisias in the light of the geological configuration. In C. Roueché and R.R.R. Smith (eds.) *Aphrodisias Papers 3: The Setting and Quarries, Mythological and*

Other Sculptural Decoration, Architectural Development, Portico of Tiberius, and Tetrapylon. Journal of Roman Archaeology Supplementary Series 20. Ann Arbor: Journal of Roman Archaeology: 105–110.

Rockwell, P. 1992. The marble quarries: a preliminary survey. In C. Roueché and R.R.R. Smith (eds.) *Aphrodisias Papers 3: The Setting and Quarries, Mythological and Other Sculptural Decoration, Architectural Development, Portico of Tiberius, and Tetrapylon.* Ann Arbor: Journal of Roman Archaeology Supplementary Series 20: 81–103.

Rothenberg, B. 1988. *The Egyptian Mining Temple at Timna.* London: Institute for Archaeometallurgical Studies.

Ruffini, G.R. 2008. *Social Networks in Byzantine Egypt.* Cambridge/New York: Cambridge University Press.

Waelkens, M. 1985. From a Phrygian quarry: the provenance of the statues of the Dacian Prisoners in Trajan's Forum at Rome. *American Journal of Archaeology* 89: 641–653.

Waelkens, M. 1990. Technique de carrière, préfaçonnage et ateliers dans les civilizations classiques (mondes grec et romain). In M. Waelkens (ed.) *Pierre Éternelle du Nil au Rhin: Carrières et Préfabrication.* Bruxelles: Crédit Communal: 53–72.

Waelkens, M., de Paepe, P. and Moens, L. 1988. Quarries and the marble trade in antiquity. In N. Herz and M. Waelkens (eds.) *Classical Marble: Geochemistry, Technology, Trade.* Boston: Kluwer Academic Publishers: 11–28.

The Herculaneum Amazon: Sculptural Polychromy, Digital Simulation and Context

Gareth Beale and Graeme Earl

Introduction

The research introduced in this paper and which forms the background to the ongoing Herculaneum Amazon project seeks to build upon ongoing work in the area of sculptural polychromy and on the simulation and analysis of sculpture in context (Happa *et al. in press*; Happa *et a.l* 2009 Earl *et al.* 2009; Earl *in press*; AmazonWeb 2009). It is focussed on creating computer-based, virtual rather than physical representations of Roman statues in simulated Roman environments. In occupying a virtual, as opposed to actual space, these reconstructions not only provide physically accurate simulations of statues but also inform considerations of space, light and sculptural polychromy that relate to environments that no longer exist and which would be difficult or impossible to recreate. Specifically, by moving into the virtual it becomes possible to contextualise – to begin to consider the ways in which environments influence the visual qualities of polychrome statuary and to consider the implications of context on the ways in which the objects may have been lit. The use of virtual objects and virtual environments provides an unrivalled opportunity for experimentation and plurality. But it has only been with the recent advent of computer algorithms derived for the film and entertainment industries, including specifically physically accurate lighting models and surface materials, that work of this type has been possible. This paper will discuss recent attempts to produce physical replicas of sculptural polychromy, consider the changing status of polychromy in the study of Roman statues, and identify the potential for digital modes of sculpting and repainting the past. This paper concentrates on marble statues and, in particular, on the Amazon discovered in the Basilica Noniana at Herculaneum (Fig. 1). However, the arguments presented here are, in many aspects, equally relevant to the study of bronze and to polychrome statuary from across the Roman world.

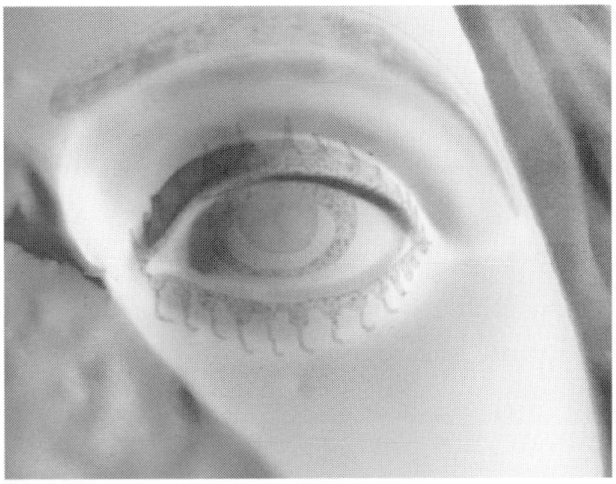

Figure 1: A virtual simulation of the Amazon head discovered at Herculaneum in 2006 (© Gareth Beale ACRG).

Visualising statues

We are used in archaeology to interpreting subtle changes in human intentionality over time. Whether carefully excavating the layers of a midden looking for changes in patterns of disposal or untangling complex urban architecture, the essence of archaeology lies in observing and constructing the changing nature of human interaction with the material world. Some of the most compelling examples of human intentionality made material can be found amongst the canon of surviving Roman statuary. These bold statements in marble frequently bear the scars of centuries of reinvention and rediscovery. In spite of this, the tendency for many years was to view the Roman statue as static, unyielding and pristine. All too often the viewer was encouraged to think in terms of ancient survivals that came into existence at the moment the chisel was put down and which found their way to us unchanged but for the wear and tear of millennia. But of course such statues have changed, as people have changed around them. The creation of the discipline of Classical Art History and subsequent definitions of lexica and modes of thinking about classical art communicated a specific range of conceptualisations of Roman statuary, conceptualisations rooted not in the Roman past but in the modern world (Stewart 2003; Østergaard 2008).

In order to develop insightful methods of considering the meanings which have shaped Roman statuary it is necessary to acknowledge our distance from the act of creation and to accept that we can only have a limited concept of the original meaning of statuary without an attempt to untangle the nexus of social, personal and inter-personal contexts that resulted in their creation and re-invention. Statues, then, are not miraculously preserved leftovers from a world which has long gone, but rather contemporary objects which have been subject to, and are records of, the interpretations and decisions of all who have come into contact with them. We argue that the creation of digital surrogates to these statues is therefore a further continuation in their life history.

If we are to begin to think about Roman statuary in these terms then it is imperative that we consider the significance of colour. Despite a traditional disinterest amongst scholars, the fact that a great deal of Roman marble statuary was artificially coloured has not only been recognised but has become the focus of research across a range of disciplines (e.g. Østergaard 2008; Elsner 2007; Bradley 2009; Potts 2008). Whilst rejecting a conceptualisation of the statue as a static object, the fact remains that marble is more hardy and stable than the painted and treated surfaces which might have adorned its surface. Developments in the study of sculptural polychromy therefore provide a window into a potentially more fluid component to a statue's life history. In turn we may consider the acts of visual perception informing the creators, from the sculptor to the painter, and all of those who engaged with and, as such, helped to form these objects.

Visualisations of various kinds have been employed by scholars for as long as polychrome statuary has been an object of study. These visualisations have taken a number of forms, including early attempts at the recreation of coloured examples such as Gibson's Tinted Venus, first displayed at the London International Exhibition of 1862 (Bradley 2009). Other examples have included the coloured engravings of Augustus from Prima Porta created by Georg Treu for Ludwig Fenger's (1886) volume *Dorische Polychromie*. A more recent work of coloured illustration can be found in Reutersward's (1960) volume *Studien zur Polychromie der Plastik: Griechenland und Rom*. These volumes made a great contribution to the study of sculptural polychromy and can provide specific insights into evidence which has now been lost. However, in terms of illustrative technique there are several factors which limit the usefulness of these volumes. Neither Fenger nor Reuterswärd had access to technology which would allow them to record or accurately represent coloured pigments or surface finishes. As such these illustrations, and the literature accompanying them, may be understood and critiqued as illustrations rather than replicas.

More recent moves to represent sculptural polychromy have employed an approach that relates the visualisation more closely to imagined Roman originals, at least in terms of physical composition and application of paint. A series of pan-European collaborations (including contributions from the Copenhagen Glyptotek, Vatican Museum, Munich Glyptotek and others) have applied advanced scientific techniques to efficiently record and analyse a series of statues with polychrome components. They have used these data to reproduce the statues physically using chemically reconstructed pigment and statues. The greatest contribution of this work has been the demonstrably accurate reproduction of colour and surface, leading to high fidelity representations (Østergaard 2008; Liverani 2004). Together these lend the representations a scientific accountability which has, up until now, been absent. Perceptually based interpretations of sculptural polychromy in context can only develop from such physically-bounded surrogates.

Our virtual approach to sculptural polychromy builds on this body of physically-accurate recreation, and has the potential to provide additional benefits. Crucially, in the world of the virtual, sculptural ambiguities can be investigated at very little additional cost. One might create eight statues, all of which are identical apart from the composition or tint of the wax used to treat the surface of the marble.

Statues in a 'pristine' state

The widely held and, in the West, culturally engrained notion of the classical white statue has been addressed by a number of authors (e.g. Østergaard 2008; Brinkmann 2004; Liverani 2004; Bradley 2009; Elsner 2007; Stewart 2003). The issue of colour is of great interest not simply because it has the potential to change our perception of statuary but because it shines a light on the past of those disciplines which have had a hand in creating the notion of a pristine, monochrome canon. As such it may give insights as to how we should advance and how we might modify the ways in which we consider statuary.

The inception of monochrome as the norm for Roman statuary can be traced back to Winckelmann (Gordon 1979; Østergaard 2008; Holscher 2004). Gordon identifies the significance of Winckelmann in the creation of Classical Art History as a formalist discipline which sought to categorise and rationalise material rather than seek to understand the conditions of its creation. To Gordon, Winckelmann's influence serves to compartmentalise all that can be considered to be classical 'art' into a discrete category, equivalent to contemporary definitions of art and often subject to the same modes of criticism (Gordon 1979:5). Furthermore, according to Østergaard, it is this separateness which allowed Classical Art History to become permeated with "neo-classical notions of a monochrome aesthetic in classical sculpture" (Østergaard 2008: 40). Essentially then, we see classical sculpture drawn in to the modern, in terms of the language and ideas which infuse its study, its analysis and in terms of the buildings within which the statues were contained (Hingley 2000: 78). The extent to which Roman statuary can be seen to have been subsumed by modern aesthetic sensibilities is demonstrated effectively by the case of the Townley Discobolus. During the restoration of this statue the restorer opted to replace the head facing forward, rather than backwards toward the throwing arm, as would have been the case in the original (Beard and Henderson 2001: 88).

At a later date Vatican restorers judged this to be the superior interpretation and later statues were restored in the same fashion.

The effect of this process on academic discourse was that the statue became divorced from polychromy in the interpretive consciousness of all but a few who continued to study in this field. The extent to which this connection was severed can be seen in the reactions of those who come into contact with examples or representations of painted classical statuary. Reactions have varied from the "causing [of a] sensation" of Gibson's Tinted Venus (Bradley 2009), to hostility to the recent repainting of a replica of the statue of Augustus from Prima Porta (Østergaard 2008:40), to media excitement surrounding the opening of the recent *Gods in Colour* Exhibition (Gopnik 2008).

Wincklemann's impact then was to make the statue something at once iconic and homogeneous. As the colour was lost so were insights into what the statue meant as an individual object with a unique past. At the same time, the aesthetic concept of the statue in white marble took hold. In failing to consider the creative influence of the painter, and subsequent restorers, alterers and manipulators, the creative process had been reduced to a single discrete act. The sculptor became an artist communicating through the medium of sculpture, and the statue ceased to be something explicitly socially constructed and defined through its enagagement with viewers and modifiers. Rather than being a socially active object the statue became a piece of art with all of the prescribed modes of interpretation and engagement implied.

Contemporary attitudes towards classical statuary demonstrate the extent to which the role and nature of statuary has relied on the social world to define the conditions of its existence. As statues had roles and were active conveyors of meaning in the Roman world, equally they were ascribed a different function in modernity. However, it is the Roman world that we wish to study and we need to adopt positions in relation to the objects which interest us to take account of this. This realisation is outlined by Gordon in his 1979 article *The Real and the Imaginary.* He speaks out against the "fictitious problems" of formalist Classical Art History, as defined by Bandinelli, but goes on to reject the Marxist approach which Bandinelli proposed as a solution (Gordon 1979:6). The conclusion arrived at by Gordon is that we must abandon positivist attempts at reaching truth and objective classification and instead engage with the social worlds within which these objects were created.

If we are to move beyond modes of understanding and analyses which have their roots in inflexible formalism and essentially abstract modes of structuring knowledge of statuary then we need to propose alternative means of interrogating the available evidence. This process must begin with attempts to re-contextualise the object and to begin to think about statues not as containers of meaning but as records of intentionality. Hopkins (1985), Stewart (2003) and Revell (2009) have all conducted socially focussed studies of different aspects of Roman society which seek to incorporate and to account for the social role of statuary. A striking example of this approach can be found in Price's (1984) account of the role of the image of the emperor and the significance of objects bearing his likeness in the reinforcing of the Imperial cult.

Sculptural polychromy

To the popular gaze colourful painted statues are compelling and, as many authors have noted, they seem to imply an imitation of life that white marble statues do not (Owen 2006; Bonn-Muller 2008). Often these reactions can be seen not to have been to the presence of colour but rather to the absence of monochrome marble. It is the difference which is startling and not the nature of that difference. The power of polychromy to engender an apparent vitality in statues seems not only to be a feature of the contemporary world. Indeed, Stewart (2003) gives a detailed account of this process in relation to wall paintings in his discussion of the image of Mars in the House of the Venus Marina at Pompeii. The colouration and situation of the subject here clearly suggests a marble statue on a pedestal; yet the subject leans to the left, much further than would be possible for a statue, displaying the absence of any strut or support, and crucially, has defined eyes, differing little in style to a depiction of a person rather than a statue. (Stewart 2003: 40). Such work explores the relationship between statue and life. Furthermore, unlike the wall painting, what underlies the painted surface of a statue is a highly refined representation in itself. Rather than considering the paint as the medium which enlivens the inanimate statue we must think of the statue as a representative whole.

Clearly colour is more ephemeral, more subject to decay than marble, and as such polychromy implies transience. Whilst the underlying stone remains static the surface may change and alter over time, and with it the meaning and social function of the object. Bradley (2009) observes this process of change taking place on the statue of Augustus from Prima Porta where the statue was probably repainted using different colours and certainly restored and altered over time. Bradley describes the Emperor's representation as "organic, subjective and interactive" (Bradley 2009: 450).

Sculptural polychromy does not merely denote the application of paint to stone. The colour of any object is defined in part by the materials chosen, and also the way in which it is constructed, the light which renders it visible, and the space which it inhabits. Therefore the appearance of the statue will be defined as much by light and the colours and forms around it as by its own composition. As such, any meaningful consideration of colour must consider both the object itself and the structures of space and light within which it might be situated.

A statue's colour is determined in the first instance by the perceived colour of the marble. To describe many marbles as monochrome ignores the richness of colour and the depth, texture and complexity of their finished surfaces. The complex surface properties of marbles mean that, when treated in different ways, they are capable of producing a vast range of visual effects. These include the high shine of a polished *Pavonazzetto* and the depth of *Parian* marble, which can be so translucent as to appear to be lit from within. Amongst the physical factors which influence these effects are the nature of the inclusions, the grain size, the orientation of the crystals, the purity of the calcite and the degree of crystal stress and twinning. Each of these variables will dictate the appearance of a marble and the way in which light behaves upon contact.

This richness of tonality and colour renders the monochrome/polychrome dichotomy rather ambiguous. Statuary which was never artificially coloured but which makes use of natural tone is a very different proposition to statuary which has been consciously altered in order to conform to a modern monochrome aesthetic. It is evident that marbles were selected, at least in part, due to their surface properties (Bartman 1991: 73; Rockwell 1993). We are able to see the selective process through the range of marbles utilised for different purposes, often within the same statue (Elsner 1998; Kousser 2008: 1). There are many similarities between the sub-surface interactions of light and human skin and the interactions between light and certain kinds of marble. We may consider that this physical similarity, and its visual correlate, suggests an understanding not only of the desirability and quality of materials but also of the visual effects which could be achieved through their use and manipulation. In turn, this informs discussions of realism and the ambiguous relationship between sculptural realism and life; a theme of modern scholarly writing and of the Roman world (Elsner 2007: 116; Stewart 2003: 262; Wheeler 1999: 155).

Perceived Greek and Roman attitudes towards marble have shaped discussions of the extent to which marble might have been supplemented through the addition of further colouration. The value of marble as a commodity within the Roman economic sphere is well documented (Oleson 2008; Peacock 1988). It is not clear whether the aesthetic and commensurate monetary value placed upon marble would have precluded it from being painted, or indeed whether the addition of pigment to a marble surface could have been seen to diminish its natural appearance. Such a position would presuppose that the addition of colour was peripheral to the identity or role of the pristine sculpture. The first and most obvious example of additive colouration applied to the marble surface is the pigment, composed from a range of materials of differing value and significance and embodying differing levels of meaning (Brinkmann 2004). It has been suggested that a visual language is evident in the use of colour applied to statuary (Holscher 2004; Bradley 2009). We must also consider the messages which would have been implicit in the use of particular colours in specific contexts to viewers of different sorts (Pollini 1995; Wallace-Hadrill 1994: 166). Both the pigment layer and undecorated marble may, in turn, have had a further layer of surface treatment. One form of this was *Ganosis* described by Pliny as a mixture of wax and oil added to the surface (Bradley 2009: 438). It functioned both as a protective layer and as a colour enhancer, considerably altering the tone of both pigment and marble. Another was *Atramentum* a brown varnish which is thought to have enhanced and softened underlying colour (Brachert 1994; Bradley 2009: 438).

Other methods of additive colour to be considered are the use of physical adornments of various kinds and the use of surface finishes. Adornments such as staffs, weapons or jewellery rarely survive but surface indentations and holes suggest these to have been commonplace. These might have been composed of a range of materials but are likely to have included the use of metal. Furthermore, there is some evidence for the draping of statues in textiles in Roman literary sources (e.g. *Eclogues 7; Metamorphosis 10*). There can be little doubt that, as well as acting as symbolic notations, such additions were also employed as visual devices drawing attention to or augmenting the statue's stylised realism. They permeate the physical boundary between statue and space and between real and unreal, whilst further adding to the statue's texture and colour (Pollini 1995: 263; Østergaard 2008; Hanfmann 1964).

Digital polychromy

The use of digital techniques loosely described as computer-generated imagery (CGI) is perfectly suited to the visualisation of statuary in context (Barceló 2000; Martinez *et al.* 2005). Computer-based reconstruction of cultural heritage – sometimes anomalously referred to as 'virtual archaeology' – is a tool that is highly suited to the meaningful representation, reconciliation and re-contextualisation of disparate data sets. Such technologies have also found applications in the interpretation of Roman archaeological data sets (Haselberger and Humphrey 2004; Earl 2007). This has not been without concerns; primarily the potential of apparently 'photorealistic' digital imagery to be viewed as an accurate recreation of the past, solely on the basis of its visual fidelity. Such concerns are discussed in the archaeological computer graphics literature and it is our belief that awareness of the origin of a particular image, coupled with the same forms of representative critiques levelled at other visual archaeological media such as photography and illustration, is sufficient. Of more interest is the potential for the computer to go beyond the appearance of visual accuracy and to employ digital methods that are themselves physically based.

The development of demonstrably accurate computer-based lighting models and simulated physical surface properties adds a new dimension to visualisation and the interpretation of images. Recent innovations in computer science mean that, for the first time, archaeological applications of CGI are able to incorporate a degree of physicality into what remains a creative process. Prior to this development, the production of hand-drawn or computer reconstructions was almost an entirely interpretive act. The inclusion of demonstrably accurate elements such as lighting models, surface properties and geometry, mean that visualisations can go beyond a merely illustrative role and can begin to function as virtual research environments. Thus, archaeological CGI becomes a process whereby interpretations are structured around an accurate representation of the available data. Because the results of such simulations are tied to physical laws they are quantitatively comparable to real-world visual perception (Happa *et al. in press*).

For the first time it becomes possible to ask questions which assume a degree of accuracy related to the behaviours of light and objects in the real world. These may be simple and abstract: for example "how would a certain paint appear in light of this type, when applied to a particular marble?" They may also be more complex: "how does the changing light caused by weather conditions effect the appearance of the statue, assuming that it was painted using a particular pigment and placed next to a wall painted with another pigment?" The images produced using these methods are not demonstrating all aspects of how a statue looked but are simply allowing the formulation of complex, contemporary, visual research questions. They incorporate the exploratory elements mentioned above, whilst introducing structural and accountable content. At the same time these representations are decidedly modern and we do not argue that by merely visualising something redolent of a Roman scene we are able better to understand how it would be observed by the Roman viewer (Elsner 2007). Rather than acting as a method for viewing the past, such scenes are a reformulation of existing data into a format which allows different questions to be addressed.

The fundamental and most crucial element of any visual scene is light. Its presence or absence not only dictates visibility but how light behaves dictates how an object appears. In order for the production of visual archaeological simulations to be considered valid it is imperative that the lighting model is accurate. By using a lighting model of this type it is possible to accurately simulate Roman sources of light, such as oil lamps, in addition to the sunlight present at a particular place, or time and date. Such lighting models can also incorporate the effects of weather conditions and particles in the air (Sundstedt *et al.* 2005, Gutierrez *et al.* 2008).

In order for the process of physically accurate modelling to be effective it is necessary to understand the different components of the scene which will affect the behaviour of light. These include, but are not limited to, the geometric form of the statue, the type and finish of marble used, the pigments and surface treatments applied, associated objects and draperies, and the context within which the statue was placed. In the case of the Herculaneum Amazon we are gathering a range of correlating data from surviving heads of the same type, better preserved in terms of form but largely lacking surviving polychromy. The surface properties of the Amazon head and similar materials are also being studied in order to better understand the way in which light is scattered across and within the surface of the marble. Digital records of these correlates enable the construction of a geometric amalgam, incorporating a digital simulation of its surface and sub-surface physical structure, over which a digital replica of the pigment may be built up and augmented. Such digital repainting is a complex process, particularly as pigments may be semi-translucent, applied with varying thicknesses and textures. Replicating the physical structure of the marble is similarly complex, with the digital simulation requiring the surface to absorb, reflect and refract light in a range of ways.

In addition, the transport of light between objects in a given scene has a dramatic impact on the appearance of all components. The virtual world provides an opportunity to experiment with context. Thus, for the Herculaneum Amazon we are constructing models of the Basilica Noniana which may have contained the statue. But the uncertainty regarding this context – the location of the statue, the architectural components, wall paintings, other statues, luminaires and so on – require a careful comparison of possibilities. It also requires an emphasis on the analysis of archaeological space as an explicitly creative practice, focussed on possibilities for interpretation rather than on impediments.

Conclusions

The possibilities of digital simulation of painted statues remain under-explored and our own project is still in its earliest stages. In addition to the technological challenges of physically accurate digital simulation of marble, pigment, surface treatment and adornment, the use of such digital simulacra remains under-theorised. However, the flexibility of interpretative practices afforded by physically accurate simulations will offer valuable new areas of research. The distinctions between physical experience and digital representation are narrowing and the role of archaeological theory will be of crucial significance. Whilst we do not yet understand fully what it is to create and to think within a wholly digital, but realistic Roman archaeological world, we look forward to the new engagements with the past that such practices will engender. As the analysis of surviving sculptural polychromy continues we may begin to see the colours and textures of the Roman world in a new light, with computation lending new eyes and new contexts for interpretation.

Archaeological Computing Research Group,
School of Humanities, University of Southampton

Acknowledgements

The Soprintendenza Speciale per i Beni Archeologici di Napoli e Pompei generously provided access to the Amazon statue and its staff were of very great assistance throughout the complex recording process. The work would be impossible without the continuing support and knowledge of members of the Herculaneum Conservation Project and in particular its director Andrew Wallace-Hadrill and its research coordinator Sarah Court. The Herculaneum Conservation Project is a partnership between the Packard Humanities Institute, Soprintendenza Speciale per i Beni Archeologici di Napoli e Pompei and the British School at Rome. The Amazon project is supported by an AHRC Collaborative Doctoral Award and by the partners – the University of Southampton, the University of Warwick and the International Centre for the Study of Herculaneum. We are very grateful to Louise Revell and David Peacock for reading and commenting upon an earlier draft of this paper, and for their continuing advice on the Amazon project.

Bibliography

Ancient Sources

Ovid (Translated by Frank Justus Miller 1984; revised by G.P. Goold). *Metamorphoses: Volume 2: 2nd Edition.* Cambridge, Mass: Harvard University Press.

Virgil (Translated by Robert Coleman 1977). *Eclogues.* Cambridge: Cambridge University Press Greek and Latin Classics.

Modern Sources

AmazonWeb 2009. *The Herculaneum Amazon Project.* http://www.southampton.ac.uk/archaeology/acrg/acrg_research_amazon.html [Accessed: 14 July 2009].

Barceló, J. 2000. *Visualising* what might be: An introduction to virtual reality techniques in archaeology In: J. Barcelo, M. Forte and D. Sanders (eds.) *Virtual Reality in Archaeology.* Oxford: ArchaeoPress: 9–36.

Bartman, E. 1991. Sculptural collecting and display in the private realm. In E.K. Gazda (ed.) *Roman Art in the Private* Sphere. Ann Arbor: University of Michigan Press: 72–73.

Beard, M. and Henderson, J. 2001. Classical Art: *From Greece to Rome.* Oxford University Press: Oxford.

Bonn-Muller, E. 2008. Carved in Living Color. *Archaeology* 61(1). http://www.archaeology.org/0801/trenches/colorgods.html. [Accessed 10 July 2009]

Brachert, T. 1994. Zum Atramentum-Firnis des Apelles *Restauro* 100(1). Munich: 50–51.

Bradley, M. 2009. The Importance of colour on ancient marble sculpture. *Art History* 32(3): 427–457.

Brinkmann, V. 2004. Colori e Tecnica Pittorica. In P. Liverani (ed.) *I Colori del Bianco: Policromia nella Scultura Antica.* Rome: De Luca: 315–324.

Earl, G.P. *in press*, Physical and Photo-Realism: The Herculaneum Amazon. *Fundamentos teóricos de la Arqueología virtual: Proceedings of Arqueologica 2.0, Seville.*

Earl, G.P., Beale, G., Happa, J., Williams, M., Turley, G., Martinez, K. and Chalmers, A. 2009. A Repainted Amazon. In A. Seal, S. Keene, J. Bowen (eds.) *Proceedings of the 2009 EVA London Conference. London*: British Computer Society.

Earl, G.P. 2007. De/construction sites: Romans and the digital playground. In J. Bowen, S. Keene and L. MacDonald (eds.) *EVA 2007 London Conference Proceedings.* Hampton Hill, UK: EVA Conferences International: 1–11.

Elsner, J. 2007. *Roman Eyes: Visuality and Subjectivity in Art and Text.* Princeton, Mass: Princeton University Press.

Elsner, J. 1998. *Imperial Rome and Christian Triumph: The Art of the Roman Empire 100-450 A.D.* Oxford: Oxford University Press.

Fenger, L. 1886. *Dorische Polychromie.* Berlin: A. Asher & Co.

Gopnik, B. 2008. Correcting a colourblind view of the treasures of antiquity. *Washington Post* (4th May 2008). http://www.washingtonpost.com/wp-dyn/content/article/2008/05/02/AR2008050200966.html?referrer=emailarticle &sid=ST2008050203083 [Accessed 14 July 2009].

Gordon, R.L. 1979. The Real and the Imaginary: Production and Religion in the Greco-Roman World. *Art History* 2: 5–34.

Gutierrez, D., Sundstedt, V., Gomez, F. and Chalmers, A. 2008. Modelling Light Scattering and Cultural Heritage. *Journal on Computing and Cultural Heritage 1. http://giga.cps.unizar.es/~diegog/ficheros/pdf_papers/2000952_LR.pdf* [Accessed 16 Nov 2009].

Hanfmann, G.M.A. 1964. *A Modern Survey of the Art of Imperial Rome.* London: Corney Adams and Mackay.

Hingley, R. 2000. *Roman Officers and English Gentlemen: The Imperial Origins of Roman Archaeology.* London: Routledge.

Holscher T. 2004. *The Language of Images in Roman Art. Cambridge*: Cambridge University Press.

Happa *et al.* in press. STAR report VAST 2009.

Happa, J., Williams, M., Turley, G., Earl, G., Dubla, P., Beale, G., Gibbons, G., Debattista, K. and Chalmers, A. 2009. Virtual Relighting of a Roman Statue Head from Herculaneum: A Case Study. In A. Hardy, P. Marais, S.N. Spencer, J.E. Gain and W. Straßer, (eds.): *Proceedings of the 6th Afrigraph 2009.* Association for Computing Machinery 2009: 5–12.

Haselberger, L. and Humphrey, J. (eds.) 2004. *Imaging Ancient Rome: Documentation, Visualisation, Imagination. Proceedings of the Third Williams Symposium on Classical Architecture.* Portsmouth, Rhode Island: Journal of Roman Archaeology Supplementary Series 61.

Hopkins, K. 1985. *Death and Renewal.* Cambridge: Cambridge University Press.

Kousser, R.M. 2008. *Hellenistic and Roman Ideal Sculpture.* Cambridge: Cambridge University Press.

Liverani, P. (ed.) 2004. *I Colori del Bianco: Policromia nella Scultura Antica.* Rome: De Luca.

Martínez, J., Finat, J., Fuentes, L.M. and Gonzalo, M. 2005. A coarse-to-fine curved approach to 3D surveying of ornamental aspects and sculptures in façades. In S. Dequal (ed.) *Proceedings.* Torino: International Scientific Committee for Documentation of Cultural Heritage: 441–446.

Oleson, J.P. 2008. *The Oxford Handbook of Engineering and Technology in the Classical World.* Oxford: Oxford University Press.

Østergaard J.S. 2008. Emerging Colours, Roman Sculptural Polychromy Revived. In R. Panzanelli, E. Schmidt and K. Lapatin (eds.) *The Colour of Life: Polychromy in Sculpture from Antiquity to the Present.* Los Angeles: Getty Research Institute: 40–61.

Owen, R. 2006. Statue reveals Roman lady with her make-up still on. *Times Online* [25 March 2008]. http://www.timesonline.co.uk/tol/news/world/europe/article695424.ece. [Accessed 10 July 2009].

Peacock, D.P.S. 1988. The Roman Quarries of Mons Claudianus, Egypt: An Interim Report. In M. Waelkens and N. Herz (eds.) *Classical Marble: Geochemistry, Technology, Trade.* Dordrecht: Kluwer ASI Series: 97–102.

Price, S.R.F, 1984. *Rituals and Power: The Roman Imperial Cult in Asia Minor.* Cambridge University Press: Cambridge.

Pollini, J. 1995, The Augustus from Prima Porta and the transformation of the Polykleitan Heroic Ideal: The rhetoric of art. In W.G. Moon and B.H. Fowler (eds.) *Polykeitos: The Doryphoros and Tradition.* Wisconsin: University of Wisconsin Press: 262–282.

Potts 2008, Colours of Sculpture. In R. Panzanelli, R. Schmidt, K. Lapatin, (eds.) *The Colour of Life: Polychromy in Sculpture from Antiquity to the Present.* Los Angeles: Getty Research Institute: 78–97.

Reuterswärd, P. 1960. *Studien zur Polychromie der Plastik: Griechenland und Rom.* Stockholm: Almqvist & Wiksell.

Revell, L. 2009. *Roman Imperialism and Local Identities.* Cambridge: Cambridge University Press.

Rockwell, P. 1993. *The Art of Stoneworking.* Cambridge: Cambridge University Press.

Stewart, P. 2003. *Statues in Roman Society: Representation and Response.* Oxford: Oxford University Press.

Sundstedt, V., Gutierrez, D., Gomez, F. and Chalmers, A. 2005. Participating Media for High-Fidelity Cultural Heritage. In M. Mudge, N. Ryan and R. Scopigno (eds.) *The 6th International Symposium on Virtual Reality, Archaeology and Cultural Heritage.* www.cs.bris.ac.uk/home/veronica/Documents/VAST05sundstedtetal.pdf [Accessed 13 November 2009].

Washington Post, 2008. Augustus of Prima Porta. *Washington Post* (Date of publication: 2008) http://www.washingtonpost.com/wp-dyn/content/article/2008/05/02/AR2008050203090.html?sid=ST2008050203083 [Accessed 14 July 2009].

Wallace-Hadrill, A. 1994, *Houses and Society in Pompeii and Herculaneum.* Princeton University Press: Princeton.

Wheeler, S.M. 1999. *A Discourse of Wonders: Audience and Performance in Ovid's Metamorphoses.* Pennsylvania: University of Pennsylvania Press.

GIS and Artefact Distribution: A Case Study on Regional Cooking Wares in Northern Gaul

Annick Lepot

Introduction

Researchers are now confronted by new technologies like Geographic Information Systems ("GIS"), but the difficulties in using such tools in archaeological interpretation are numerous. GIS offers a way of moving interpretation beyond 'black dots on a map' by placing settlements or artefacts in their geographical, socio-political and cultural contexts.

Artefacts, such as consumption goods, can provide information about socio-cultural contexts, exchange patterns and mechanisms. In artefact studies, GIS can be used as a precise cartography tool which allows the re-interpretation of data collected on consumption sites. However, behind the finished maps lies a great deal of work collecting and reflecting on the data before it is used in the software, in order to avoid producing completely unusable maps. GIS can produce visually spectacular maps, but not always intellectually elaborate analysis. This paper explores the importance of GIS as an analytical tool in the understanding of artefact distribution, through an examination of regional cooking wares in areas of Northern Gaul.

GIS and artefacts

Geographic Information Systems are computer programs which integrate operating procedures to store, manipulate, analyze and visualize spatial information. GIS in archaeology can work at different levels, from a micro level for intra-site studies to the large scale distribution of settlements (for more details of GIS and archaeology see Lock and Stancic 1995; Maschner 1996; Kvamme 1999; Wescott and Brandon 2000; Harris 2002; Wheatley and Gillings 2002; Conolly and Lake 2006).

Intra-site distribution studies are characteristic of current research that combines GIS-use and artefact distribution , focusing on the spatial analysis of objects across a site. The objective is to geo-reference artefacts on archaeological sites in order to determine functional zoning. This is an ideal approach for prehistoric habitat reconstruction (Spikins *et al.* 2002; Williams 2004) or underwater archaeological excavations (Oxley 2001; Mather and Watts 2002). An extension of this application is to create an on-site geo-referenced database for archaeological artefacts (e.g. Zahab and Sawada 2005). GIS also has great potential within rescue archaeology, and in archaeological surveying, to map the distribution of artefacts and define the archaeological potential of an area or site.

However, the main use of GIS-based analysis for artefacts is probably in visualizing their relationships with political boundaries, socio-economic contexts and environmental factors within a large region. More than just indicators of the economy, artefacts can inform us about the cultural preferences of the populations who produced and used them. Using GIS to map artefact distribution has been used effectively by Anglo-Saxon scholars such as Jason Lucas (2001) on the distribution of Roman military sites and stamped brick and tiles, whilst Allison (2006) has examined the distribution of 'gendered' artefacts at Roman military sites.

GIS and artefact distribution in Northern Gaul

The research presented here is a case study of GIS use in artefact distribution research. This paper is related to studies undertaken by the Centre de Recherches d'Archéologie Nationale (CRAN) of the Catholic University of Louvain-la-Neuve (Belgium) on Gallo-Roman civilization in Northern Gaul, principally Gallia Belgica. Whilst this is not the place to discuss the concept of Romanisation (e.g. Woolf 1992; 1997; Hingley 2005), this study forms part of the debate about the diversity within the overall unity of the Empire and further explores the evidence for cultural multiplicity beyond a simple Roman/native dichotomy.

The study focuses on geographic areas of countryside within about thirty kilometres of three cities in Belgium and France: Tongres, Bavay and Tournai (Fig. 1). The borders of the mapped areas were defined on the basis of modern Belgian communes and French Cantons.The zones cover sections of four *civitates* territories; the *civitas Tungrorum*, the *civitas Nerviorum*, the *civitas Menapiorum* and a small part of the *civitas Atrebatum*. This geographic framework and the use of GIS allows for more detailed studies than previously, providing a new interpretation of space.

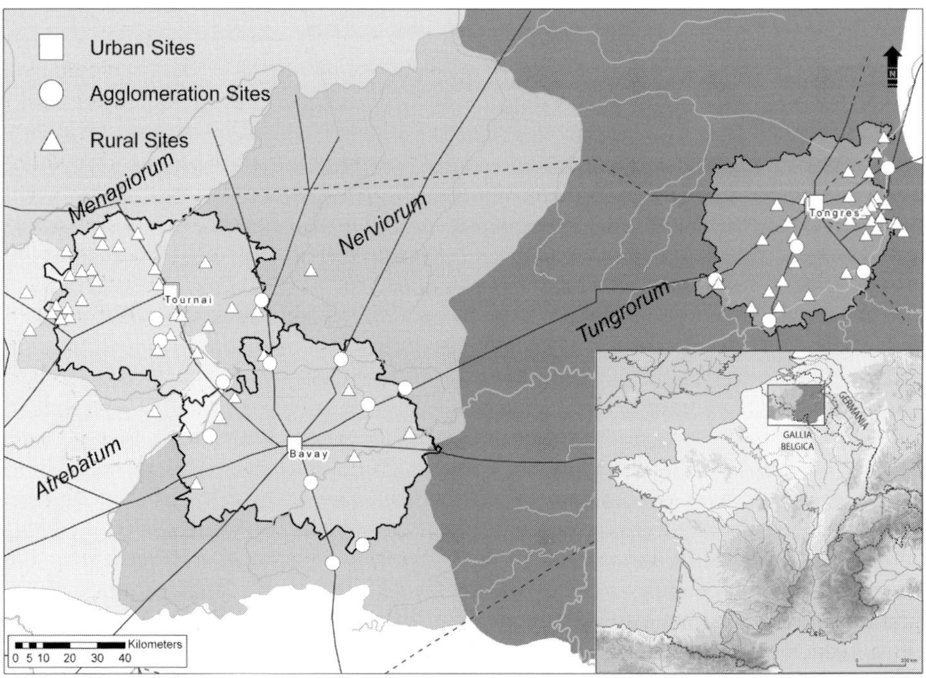

Figure 1: Location of the areas under investigation. The plots represent sites with potential for pottery studies (square: urban sites, circle: agglomeration sites, triangle: rural sites).

The overall collective project explores the process behind, and the impact of, Romanisation in Northern Gaul within both urban and rural contexts. Its objectives are to understand landscapes, land use, and the density, chronology and typology of settlements within the regions. The research project also aims to identify the timing of the infiltration of a variety of

Roman habits into daily life (e.g. architecture and material culture), and to understand the relationships between towns, agglomerations and the countryside, through exchange patterns relating to the production, distribution and consumption of goods such as pottery and food (Lepot 2008). The overall project has an archaeological catalogue as a relational database imported into GIS (for a synthesis of GIS and DBMS software in archaeology see Djindjian 1998), thus creating A.P.I.S., the Archaeological Project of Interconnected Studies for Roman Northern Gaul. A.P.I.S. is kept up-to-date through the use of an electronic user input form, onto which researchers can enter data whilst they work. Through this approach a systematic register of Roman sites in the three regions has been created, integrating many different types of information. These include location coordinates, occupation phase, site type, structure type, description, type of excavation, author of the excavation and bibliography. This archaeological database project connects the varied fields of study on Romanisation in Northern Gaul, linking different databases relating to villa sites, functional zoning within cities and agglomerations, and especially pottery.

Specificity of pottery studies

The artefact study in progress at CRAN focuses principally on pottery, as it is the most abundant archaeological material. The aim of our pottery studies is to move beyond the limited view that pottery is only useful in dating a site or exploring economics (Hawthorne 1997, Hawkes 2000; 2001), to explore other avenues such as the regional economy, socio-cultural contexts, pottery supply and demand or phenomena relating to consumption and food habits. Regional ceramics – particularly cooking wares – are an ideal pottery class through which to examine artefact distribution. Often overlooked in pottery studies, cooking wares are good indicators of the degree of dissemination of Roman material culture, the persistence of indigenous pottery use and the creation of a new repertory. Due to their technical and typological characteristics, and because they are less affected by fashion trends, this category of pottery has many advantages in the study of acculturation.

The method of analysis of sherds from consumption sites is based on the model defined by the CRAN Ceramic Laboratory. On the basis of technological and typological characteristics, the main ceramological categories of Northern Gaulish cooking wares have been defined for the three regions. Briefly, the most important categories are: Modelled Cooking ceramic (MC), Reduced Cooking ceramic (RC), Oxidized Cooking ceramic (OC), Smocked Cooking ceramic (SC) and Colour-Coated Cooking ceramic (CC) (Fig. 2). Modelled cooking wares are traditional pre-Roman cooking ceramics fired at low temperatures and presenting coarse inclusions. Reduced Cooking wares were an evolution of traditional cooking ceramics, integrating Roman technological innovations such as throwing and firing at high temperatures, but in a reducing atmosphere. Oxidized cooking ceramics present the same technological innovations but were fired in an oxidizing atmosphere. Smocked Cooking ceramics are a category within which the wares present a smocked surface and an oxidized matrix, an effect due to a particular post-firing atmosphere (Picon 1973: 67). Finally Colour-Coated wares, which appear to have been a marginal phenomenon, present an argillaceous glaze and an oxidizing firing.

Sherds were examined at macroscopic level and attached to paste groups before undergoing petrological examination, which identifies particular fabrics attributable, in certain cases, to individual workshops. This analysis was followed up with reference to published typologies, where available, and the total number of pots was identified through sherd counts and the estimation of the Minimal Number of Individuals (MNI), based on counting the number of rims. The study model is based on examination of sufficiently well-dated pottery assemblages. These assemblages were collected from publications, old excavations and current researches, and have been classified by chronological horizons through the analysis of whole ceramics, context, and other supporting data such as coin issues (for chronological horizons valid in Northern Gaul see Brulet 2008: 20–21).

Figure 2: The main ceramological categories represented within the site assemblages:(from left to right) Reduced, Oxidized, Smocked and Modelled cooking ceramics.

In the field of ceramology, GIS offers a significant deviation from the more traditional approaches of find-spot maps, providing a tool to search and map spatial queries based on pottery categories, pottery fabrics or pottery types. Three factors can expand our understanding of the distribution of pottery. The first is the recognition of ceramological categories, where maps can characterize a particular ceramic supply to the different sites. The second factor is the recognition of pottery types, with maps representing the areas where particular types were in use. The final factor is the differentiation of pottery fabrics, and maps based on this factor represent the diffusion of a particular kiln production. If the production centre is not localised, such maps can define an area where a particular fabric is strongly represented and, in certain cases, associations with a geological outcrop.

To link the ceramic form in the A.P.I.S. database with the site data, each assemblage was identified by both site and trench locations. The objective in using GIS technology in Roman pottery studies is to generate a computer-based system that allows researchers to carry out a series of spatial analyses. The system can be used to view ceramic distributions according to culture, group, time period and/or region in relation to historical, political, cultural or topographical contexts, as well as soil types. A map plotting the ceramic types can then chart local, regional and supra-regional movements, or identify homogeneous cultural groups.

Possibilities and limits of GIS-use in pottery artefact distribution

According to Ressler (1989), GIS analysis demands a structure consisting of problem definition, data acquisition, data manipulation and report or map generation. Creating a database is not difficult in itself, but the researcher must be aware of the final objectives of the research in order to create the appropriate fields. What types of requests are needed, and which questions should be answered? Limitations with GIS are also due to the current state of research and the specific characteristics of pottery. The first problem is with data standardization. The difficulty in compiling fully quantitative distribution maps from published sources is well known (Orton *et al.* 1993). Difficulties also lie in non-standard vocabularies, reports without quantitative analysis or with minimal study of ceramic fabrics. The second problem is time management. Geographic Information Systems cannot manage the fourth dimension, so that the only way to deal with the temporal is at a thematic level, by creating diachronic maps using chronological periodization. Another primary difficulty with the application of GIS to pottery studies is the multiple expressions of pottery. In order to analyze the material successfully, the researcher needs to classify it into ceramological categories, paste groups, fabrics, types or functions. All these aspects are important in analyzing sherds, so must be integrated within the GIS database before creating a map. The final difficulty is linking GIS visualization with quantitative analysis. Quantity of ceramics is an important factor in comparing sites, and the plotting of pottery does not mean that there will be the same percentages at each site.

Mapping cooking wares

In total, data were analyzed in a homogeneous way for twenty percent of the sites. These assemblages enable comparisons both within a site and between sites. The initial results below are based on three simple models of GIS-based requests. The first model illustrates the supply of sites based on the proportion of different ceramological categories. The second model illustrates the regional specificity through the technological aspects of fabrics. The final model illustrates regional characters based on typological patterns.

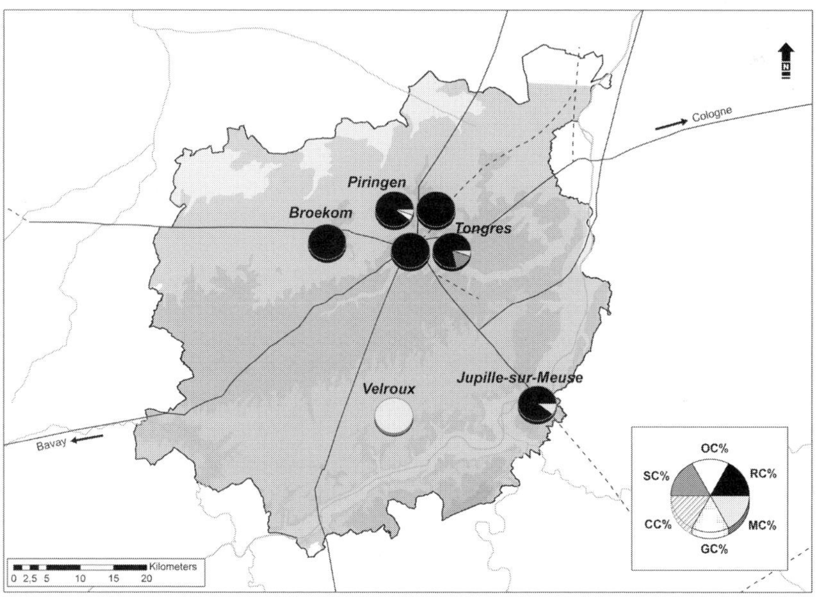

Figure 3: First century A.D. pottery assemblages in the area of Tongres.

The GIS-based maps are the result of information regarding the percentage of MNI of each ceramological categories. In the Tongres areas, both urban and agglomeration sites evolved in the same way, with assemblages from Tongres (Vanderhoeven *et al.* 1992; 2006) and Jupille-sur-Meuse showing Reduced Cooking ceramics predominating over traditional Modelled wares from the pre-Flavian period (Fig. 3). In contrast, Reduced Cooking ceramics appear on rural sites, such as the *villae* at Piringen and Broekom, slightly later during the second half of the first century A.D.

In the areas of Tongres and Bavay-Tournai, the cooking ware supply shows a difference at second century A.D. sites. Within the Tongres area, the pie charts (Fig. 4) show a multiplicity of different cooking ware production techniques, with Smocked ceramic prevailing. Smocked ceramic is characteristic of the *civitas Tungrorum* and appeared during the last decades of the first century A.D. Oxidized Cooking wares also appear on sites at the end of the first century and then increase in number, particularly in the second century A.D. assemblages from the villa at Velroux. Oxidizing firing applied to cooking wares is also attested for production in the second century A.D. at Cologne (Höpken 2006: 115).

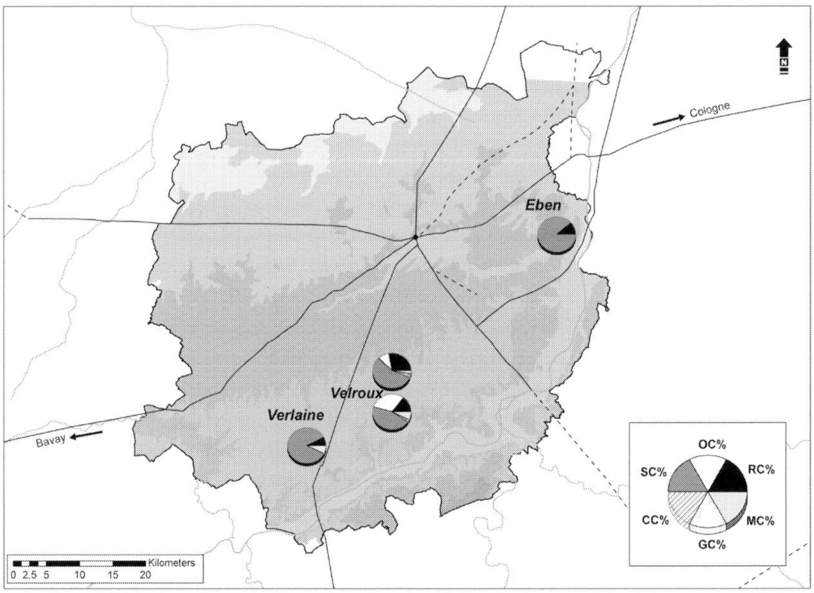

Figure 4: Second century A.D. pottery assemblages in the area of Tongres.

During the third century A.D., the assemblages from sites in the region of Tongres underline the preference for Smocked Cooking ceramics, with assemblages from Tongres and the agglomerations of Braives and Amay, as well as rural sites, being dominated by this category (Fig. 5). The map shows that Oxidized Cooking ceramics are well represented on sites located along the River Meuse, which suggests that the river had an important role in the diffusion of pottery goods.

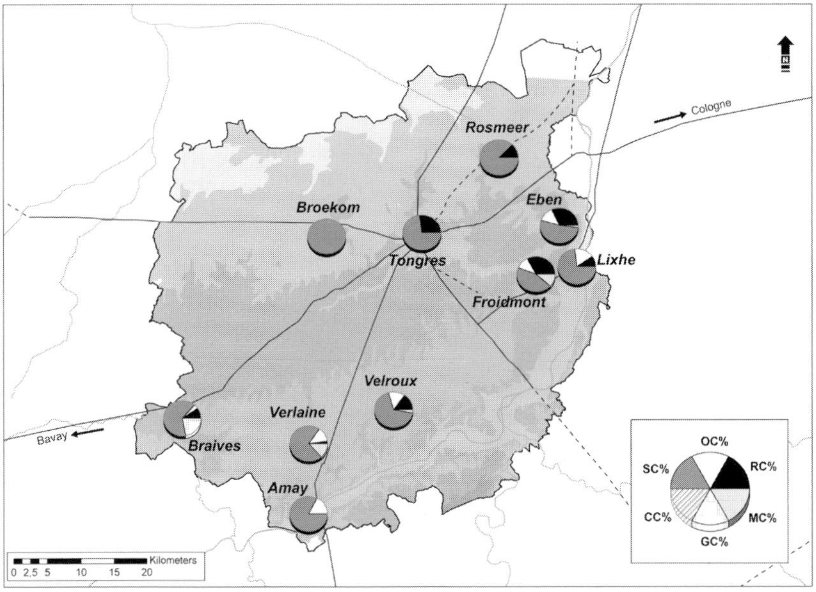

Figure 5: Third century A.D. pottery assemblages in the area of Tongres.

The two remaining study areas of Bavay and Tournai indicate a consistent level of continuity. Both places were supplied with Reduced Cooking ceramics during the second century A.D., which prevailed over Modelled ceramics (Fig. 6). This pattern may suggest that these areas retained a tradition of, or preference for, pre-Roman dark aspect cooking wares.

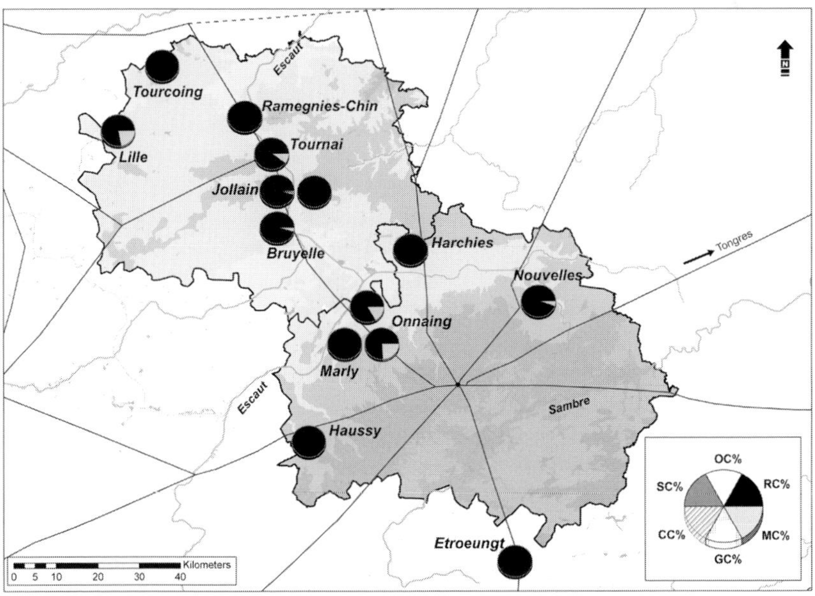

Figure 6: Assemblages of the second century A.D. in the areas of Tournai and Bavay.

The first occurrences of Smocked Ceramic within the Bavay and Tournai regions were during the third century A.D. in the agglomeration site of Waudrez, and in rural contexts such as Merbes (Fig. 7). Examination of the sherds shows that they were importations from *civitas Tungrorum*. Based on a movement from east to west, this dispersion pattern follows the Roman road connecting Bavay to Cologne and the river Sambre, which flows into the Meuse.

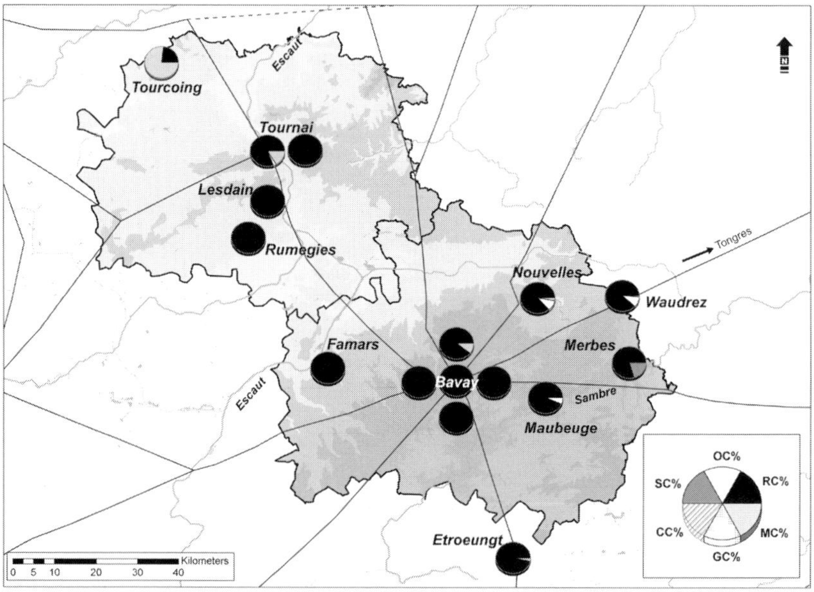

Figure 7: Assemblages of the third century A.D. in the areas of Tournai and Bavay.

Technological characteristics of pottery, especially cooking wares, are significant in understanding production, exchange patterns and exchange mechanisms. It is now well demonstrated that Gallo-Roman potters applied new technologies to produce wares with specific technological characteristics, such as shock resistance or thermic resistance (Picon 1997, Desbat and Batigne 1996). This can be identified in the study of cooking ware, as its use requires resistance to both environmental factors and high temperatures. For example, kaolin-type clays, used in the production of Roman cooking wares, are a shock and heat-resistant raw material (Picon 1992–1993). During the third century A.D., the sites in the Tongres area show that several productions of both Oxidized and Smocked ceramics were made from white pastes, similar to kaolin-type clays, which correspond to the MOSA fabric from the *vicus* of Liberchies (Vilvorder 2001: 121–122). The distribution of this fabric type (Fig. 8) shows a strong representation at rural sites within the Meuse valley and in the agglomeration sites located along the river, suggesting that both production and diffusion were closely related to the river or to the Meuse valley. The only Roman workshop so far attested within this area which produced Oxidized cooking wares using kaolinitical clays was located at Amay, but its diffusion is quite limited (Vilvorder and Rekk in press). The link between this type of clay and the Meuse valley is further supported by the presence of kaolinitical outcrops, more common in this geographical area than in the more sandy northern part of the *civitas Tungrorum* (Calembert 1945).

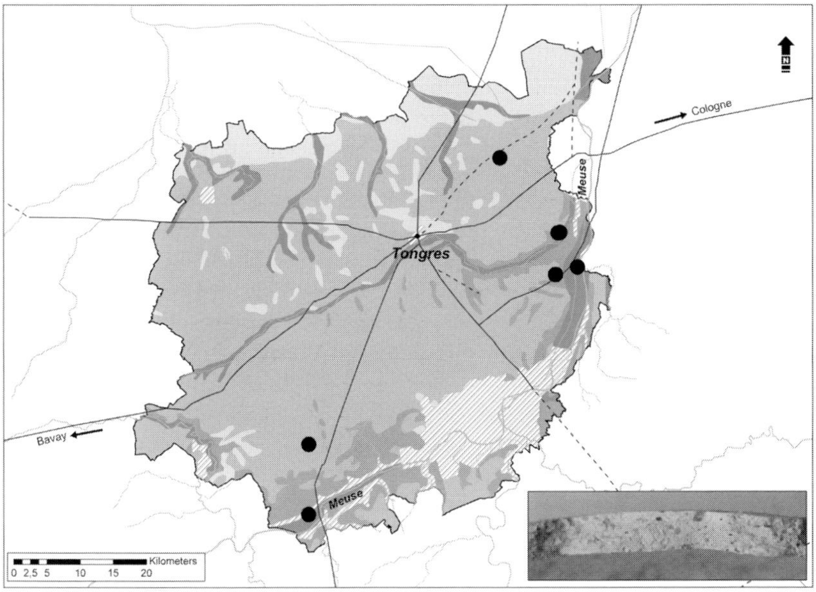

Figure 8: Sites with assemblages having more than 50% MNI of the cooking wares in MOSA fabric.

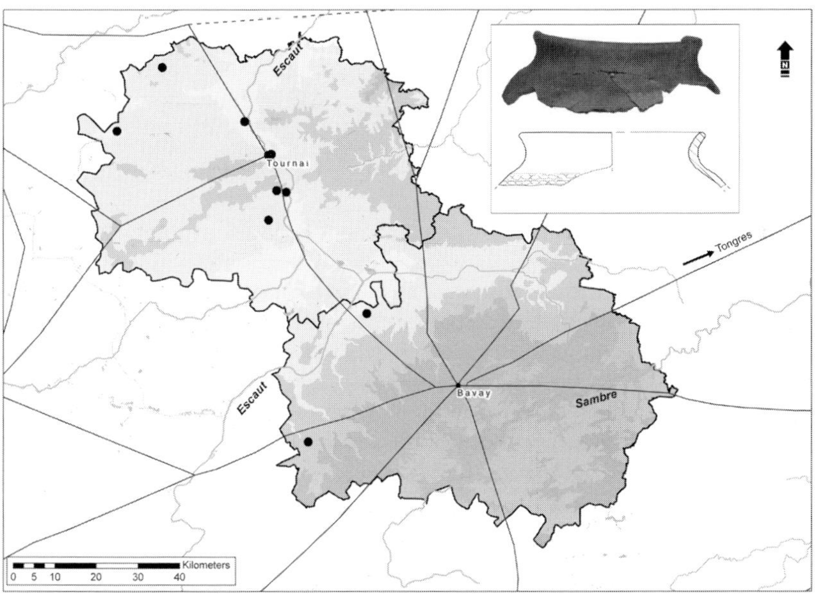

Figure 9: GIS map recording the presence of the Reduced ceramic "Menapian" cooking pot during the second century A.D.

Ceramological studies are increasingly focused on understanding population groups or boundaries through the definition of *facies*. *Facies* means the appearance of an object group and reflect its morphological, technological, regional and/or chronological coherence (D'Anna *et al.* 2003: 277; Lepot and Brulet 2007). The definition of ceramological *facies*, as a homogeneous regional sequence of ceramics, allows areas of expansion or cultural interaction between population groups to be identified. These *facies* can be defined on the bases of typology, with specific types representing a population group. The adoption of Roman forms and the creation of new repertories are indicators of the acculturation or assimilation of Roman habits. This assimilation is perceptible in cooking wares through the use of Roman techniques, such as throwing and improved firing, whilst still preserving indigenous traditional forms. Fig. 9, for example, shows the diffusion of the "Menapian" globular cooking pot, derived directly from an indigenous type (Vermeulen 1992), but produced using the Roman technique of Reduced ceramic. The GIS mapping of this pottery type shows a concentration within the eastern part of the *civitas Menapiorum* territory and at the sites situated along the River Escaut and its tributaries, suggesting that the river created a natural frontier which corresponded to the *civitas* territory limits.

Conclusion

The effect of Romanisation on the northern provinces of the Empire can be seen through different themes, including economic and architectural changes, or through the variation in material culture. The use of GIS in mapping these changes requires confidence in its applicability to the strand of artefact research being undertaken on an inter-site basis. By developing GIS at a regional level, the objective is to create a dynamic reading of regions by combining social, cultural, environmental and material data. Whilst the difficulties of GIS, outlined above, and the problem of time and monetary constraints in training archaeologists to handle the new technologies, are a current limitation, the benefits of GIS are evident. The use of GIS in artefact distribution, particularly pottery studies, provides a tool to test ideas or models, and the acquisition and creation of the data layers allows a more detailed interpretation of spatial, economic and cultural relationships. Archaeologists must first collate the data, frame ideas and then test them to find out if they are correct. The 'reality' of the maps depends on the state of research, number of sites and scales of analysis, as determined by the researcher. If these factors are taken into account, GIS holds exciting possibilities for further understanding cultural variation within the Roman Empire.

GIS can help bring out the regional patterns in pottery consumption. The effects of Romanisation are not uniform within these three regions and the differences in ceramological categories, fabrics and typology, highlighted in this paper, underline the regional variation. The specificity of ceramics in the Tongres region appears to be a consequence of the influence of the Rhenan Limes, which reached this area early and had a large impact on the technological and typological evolution of cooking wares. In contrast, the regions of Bavay and Tournai, geographically closer to one another and with a pre-Roman cultural background deeply rooted in the *civitas Menapiorum*, evolved under more diverse influences. Moreover, these GIS-based samples clearly show the importance of the topography, whether it is rivers or roads, in the production, distribution and consumption of pottery. Further GIS research will be focused towards identifying distinctive local identities through pottery, as well as the exchange patterns and mechanisms, which characterize these regions of Northern Gaul.

Centre de Recherche d'Archéologie Nationale, Université Catholique de Louvain

Acknowledgements

This paper derives from my PhD thesis, as Research Fellow F.R.S.-FNRS, which focuses on 'Food and Vessels as Evidence of the Phenomenon of Acculturation'. Both are part of an International Research Project, Interuniversity Attraction Poles - Phase VI, titled *Transition from Republic to Empire: the Impact of Romanisation on Cities and Countryside in Italy and the Provinces (Second/first century B.C. – second/third century A.D.)* (Belgian Science Policy-Belgian State 2007–2011). I would like to thank Kate Marino and Lisa Anderson, the organizers of the TRAC session at Ann Arbor, Michigan, for their themed session, 'Technologies of Roman Archaeology and its Theoretical Implications'. I would also thank the anonymous referees for their advice, as well as the people who have had the kindness to correct my English.

Bibliography

Allison, P.M. 2006. Mapping for gender: Interpreting artefact distribution inside first and second century A.D. forts in Roman Germany. *Archaeological Dialogues* 13(1): 1–20.

Brulet, R. 2008. *Les Romains en Wallonie. Atlas topographiques des sites*. Bruxelles: Racine.

Calembert, L. 1945. *Les gisements de terres plastiques et réfractaires d'Andenne et du Condroz*. Sine loco: Vaillant-Carmanne.

Conolly, J. and Lake, M. 2006. *Geographical Information Systems in Archaeology*. Cambridge: Cambridge University Press.

D'Anna, A., Desbat A., Garcia D., Shmitt A. and Verhage F. 2003. *La Céramique. La Poterie du Néolithique aux Temps Modernes*. Paris: Errance.

Desbat, A. and Batigne, C. 1996. Un type particulier de "cruche": les bouilloires en céramique d'époque romaine (Ier-IIIème siècles). In *Actes de la Société Française d'Étude de la Céramique Antique en Gaule, Dijon 1996*. Marseille: SFECAG: 381–394.

Djindjian, F. 1998. *GIS usage in worldwide archaeology*. http://www.progettocaere.rm.cnr.it/databasegestione/open_oai_page.asp?id=OAI:www.progettocaere.rm.cnr.it/databasegestione/A_C_oai_Archive.xml:20. (accessed June 20 2009).

Harris, T.M. 2002. GIS in archaeology. In A.K. Knowles (ed.) *Past Time, Past Place: GIS for History*. Redlands: ESRI Press: 131–144.

Hawkes, G. 2000. An archaeology of food: A case study from Roman Britain. In G. Davies, A. Gardner and K. Lockyear (eds.) *TRAC 2000: Proceedings of the Tenth Annual Theoretical Roman Archaeology Conference, London 2000*. Oxford: Oxbow Books: 94–103

Hawkes, G. 2001. Wolves' Nipples and Otters' Noses? Rural foodways and Roman Britain. In M. Carruthers, C. van Driel-Murray, A. Gardner, J. Lucas, L. Revell and E.V. Swift (eds.) *TRAC 2001: Proceedings of the Eleventh Annual Theoretical Roman Archaeology Conference, Glasgow 2001*. Oxford: Oxbow Books: 45–50.

Hawthorne, J.W.J. 1997. Pottery and paradigms in early western Empire. In C. Forcey, J. Hawthorne and R. Witcher (eds.) *TRAC 97: Proceedings of the Seventh Annual Theoretical Roman Archaeology Conference, Nottingham 1997*. Oxford: Oxbow Books: 160–172.

Hingley, R. 2005. *Globalizing Roman Culture*. London: Routledge.

Höpken, C. 2006. Die Römische keramikproduktion in Köln. Kölner Forshungen 8. Mainz am Rhein: Philipp Von Zabern.

Kvamme, K. 1999. Recent Directions and Developments in Geographical Information Systems. *Journal of Archaeological Research* 7(2): 153–201.

Lepot, A. 2008. Regional influences, economies and culture in Northern Gaul: The interest of ceramics. *Poster for TRAC 2008 Amsterdam.*

Lepot, A. and Brulet R. 2007. Faciès et chronologie. In *Actes de la Société Française d'Étude de la Céramique Antique en Gaule, Langres 2007*. Marseille: SFECAG: 61–69.

Lock, G.R. and Stancic, Z. 1995. *Archaeology and Geographical Information Systems: a European Perspective.* Bristol: CRC Press.

Lucas, J. 2001. Material Culture Patterns and Cultural Change in South-West Britain. In C. Carruthers, C. van Driel-Murray, A.J. Lucas, L. Revell and E.V. Swift (eds.) *TRAC 2001: Proceedings of the Eleventh Annual Theoretical Roman Archaeology Conference, Glasgow 2001.* Oxford: Oxbow Books: 51–72.

Maschner, H.D.G. 1996. *New Methods, Old Problems: Geographic Information Systems in Modern Archaeological Research.* Carbondale: Southern Illinois University Occasional Papers.

Mather, I.R. and Watts G.P. 2002. Geographic Information Systems. In C.V. Ruppe and J.H. Bastard (eds.) *International Handbook of Underwater Archaeology.* New York: Kluwer Academic/Plenum Publishers: 679–696.

Orton, C., Tyers P. and Vince A.G. 1933. *Pottery in Archaeology.* Cambridge: Cambridge University Press.

Oxley, I. 2001. Towards the Integrated Management of Scotland's Cultural Heritage: Examining Historic Shipwrecks as Marine Environmental Resources. *World Archaeology* 32(3): 413–426.

Picon, M., 1973. *Introduction à l'étude technique des céramiques sigillées de Lezoux.* Dijon: Université de Dijon.

Picon, M. 1992–1993. Les céramiques culinaires de la Graufesenque: introduction technique. *Annales de Pegasus* 2: 42–48.

Picon, M. 1997. Le passage des céramiques culinaires gauloises aux céramiques culinaires romaines, à La Graufesenque (Aveyron F): résultats et questions. In S. Santoro Bianchi and B. Fabbri (eds.) *Il Contributo delle Analisi Archeometriche allo Studio delle Ceramiche Grezze e Communi: Il Rapporto Forma/Funzione/Impasto. Atti della 1a Giornata di archeometria della ceramica-Bologna, 28 Febbraio 1997 (Studi e Scavi, 4).* Bologna: Bologna University Press: 71–74.

Ressler, J.Q. 1989. *The GRASS Problem-Solving Manual.* Washington University: Department of Geography.

Spikins, P., Connelle C., Avestaran H. and Scaife B. 2002. GIS Based Interpolation Applied to Distinguish Occupation Phases of Early Prehistoric Sites. *Journal of Archaeological Science* 29: 1235–1245.

Vanderhoeven, A., Vynckier G., Ervynck A. and Cooremans B. 1992. Het oudheidkundig bodemonderzoek aan de Kielenstraat te Tongeren (prov. Limburg). *Archeologie in Valnderen* II: 89–143.

Vanderhoeven A., Vynckier G., Ervynck A., Cooremans B. 2006. Het oudheidkundig bodemonderzoek aan de Mombersstraat te Tongeren (prov. Limburg) Eindverslag 2005. *Relicta* 3: 93–158.

Vermeulen, F. 1992. Céramique non tournée du Haut et du Bas-Empire en Flandre sablonneuse (Belgique). In *Actes de la Société Française d'Étude de la Céramique Antique en Gaule, Tournai 1992.* Marseille: SFECAG : 279–290.

Vilvorder, F. 2001. Les contextes de references et les horizons chronologiques. In R. Brulet, J.P. Dewert, and F. Vilvorder. *Liberchies IV: Vicus Gallo-Romain, Le travail de rivière.* Louvain-la-Neuve: Publication d'Histoire de l'Art et d'Archéologie de l'Université Catholique de Louvain: 359–377.

Vilvorder, F. and Rekk, S. *In press.* Caractérisation de la production d'Amay. *Documents d'Archéologie Régionale 5,* (Collection d'archéologie Joseph Mertens, XIV). Louvain-la-Neuve: Université Catholique de Louvain.

Wescott, K. and Brandon R.J. 2000. *Practical Applications of GIS for Archeologists.* Bristol: CRC Press.

Wheatley, D. and Gillings M. 2002. Spatial Technology and Archaeology. Bristol: CRC Press.

Williams, M.L. 2004. *Interpreting Prehistoric Patterns: Site-Catchment Analysis in the Upper Trinity River Basin of North Central Texas.* Denton: University of North Texas.

Woolf, G. 1992. Imperialism, Empire and the integration of Roman economy. *World Archaeology* 23(3): 283–293.

Woolf, G. 1997. Beyond Romans and natives. *World Archaeology* 28(3): 339–350.

Zahab, M. and Sawada, M. 2005. *Artefacts of Maas Distinction: Onsite Program for Archaeological Artefact Data Catalogue and Mapping in ArcGIS.* http://www.geomatics.uottawa.ca/ CIGConference_pdf/ Zahab_CIG2005.pdf. (accessed July 15 2009).

The Advantages and Limitations of Coring Survey: An Initial Assessment of the Poggio Colla Coring Project

Ivo van der Graaff, Robert Vander Poppen, and Thijs Nales

Introduction

It is a truism that archaeology is more than excavation. Archaeological survey, in particular, explores the interactions and relationships of past peoples with landscapes. Under ideal circumstances, the theoretical tools used in field-walking surveys are powerful instruments in revealing patterns of use and settlement across large swathes of territory. As part of multi-stage projects, the relatively non-destructive techniques of survey create opportunities for increased efficiency in terms of money and labour in subsequent excavations. Unfortunately, not all landscapes and research questions are ideal for exploration via traditional field survey methods, as factors such as high degrees of sedimentation, geopedological change and low surface visibility significantly hamper the ability to produce viable datasets for analysis. Nevertheless, landscapes with compromised visibility often represent areas of high archaeological interest.

Although a set of minimum standards or best practices in record keeping and data collection are useful and necessary developments of the discipline, survey methodologies are most powerful when tailored to local conditions (Terrenato 1996: 216). This paper assesses coring as a survey methodology using the preliminary results of a six week campaign, conducted over two seasons at the Etruscan site of Poggio Colla in association with the Mugello Valley Archaeological Project in Tuscany, Italy. The coring project carried out a regional and site-specific survey campaign aimed at overcoming the difficulties of terrain and surface visibility. The preliminary results of the Poggio Colla Coring Project suggest a way forward in survey methods for highly problematic landscapes. This article also briefly assesses data comparability problems between coring and field-walking results.

Located in northern Tuscany, the site of Poggio Colla fits into the landscape of pre-Roman native fortified hilltop settlements known as *castella* or *oppida.* Such sites played key roles in the process of territorial definition in pre-Roman polities, and served as focal points for the negotiation between indigenous populations and the Celtic and Roman expansions into the Italian peninsula (Terrenato 1998; Becker 2002; Vander Poppen 2008). Traditionally, excavation has formed the primary lens of exploration for such sites. Yet, in most cases, only the walled *arces* formed the object of study, rather than the settlements as a whole. As such, most studies have taken these fortified citadels as a proxy for the entirety of the settlement associated with such sites (Judson and Hemphill 1981; Barker 1988). The very nature and location of hilltop sites, fortified high places subject to erosion in often uncultivable terrain, precludes the application of field-walking techniques otherwise used to investigate the extramural settlements surrounding these centres. Rather, such sites form the ideal venue for coring survey techniques to assess the archaeological potential, settlement patterning, and diachronic development of fortified hilltop centres at a minimal investment of time and resources.

Settlement Development and Research History at Poggio Colla

Since 1995, the Mugello Valley Archaeological project has conducted excavations at Poggio Colla (Fig. 1), an Etruscan site some 40 km northeast of Florence (Warden 2007). Research has focused primarily on a hilltop plateau defining the *arx* of the settlement. A multitude of votive offerings, including inscribed statue bases, gold jewellery, silver Republican coins, and various bronze objects, suggest that the *arx* served primarily as a regional religious sanctuary (Warden 2009). The location of the site suggests that it also controlled the Apennine passes connecting Etruscan Tuscany with the region of the Po Valley. With the Gallic expansion in the Po Valley during the fourth century B.C., the area functioned as a contact zone between Etruscan and Celtic spheres of influence.

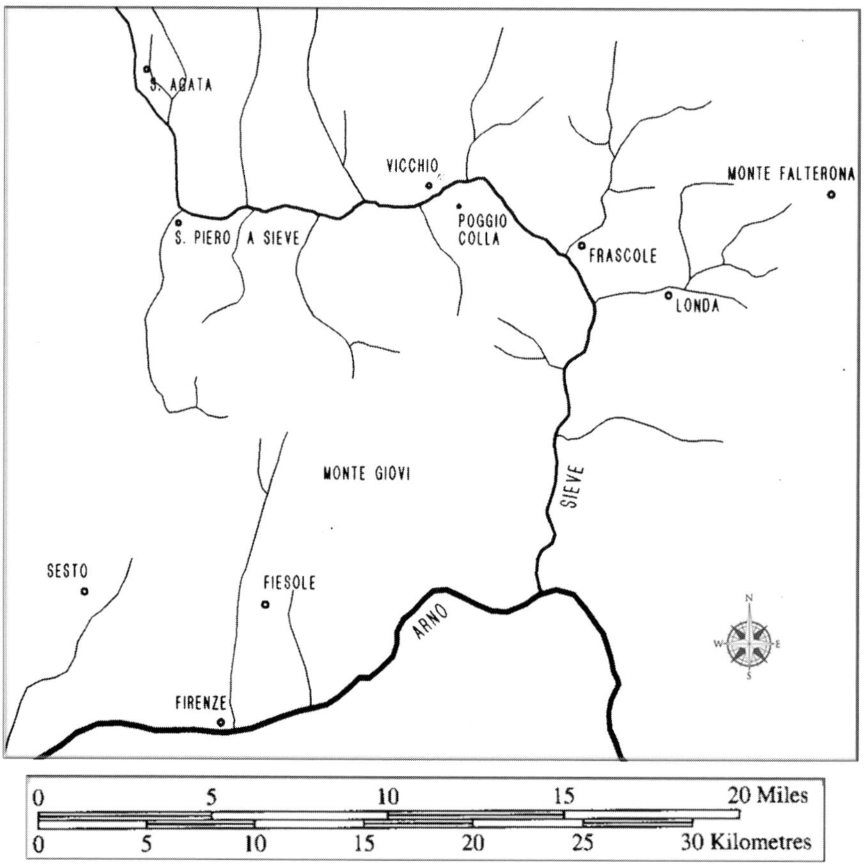

Figure 1: Archaeological Sites in the Mugello Valley (Map by Jess Galloway after Warden et al. *1999: Fig. 1).*

Excavation results point to at least four phases of human activity between the seventh and second centuries B.C. (Fig. 2). A series of postholes mark the first occupation event at the site, followed closely by a temple constructed sometime between the sixth and fifth centuries B.C. During the fourth century B.C., a further reorganization altered the *arx* into an open-air courtyard building with a central altar and hearth. The last phase, dating from the third to early second centuries B.C., saw the addition of fortifications, a terracing wall, and a series of storage areas, transforming the plateau into a fortified stronghold (Warden 2007). Such settlement types typically functioned as defensive border outposts in the territory of larger north Etruscan settlements, such as nearby Fiesole (Capecchi 1996; Becker 2002; Vander Poppen 2003; Van der Graaff 2006; Maggiani 2008: 368–371).

Figure 2: Archaeological remains from the Arx at Poggio Colla through 2009 (Plan by Jess Galloway, courtesy of Mugello Valley Archaeological Project).

From its inception, the Mugello Valley Archaeological Project applied a broad methodological spectrum to the study of the settlement. These approaches included a desire to explore the landscape around the fortified *arx*. Mark Corney of the University of Bristol conducted an initial topographic survey of the territory surrounding Poggio Colla using hachures, the shading applied on relief maps as gradient markers, to demarcate extant landforms (Warden *et al.* 1999: 235). This survey suggested the presence of a number of man-made terraces, but the lack of archaeological material led to inconclusive results about their type and historical use. In an effort to further assess the terrace structures, and verify local reports of substantial pottery surfacing on a nearby field, the Mugello Valley Archaeological Project initiated a pair of small-scale surveys in 1997 and 1999. The projects aimed to test both the viability of various survey methodologies and to obtain data on zones of interest. Preliminary results of the Poggio Colla Coring Project allow a revision of these results and include the systematic assessment of areas unexplored due to time, visibility, and manpower constraints.

Initial results of a limited field-walking survey in the Podere Funghi, one of the few ploughed fields in the vicinity of the *arx,* revealed a dense concentration of residual ceramics southeast of Poggio Colla (Warden and Thomas 1999: 119–120). Subsequent excavations uncovered the structural remains of a Hellenistic pottery production facility, including at least three kilns and a waster midden (Warden *et al.* 2005: 258–262). The recovery of vessels identical to those uncovered in a destruction layer on the *arx* suggests that the facility catered primarily to a local market. The Mugello Valley Archaeological Project also conducted a second limited survey on some of the man-made terraces identified by the landform study, employing shovel test-pits to investigate the area. The survey established the limit of a series of Etruscan terraces on the southeast slope of the hill, but the labour-intensive methodology discouraged further systematic use. Nevertheless, these early results prompted the directors of the excavations to state:

> '[I]nitial survey suggests that the lower slopes of Poggio Colla may preserve numerous rural structures, perhaps part of a farming community associated with the town above (Warden *et al.* 1999: 245).'

The importance of the site as a regional outpost, coupled with the early success of the limited surveys, led the directors at Poggio Colla to call for a 'large-scale field survey' campaign around the *arx* (Warden *et al.* 1999: 235).

The hilltop of Poggio Colla consists mainly of sandstone marked by unstable rocky slopes, bedrock outcrops and little soil. Heavy forestation limits surface visibility, while the steep slopes, heavy erosion and sedimentation washed away or buried occupation horizons. The lack of high visibility land rendered field-walking problematic, while limited time prevented a systematic shovel test-pit campaign. Under these conditions, the coring survey presented a unique opportunity to map the effect of post-depositional processes and assess the *anthrosols* (soils created or profoundly influenced by human activity) remaining on site. This simple, cost-effective methodology is capable of creating a substantial local landscape narrative unconstrained by limited surface visibility.

Low Surface Visibility and the Potential of Coring Surveys

In order to sufficiently understand the problems that low visibility landscapes pose for field-walking, it is helpful to trace their treatment in past survey programs (Banning 1996: 46–60). The pioneering survey projects of the decades immediately after the Second World War focused on site identification, regardless of visibility issues (Willey 1953; Wright and Johnson 1975; Potter 1979; Adams 1981). Despite their groundbreaking nature, many projects either included tracts of land without calibrating for surface visibility, or avoided such zones altogether (Terrenato and Ammerman 1996; Terrenato 2000: 60). As a result, the vast majority of archaeological surveys systematically underreported the number of sites in areas of low visibility (Terrenato 2000). With sophisticated sampling methodologies at the heart of basic research designs, visibility issues become all the more important as archaeologists attempt to populate whole landscapes on the basis of surveyed fractions. Within such designs, the lack of site identification in low visibility zones can potentially skew the extrapolated data.

Surveyors first recognized these difficulties while working in the temperate forests of the United States and Canada. In an attempt to correct the error, researchers developed subsurface testing methodologies, such as shovel test-pits, to recognize sites in heavily wooded areas. The processual tradition of New Archaeology further developed early subsurface experiments, concerning themselves primarily with establishing site detection probabilities within given sets of search parameters. The surveys were largely successful in predicting the likelihood of intersecting archaeological sites, thereby providing a reliable statistical basis for the extrapolation of data based on sampling designs (Lovis 1976; Nance 1979 & 1981; Nance and Ball 1986). Nevertheless, extremely low artefact scatter intersection probabilities coupled with heavy labour inputs formed a recurrent methodological criticism on such techniques (Lynch 1980; Krakker *et al.*1983: 478; Shott 1985; Kintigh 1988). The low absolute numbers of identified sites allowed for significant error in landscape reconstruction due to often infinitesimally small sample size. Test-pits were just too inefficient to identify sites on the basis of artefact recovery. More recent field-walking projects struggled with this problem further. Some, such as the Cecina Valley Survey, attempted, with limited success, to develop algorithms to cope with visibility effects (Terrenato 1992; Terrenato and Ammerman 1996; Terrenato 2000).

Although laudable in their intent, all these methodologies employed the site as the basic unit of study and ignored the evidence supplied by *anthrosol* analysis. The Poggio Colla Coring Survey alters two key components of the standard research design for subsurface testing: the employment of the two stage gouge/auger method to determine archaeological activity, and the shift from the site to the *anthrosol* as the basic unit of study. The adoption of an extensive core sampling program allows such conceptual shifts, creating a far more economical and efficient method for deriving subsurface data. Systematic campaigns of coring also yield datasets that, when combined with larger survey projects, allow for the inclusion of low visibility tracts.

Despite the application of such techniques across northern Europe, the United States, and Canada, academic surveys in the Mediterranean tend to ignore coring as a large-scale prospection method. Instead, such campaigns employ coring to evaluate stratigraphy at already identified sites (*cf.* Ammerman 1990 & 1996). Furthermore, even when employed, the vast majority of systematic subsurface testing campaigns simply assume that sites form ideal evaluation units. Given the low probabilities of site recovery mentioned above, single sites as study units seem wholly inappropriate to the regional scales under consideration. The low minimum threshold of indicators needed to discern the presence of an activity surface suggests that *anthrosols,* rather than artefact clusters, are more useful in recognizing past interventions (Valentine *et al.* 1980; Stafford 1995). The use of *anthrosols* as basic study units eliminates the complicating factor of artefact density from the calculus of site recognition probability. Such a shift allows the recognition of surfaces altered by human activity, even when these layers contain few of the archaeological indicators otherwise designating sites in traditional field-walking and test-pit surveys. The switch also provides an additional level of information beyond artefact scatters by conveying details about the state of preservation of underlying archaeological layers, a notoriously problematic factor for field-walking surveys (Odell and Cowan 1987: 456–457; Orton 2000: 57–60). In some cases, however, the shift to *anthrosols* as the basic study unit sacrifices the tighter chronological resolution offered by ceramics in artefact based projects. In contrast to such surveys, few or no chronological markers mark many of the identified traces of human intervention upon the landscape.

Not every region is suitable to such a methodological shift, but for landscapes like that surrounding Poggio Colla, where a significant central monumental complex suggests further habitation, it is ideal. As the pioneering work of Ammerman shows, coring evaluated on stratigraphy is a minimally intrusive method useful to construct site-specific narratives detailing size and history (Ammerman 1990 & 1996; Ammerman *et al.* 2008). Extending such a methodology into the broader landscape enhances survey results in specific environmental and post-depositional situations. Such an expansion allows for the creation of regional data amenable to spatial analysis of the sort employed in most field-walking surveys. Coring also provides an opportunity to analyze the long term environmental changes in geopedology, hydrology, and land–use. Other suites of archaeological techniques seem incapable of answering such questions. Field-walking, for example, obtains only a limited dataset related to surface scatter analysis while excavation, even on a large scale, inevitably provides a smaller landscape sample than achievable through coring. As a method, therefore, coring survey supplies another layer of enquiry, allowing the scrutiny of environmental and anthropogenic evidence within the same dataset. This type of analysis creates the opportunity to study human and environmental processes in a dialectical relationship.

Project Methodology at Poggio Colla

The full analysis of the *anthrosols* surviving in the vicinity of Poggio Colla required the application of a systematic survey campaign placing cores according to a fixed grid. A 20x25m base grid dictated the placement of cores at 20 meters intervals on lines 25 meters apart (Fig. 3). This spacing reflected the expected size of archaeological layers associated with small Etruscan dwellings and outbuildings, such as the one excavated in the Podere Funghi near Poggio Colla (Warden *et al.* 2005: 258–262). Such structures, often 5–10m in length, produce recognizable activity areas in the soil profile between 10–20m in extent (*cf.* Attolini and Perkins 1992; Esposito 1999: 25–26; Terrenato 2001: 13–14). The grid, therefore, maximized the potential of encountering the majority of sites within the survey zone (*cf.* Krakker *et al.* 1983; Kintigh 1988 on the potential of intersecting archaeological sites of similar size to those predicted). Compared to a square model the irregular staggered grid and its offset pattern reduced the probability of missing regularly spaced features within the study zone, and increased the potential of intersecting archaeological remains (*cf.* Krakker *et al.* 1983: 474–476; Kintigh 1988: 688).

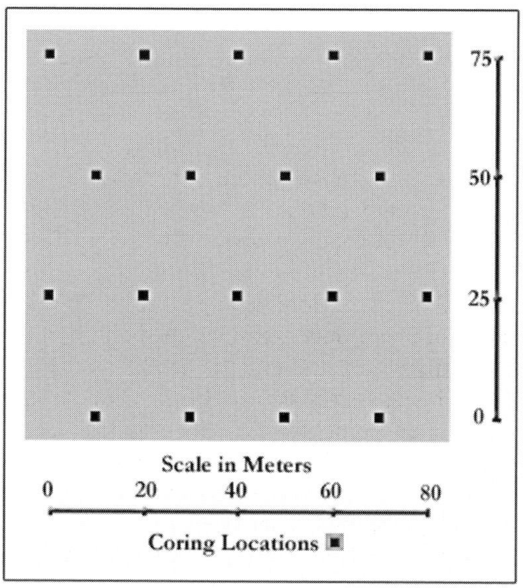

Figure 3: Sample grid for coring locations (Illustration by authors).

The frequency of cores increased to define the edge of layers and architectural features, while steep slopes, roadways, modern architecture, and land inaccessible due to a lack of landowner permission, required grid expansion or relocation of cores to adjacent areas. On occasion, the project also increased the frequency of cores to reduce the inherent probability error related to hitting or missing *anthrosols* in individual cores. The heavy forest surrounding Poggio Colla produces a considerable bioturbation factor, sometimes resulting in unclear core profiles. The use of the auger or the placement of extra cores in the vicinity of points where the gouge produced confusing or unclear results helped further clarify ambiguous stratigraphic matrices.

A TOPCON GMS-2 Geographic Positioning Satellite (RT-GPS) unit recorded the core locations using the UTM Zone 32 N coordinate system on the Rome 1940 datum and uploaded the points into an ESRI, ArcGIS geo-database. A topographical dataset acquired from the Rete Toscana provided a platform to develop a detailed Digital Elevation Model (DEM). In addition to calculating landscape characteristics, such as slope angles and natural drainage arteries, the DEM allowed the precise placement of core locations and three dimensional projections of the results on soil texture, stratigraphy and associated archaeological finds.

Each core used a cast iron open ended 3cm wide and 100 cm long ramming gouge. The inherent strength, versatility of use in most soils, and capability to produce an exact localized soil profile, led to the choice of this instrument. Furthermore, 100cm extensions reached deeper into the subsoil when required. In order to gain the most accurate readings of stratigraphic profiles, we recorded 10cm section intervals using USDA soil guidelines and Munsell colour charts. Only upon encountering intact anthropogenic layers did a 10cm sand auger supplement the gouge to retrieve associated archaeological indicators. Each 10cm soil sample was passed through a 5mm sieve, and associated artefacts were separated into bags according to core, stratum, and depth. The use of this two-stage methodology created significant time savings when compared to the one-stage process of test-pitting. The primary gouge supplied the stratigraphic information, while the secondary auger expanded the core only after the positive recognition of *anthrosols*.

Preliminary Results

Ideally, the spatial analysis of the recovered archaeological indicators would produce a diachronic history of the site. Unfortunately, the prevalence of coarse ware types in the archaeological assemblage at Poggio Colla has, as yet, undermined such attempts due to their long chronological range. Occasional datable wares, such as Etruscan *Bucchero*, *Vernice Nero*, Attic black glaze, and local Hellenistic fine and coarse wares, however, allow a tentative chronology of the settlement *anthrosols*. More detailed results of the temporal spread at Poggio Colla await further evaluation of the ceramics, and will be published elsewhere.

Depending on terrain conditions and stratigraphic depth, the two research seasons averaged between 15–25 cores a day to cover a total area of 35 hectares with almost 700 units. Starting from the *arx,* the survey expanded to include the neighbouring hilltop of Montesassi and the fields surrounding the Podere Funghi. The cores universally revealed bedrock composed of sandstone and/or clay at depths between 10cm and 250cm (Fig. 4). The sandstone consists mainly of quartz and feldspar with a high content of mica. The gouge easily penetrated the interface between weathered sandstone and the soil profile. The fields surrounding the Podere Funghi, and the area along the northeast and east slopes of Poggio Colla present clay, or nearly-lithified clay, above the bedrock. The clay is typically bluish-gray in colour and includes locally lithified fragments with minor percentages of silt and sand. The clay likely acts as an agent facilitating mass slope movements and soil creep, causing trees to show tell-tale S-curved trunks. In contrast, the predominantly sandstone areas southeast and northwest of the *arx* prevent creep and solifluction processes.

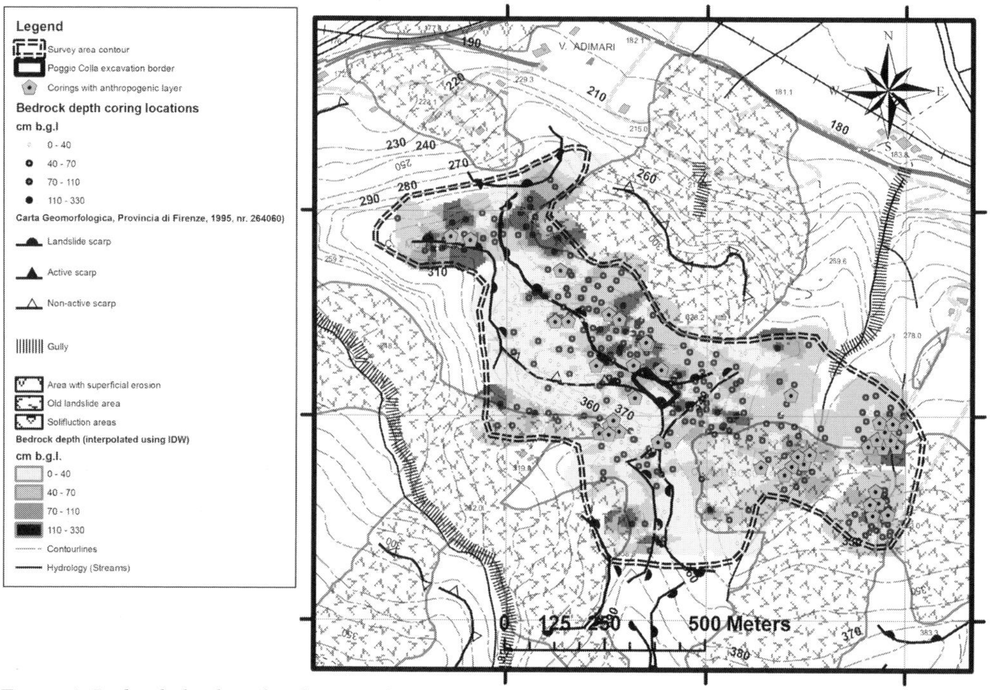

Figure 4: Bedrock depth and soil accumulation (Map by John van Tol).

A yellowish brown layer of sandy loam containing significant quantities of archaeological material covers much of the study area. The layer is far sandier and less compact than typical anthropogenic layers, and the small and abraded artefacts suggest mass displacement from their original location. Also known as colluvium, this soil fits into the regisol family, and consists of weathered bedrock washed down slope by rainfall and snowmelt. In some cases this process buried archaeological deposits, thereby preserving them to an exceptional degree against the effects of bioturbation and ploughing.

Initial results supplied a rough gauge of the extent of the surviving anthropogenic layers. The cores provided evidence for active habitation strata associated with fills and architectural remains, and more generic passive occupation accumulations such as walking surfaces and agricultural use layers (Fig. 5). These strata divide into two primary types of anthropogenic accumulations: passive prolonged silt sedimentations created through irrigation or habitation, known as *cumulic anthrosols* (ATc), and active *urbic anthrosols* (ATu) resulting from admixtures of refuse wastes or urban development fills (Valentine *et al.*1990; Driessen and Dudal 1991).

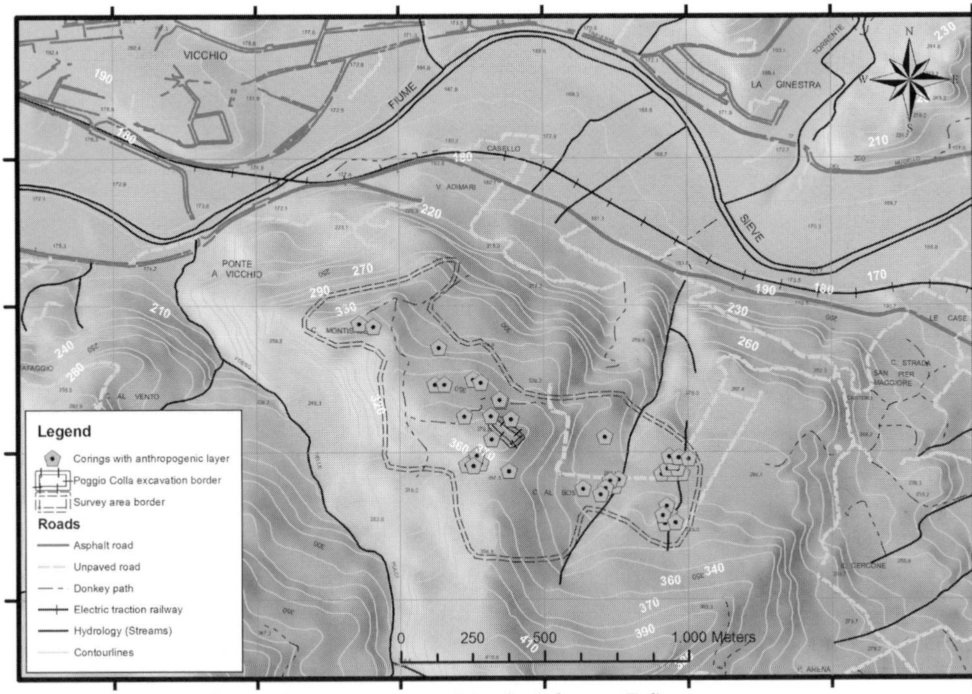

Figure 5: Cores revealing anthropogenic layer (Map by John van Tol).

A number of terraces present a dark yellowish brown layer with high clay content, frequently dotted with Etruscan ceramics and mudbrick. This heterogeneous layer appears to be a gradually accreting Etruscan habitation layer or *cumulic anthrosol* (ATc). An extended occupation event, probably related to walking surfaces or agricultural horizons, explains the tight packing and high degree of clay and carbon within the layer. The presence of this stratum across the landscape reveals the presence and extent of human occupation around the *arx*.

The *urbic anthrosols* vary in type and appearance according to their presence in the landscape and archaeological context. The most common type appears on several locations along the northeast slope of the hill as dark grey sediment of very sandy loam. The completely decalcified sediment produces a sulphuric odour when brought into contact with dilute hydrochloric acid. Green spotting within the layer suggests heavy phosphate content typical of midden activity (ATu). Cultural material dates the stratum to the Hellenistic period. Strikingly, the presence of hydrophilic vegetation, suggesting the surfacing of groundwater, correlates directly to the middening zones. The natural drainage characteristics of these areas probably invited intentional waste dumping.

The two layers mentioned above form the chief indicators connecting the cores to the occupation horizons related to the settlement. Within this broad matrix the cores revealed some clear examples of anthropogenic depositions such as levelling fills, floor levels, and possible destruction horizons associated with individual buildings. The characteristics of such soils, however, warrant more detailed attention than can be given here and will be published elsewhere.

Relatively flat terrace levels usually protected the layers just described from erosion processes. In contrast, the steep locations situated primarily on the north-eastern and western slopes of Poggio Colla present bedrock under a thin colluvium cover. Some terraces along the ridge south of the *arx*, however, appear to be naturally filled drainage gullies. At first, the mixed nature of the soil and finds suggested human construction of the terraces, but further coring yielded an eclectic mixture of medieval and Etruscan sherds resulting only from the occurrence of mass soil movements. Geological and geomorphologic maps obtained from the Comune di Vicchio confirmed our hypothesis that massive landslides created these natural terraces (Fig. 5).

Post-depositional processes and human activity have taken an enormous toll on the remains of a once significant settlement. The activities of a number of quarries, intense deforestation, and cultivation during the twentieth century A.D. have proved particularly destructive. The absence of vegetation caused extensive erosion, locally removing colluvium decks, and turning some areas into barren badlands. We must therefore recognize that our results do not project the full extent of occupation in antiquity, which will irreparably remain lost to conjecture. Nevertheless, the Poggio Colla Coring Survey revealed the remaining expanse of a once extensive habitation surrounding the monumental centre on the fortified *arx*.

The detailed analysis of the recovered ceramics will eventually reconstruct the diachronic depositional history of the surviving anthrosols related to the settlement. Despite this time lag in result processing, the evidence already pinpoints and suggests further exploration in several zones of high archaeological potential (Fig. 5). The application of geophysical survey techniques and test sondages could confirm the presence of substantial archaeological remains, refine chronological use patterns, and further decipher the stratigraphy found in the cores. This combination of techniques can follow up on the coring survey to produce a detailed and dynamic narrative of the heavily exploited landscape in the vicinity of Poggio Colla.

Strategies for Employing Coring as a Tool in Survey Projects

Moving beyond the survey results, a few further remarks concerning the integration of coring studies into larger survey projects are appropriate. The analytical unit shift from the site to the *anthrosol* renders any direct quantitative data comparison between field-walking and coring fruitless. On the surface, this seems an insurmountable difficulty, since the former employs artefacts rather than archaeological layers as basic analytical units. As yet, no consensus exists on the integration of data obtained from different survey projects, even when they employ similar analytical units and primary techniques. The micro-narrative of local landscapes obtained through coring can, however, qualitatively compare to broader surveys (Terrenato 2004: 44–47). By supplementing the picture derived from other survey methods, the narrative of formerly archaeologically invisible zones will add to the richness of our understanding of past landscapes.

On a regional level, geologists and geomorphologists use coring to reconstruct paleogeographic landscapes, but the archaeological utility of coring remains largely unnoticed. Within coring surveys, such reconstructions are crucial to understand the nature of the soils encountered in the profiles. As a result, coring also helps assess environmental factors influencing landscape exploitation, settlement location and regional relationships amongst communities. Furthermore, by understanding the circumstances of *anthrosol* conservation, coring also assesses the effects of post-depositional processes upon site preservation. Thus, coring can play an instrumental role in the research design of any regional landscape survey.

Both field-walking and subsurface testing, as site-based survey techniques, successfully quantify site identification probabilities on the basis of artefact assemblage recovery. Detecting and evaluating sites upon surface scatters in situations of low visibility, high degrees of geopedological change, or intensively layered paleo-landscapes, remains problematic. Once researchers obtain the necessary background for recognizing their presence in soil profiles, coring survey, using *anthrosols* as the basic analytical unit, represents a suitable and cost-effective procedure in landscape analysis (Valentine *et al.* 1980). This method allows the identification of areas preserving archaeological remains, and disqualifies regions unfruitful for further study.

Finally, coring generates regional and site-specific archaeological potential maps at a minimal investment of time and equipment. The two stage gouge and auger system allows a significant temporal gain, as the latter is only used when the former produces relevant stratigraphic information. Furthermore, researchers can use coring as a guide to pinpoint locations for future excavation or geophysical survey, while stratigraphic recognition and depth assessment within core profiles can expedite the excavation process. The minimally intrusive nature of the cores, however, does not supply a full picture of anthropogenic depositional events. Although coring can stand as an individual method for landscape analysis, it is not a panacea in conducting every survey. This paper suggests that coring works best when combined with other survey techniques and excavations. The procedures employed in any survey should reflect their suitability toward the landscape under consideration. In conditions such as those surrounding the Etruscan site at Poggio Colla, coring makes an ideal addition to the survey techniques available to archaeologists.

Department of Art and Art History, University of Texas at Austin
Department of Art History, Rollins College
Becker & Van de Graaf, B.V. (NL)

Acknowledgements

We wish to thank John van Tol for his invaluable work producing the maps contained in this paper and managing the GIS database. We also wish to acknowledge directors P. Gregory Warden and Michael L. Thomas, and research director Ann Steiner, of the Poggio Colla Excavations for supporting and advising our project. Kathy Windrow, Jess Galloway, Michael L. Thomas, and P. Gregory Warden generously provided permission to reproduce or use images within the text above. The Rete Toscana produced the original maps used to create the DEM. Finally, we extend our gratitude to the numerous student volunteers who drilled cores in the forests of the Mugello.

Bibliography

Adams, R. McC. 1981. *Heartland of Cities: Surveys of Ancient Settlements and Land Use of the Central Floodplains of the Euphrates*. Chicago: University of Chicago Press.

Alexander, D. 1983. The Limitations of Traditional Surveying Techniques in a Forested Environment. *Journal of Field Archaeology* 10(2): 177–186.

Ammerman, A.J. 1990. On the Origins of the *Forum Romanum*. *American Journal of Archaeology* 94(4): 627–645.

Ammerman, A.J. 1996. The *Comitium* in Rome from the Beginning. *American Journal of Archaeology* 100(1): 121–136.

Ammerman, A.J., Efstratiou, N., Ntinou, M., Pavlopoulos, K., Gabrielli, R., Thomas, K.D. and Mannino, M.A. 2008. Finding the Early Neolithic in Aegean Thrace: The Use of Cores. *Antiquity* 82:139–150.

Attolini, I. and Perkins, P. 1992. The Excavation of an Etruscan Farm at Podere Tartuchino. *Papers of the British School at Rome* 60: 1–76

Banning, E.B. 1996. Highlands and Lowlands: Problems and Survey Frameworks for Rural Archaeology in the near East. *Bulletin of the American Schools of Oriental Research* 301: 25–45.

Barker, G. 1988. Archaeology of the Etruscan Countryside. *Antiquity* 62(237): 772–785.

Becker, H.W. 2002. The Etruscan *Castellum:* Fortified Settlements and Regional Autonomy in Etruria. *Etruscan Studies* 9: 85–95.

Capecchi, G. 1996. Le 'pietre fiesolane': nuova carta delle segnalazioni. In G. Capecchi (ed.) *Alle Origini di Firenze. Dalla Preistoria alla Città Romana. Firenze 25 giugno 1996 – 19 gennaio 1997.* Florence: Edizioni Polistampa Firenze: 154–167.

Driessen, P.M. and Dudal, R. 1991. *The Major Soils of the World: Lecture Notes on their Geography, Formation, Properties and Use.* Wageningen: Institute for Land and Water Management.

Esposito, A.M. 1999. *Principi Guerrieri: La Necropoli Etrusca di Casale Marittimo.* Milan: Electa.

Judson, S. and Hemphill, P. 1981. Sizes of Settlements and in Southern Etruria, 6th–5th Centuries BC. *Studi Etruschi* 49: 193–202.

Kintigh, K.W. 1988. The Effectiveness of Subsurface Testing: A Simulation Approach. *American Antiquity* 53(4): 686–707.

Krakker, J.J., Shott, M.J. and Welch, P.D. 1983. Design and Evaluation of Shovel-Test Sampling in Regional Archaeological Survey. *Journal of Field Archaeology* 10(4): 469–480.

Lovis, Jr. W.A. 1976. Quarter Sections and Forests: An Example of Probability Sampling in the Northeastern Woodlands. *American Antiquity* 41(3): 364–372.

Lynch, B.M. 1980. Site Artifact Density and the Effectiveness of Shovel Probes. *Current Anthropology* 21(4): 516–517.

Maggiani, A. 2008. Oppida e Castella: La Difesa del Territorio. In G. Camporeale (ed.) *La Città Murata in Etruria: Atti del XXV Convegno di Studi Etruschi ed Italici, (Chianciano Terme, Sarteano, Chiusi, 30 marzo–3 aprile 2005).* Atti di Convegni Istituto Nazionale di Studi Etruschi ed Italici 25. Pisa/Rome: Istituto Nazionale di Studi Etruschi ed Italici: 355–372.

Nance, J.D. 1979. Regional Subsampling and Statistical Inferenrce in Forested Habitats. *American Antiquity* 44(1): 172–176.

Nance, J.D. 1981. Statistical Fact and Archaeological Faith: Two Models in Small-Sites Sampling. *Journal of Field Archaeology* 8(2): 151–165.

Nance, J.D. and Ball, B.F. 1986. No Surprises? The Reliability and Validity of Test Pit Sampling. *American Antiquity* 51(3): 457–483.

Nance, J.D. and Ball, B.F. 1989. A Shot in the Dark: Shott's Comments on Nance and Ball. *American Antiquity* 54(2): 405–412.

Odell, G.H. and Cowan, F. 1987. Estimating Tillage Effects on Artifact Distributions. *American Antiquity* 53(3): 456–484.

Orton, C. 2000. *Sampling in Archaeology.* Cambridge/New York: Cambridge University Press.

Potter, T.W. 1979. *The Changing Landscape of South Etruria.* London: St. Martin's Press.

Shott, M. 1985. Shovel-Test Sampling as a Site Discovery Technique: A Case Study from Michigan. *Journal of Field Archaeology* 12(4): 457–468.

Stafford, C.R. 1995. Geoarchaeological Perspectives on Paleolandscapes and Regional Subsurface Archaeology. *Journal of Archaeological Method and Theory* 2: 69–104.

Terrenato, N. 1992. La Ricoginzione della Val di Cecina: L'Evoluzione di una Metodologia di Ricerca. In M. Bernardi (ed.) *Archeologia del Paesaggio, IV Ciclo di Lezioni sulla Ricerca Applicata in Archeologia, (Certosa di Pomignano (Siena), 14–26 gennaio 1991).* Florence: All'insegna del giglio: 561–596.

Terrenato, N. 1996. Field survey methods in Central Italy: Between Local Knowledge and Regional Traditions. *Archaeological Dialogues* 3(2): 216–230.

Terrenato, N. 1998. The Romanization of Italy: Global Acculturation or Cultural Bricolage? In C. Forcey *et al.* (eds.) *TRAC 1997, Proceedings of the Seventh Theoretical Roman Archaeology Conference, Nottingham 1997*. Oxford: Oxbow Books: 20–27.

Terrenato, N. 2000. The Visibility of Sites and the Interpretation of Field Survey Results: Towards and Analysis of Incomplete Distributions. In R. Francovich and H. Patterson (eds.) *Extracting Meaning from Ploughsoil Assemblages*. Oxford: Oxbow Books: 60–71.

Terrenato, N. 2001. The Auditorium Site and the Origins of the Villa. *Journal of Roman Archaeology* 14: 5–32.

Terrenato, N. 2004. Sample Size Matters! The Paradox of Global Trends and Local Surveys. In S.E. Alcock and J.F. Cherry (eds.) *Side-by-Side Survey Comparative Regional Studies in the Mediterranean World.* London: Oxbow Books: 36–48.

Terrenato, N. and Ammerman, A.J. 1996. Visibility and Site Recovery in the Cecina Valley Survey, Italy. *Journal of Field Archaeology* 23(1): 91–109.

Valentine, K.W.G., Fladmark, K.R., Spurling, B.E. 1980. The Description, Chronology, and Correlation of Buried Soils and Cultural Layers in a Terrace Section, Peace River Valley, British Columbia. *Canadian Journal of Soil Science* 60: 185–197.

Van der Graaff, I. 2006. *Fortifications of Northern Etruria in the Fifth Century B.C.: A Preliminary Research into the Archaeological, Anthropological, Historical and Military Aspects of Fortifications in Northern Etruria.* M.A. Thesis. University of Amsterdam.

Vander Poppen, R.E. 2003. *A Convergent Process Model for State Formation in the Mugello Valley.* M.A. Thesis. University of North Carolina at Chapel Hill.

Vander Poppen, R. E. 2008. *Rural Change and Continuity in Etruria: A Study of Village Communities from the 7th Century B.C. to the 1st Century A.D.* Unpublished Doctoral Dissertation. University of North Carolina.

Warden, P.G. 2007. Vicchio (FI). Poggio Colla. Campagna di scavo 2006. *Notiziario della Soprintendenza per i Beni Archeologici della Toscana.* Florence: All'Insegna del Giglio: 38–40.

Warden, P.G. 2009. Remains of Ritual at the Sanctuary of Poggio Colla. In M. Gleba and H. Becker (eds.) *Votives, Places, and Rituals in Etruscan Religion: Studies in Honor of Jean MacIntosh Turfa.* Leiden: Brill Academic Publishers: 107–122.

Warden, P.G. and Thomas, M.L. 1999. Excavations at Poggio Colla: the 1998 Season. *Etruscan Studies* 6: 111–122.

Warden, P.G., Thomas, M.L. and Galloway J. 1999. The Etruscan Settlement of Poggio Colla (1995–98 Excavations). *Journal of Roman Archaeology* 12: 231–246.

Warden, P.G., Thomas, M.L., Steiner, A., and Meyers, G. 2005. Poggio Colla. An Etruscan Settlement of the 7th–2nd c. B.C. (1998–2004 excavations). *Journal of Roman Archaeology* 18: 252–266.

Willey, G. 1953. *Prehistoric Settlement Patterns in the Virù Valley, Peru.* Bureau of American Ethnology Bulletin155. Washington, DC: Smithsonian.

Wright, H.T., and Johnson, G.A. 1975. Population, Exchange, and Early State Formation in Southwestern Iran. *American Anthropologist* 77: 267–289.

Performativity of Place: Movement and Water in Second Century A.D. Ephesus

Cecelia Feldman Weiss

Introduction

To say that people and things move in space is not a particularly groundbreaking statement. It seems obvious, a taken-for-granted. However, only recently have the concepts of movement, performativity, and the experience of place been truly incorporated into archaeological thought and practice (Rogers 1991; Bergmann and Kondoleon 1999). For example, much of the discussion of urban space in Ephesus, one of the principal cities in western Asia Minor, has focused primarily on the formal elements of the city's architectural and artistic programs (Koester 1995; Thür 1995; Sherwood 2000; Scherrer 2001; Longfellow 2005). However, these architectural and art historical approaches have a tendency to foreground material remains and treat them as static entities, at the expense of investigating the changing and phenomenological aspects of lived space. Too often, such examinations fail to consider the dynamic and moving parts of cityscapes and the ways in which these aspects were integral to urban life in antiquity. I argue that the investigation of movement within the urban landscape can deepen our understanding of life in antiquity and contribute insight into the processes that make the city a lived and experienced place.

Drawing on the idea of 'flows,' (Appadurai 1986, 1994; Latour and Yaneva 2008) this paper explores movement within the urban environment of Ephesus as a means of re-imagining the dynamism of the city in antiquity. In an effort to break down the notion of a natural/cultural dichotomy, the two case studies presented in this paper were chosen as an illustration of the ways in which the city as place integrates these elements. First, I will discuss water use and management as exemplified in the Nymphaeum Traiani, and then examine the ritual procession recorded in the dedication of C. Vibius Salutaris. Thinking about what flows through the city – both things and people – promotes a more nuanced understanding of the performativity of a place.

For my purpose here, I define performativity broadly as the actions and movements of things and people, on scales from monumental to mundane. Much ink has been employed engaging with questions of what constitutes performance and how it can be identified in the archaeological record (Inomata and Coben 2006). Scholars from a variety of disciplines have positioned themselves on either side of a theoretical fence. Some define performance as ordinary and daily actions (Bourdieu 1977; Butler 1990; 1993; Hodder 2006), while others utilize the term performance to refer to large-scale public spectacle (Connerton 1989; Inomata and Coben 2006). Instead of positioning myself on one side or the other, I submit that both daily actions <u>and</u> monumental spectacle should be considered performance, with each operating in different ways to different ends. Further, all of these theoretical approaches are concerned with the transmission of culture, and therefore conceive of performance as a uniquely human action. In contrast, I suggest that action of both things and people should be considered to operate in a performative manner. Both human and non-human actors contribute to movement and action in the world which, in turn, are integral to place-making (Ingold 2000).

Bodily action and performance have long been considered of primary importance to those processes that make 'place' (Casey 1996, 2001; Smith 1987). As I have suggested, the action and movements of both things and people in mundane and extra-ordinary circumstances should also be considered within the milieu of place and place-making within urban environments. The humanist geographer Y-F Tuan (1977: 6) contrasts movement and pause to illustrate his understanding of place-making. '…If we think of space as that which allows movement, then place is pause; each pause in movement makes it possible for location to be transformed into place.' Here, approaching 'place' as that which arises from the cessation of action, Tuan emphasizes how movement is a necessary component in the place-making process. However, unlike Tuan, who suggests that place grows out of a suspension of movement, I believe that active engagement with the world makes place. This theoretical perspective offers insight into the ways in which we conceptualize ancient urban environments and presents a means to examine cities in antiquity as dynamic and experienced places.

Ephesus serves as an instructive case study because it has been thoroughly investigated and published. However, like many examples from the Roman world, the study of these urban environments has largely neglected the centrality of movement and human engagement as integral to the urban landscape. Admittedly, there are undeniable challenges implicit in a project that attempts to invoke impermanent actions and movements through the evidence that remains – namely architecture and the literary and epigraphic record. However, the detailed instruction of the Salutaris inscription, coupled with the extraordinary preservation of the urban fabric of Ephesus, provides a productive starting point.

Water and Movement in Ephesus

Ephesus is a city surrounded by water. West of the city, the harbour fed into the wide expanse of the Mediterranean Sea. On the eastern side of the urban centre the Selinos, Marnas, and Kaystros Rivers all flowed through a low valley around the city. The Marnas River, in particular, was a major source of water for the city and also appeared on several of the coinages produced by the Ephesian mint (Rogers 1991; Karwiese 2006). In addition to the abundant sources of water in the immediate vicinity of the city, an extensive system of aqueducts piped fresh water into the urban centre (Wiplinger 2006). Of particular consideration in this paper is the water that flowed into the city as the result of large-scale aqueduct construction. This water, as opposed to the self-propulsion of the sea and rivers, moved as a result of human engineering.

Because water is elemental – in all senses of the word – it is simultaneously pervasive, highly symbolic, and lends itself to being aesthetically manipulated. In a study of movement within an urban environment, water provides a productive case for study as it is essential for life and is consciously employed in urban design and civic benefaction.

The performative nature of water was harnessed in many monumental fountains and *nymphaea* throughout the Roman world. However, the use of water as a decorative element was a major innovation of the Hellenistic east. Their early hydraulic displays used water primarily as a landscaping element to provide a particular setting for sculpture (Longfellow 2005: 23). Although water was first utilized aesthetically in the east, it was in Italy that monumental artistic water displays first appeared in urban spaces, in addition to their more common uses in sanctuaries, baths, and residences. By the period under consideration here – namely the second century C.E. – the supply of water to cities, through aqueduct construction and the erection of monumental fountains, was a well-developed form of civic benefaction and elite competition throughout the Roman world (Rogers 1991; Longfellow 2005: 23; Ng 2007).

The Nymphaeum Traiani, or Trajan's Fountain, was the monumental terminus of a large-scale hydraulic project sponsored by the civic benefactors Claudius Aristion and his wife Julia Lydia Laternae (Fig. 1). The pi-shaped fountain was located on the Embolos, one of the major thoroughfares in the city, running between the heavily-trafficked State Agora and market district. The back wall of the *nymphaeum* was formed by a two-storied *aedicula* (an architectural frame consisting of columns or pilasters supporting a pediment), topped by a triangular pediment, which framed the space above which the water flowed. In the centre of the back wall stood a partially nude statue of Trajan in the guise of a hero. In addition, various other statues of divine, imperial, and Ephesian notables occupied the surrounding *aediculae* (Quatember 2006). Although none of the statues now survive, from the size of their bases it is possible to discern that they were most likely life-size on the first story and just under life-size on the upper story (Ng 2007: 201).

Figure 1: Nymphaeum Traiani, Ephesus (Photo by author).

An inscription on the entablature of the fountain records this gift to the city of Ephesus and its citizens (Ng 2007: 199). The inscription indicates that the water to the *nymphaeum* was provided by a 210 *stadia* (*c*. 32 km) long supply conduit. Recent research by Wiplinger has identified the source of this aqueduct near the modern village of Büyükkale, northeast of Ephesus (Quatember 2006: 73; Wiplinger 2006). In addition, a surviving statue plinth dedicated to the emperor reads, 'To the Emperor Caesar Nerva Sebastos Germanicos Dacius son of a god.' Based on the titulature, which is again repeated in the dedication by Aristion, the *nymphaeum* is dated to between 102 and 114 C.E. (Ng 2007: 201).

Analysis of the hydraulic management and delivery system by Ursula Quatember (2006: 74–76) provides insight into the movement of water into, around, and out of the Nymphaeum Traiani. She has identified the location at the back of the fountain where the conduit met with the building. A pipe system carried water from the main channel of the aqueduct to openings in the back wall of the *nymphaeum*. In at least three of the four *aediculae* in the rear wall, a small opening in each bay can be seen at about 25 to 30 cm above the floor level, probably for housing lead pipes. Quatember suggests that a low wall, which acted as a dam, would have provided sufficient hydrostatic pressure to push the water to the level of the pedestals on which statues rested.

The organization of pipes in Trajan's Fountain would have provided the necessary pressure so that water could flow into the main pool in a strong and constant stream. The statue of Trajan as hero was positioned in the centre of the back wall, beneath which the water gushed into the large central basin. It is probable that the water flowed from this large collecting basin over a parapet wall into a smaller, secondary basin. It was most likely from this shallower, narrower basin that the inhabitants of Ephesus collected their water.

The main drain of the fountain was located in the eastern end of the secondary pool. The unused water from the fountain was carried to the primary sewer underneath the Embolos, and was probably used as 'grey water' elsewhere in the city. When the secondary basin overflowed it presumably flowed over the parapet wall. Quatember suggests that there was probably a shallow channel in front of the *nymphaeum* that would take the excess water into another drain to avoid flooding in the street. This assumption is based on a similar installation at the Antonine *nymphaeum* in the Upper Agora at Sagalassos, although this cannot be confirmed at Ephesus due to the extant preserved paving dating to the late antique period. If her assumption is correct, the water used here as a decorative element and a resource for consumption literally spills out into the city.

Wiplinger and Quatember's work allows us to trace the movement of the water from its source outside the city, to the monumental fountain, and along the street. Using the raw materials they provide, it is possible to begin to re-imagine the activity of the water within the city. The *nymphaeum* engendered interplay between water and architecture, so that one was inextricably part of the other. The action of the water in the fountain as it gushed out of the opening, bubbled in the basin, spilled over the parapet wall, was scooped up by the inhabitants of Ephesus, gargled down the drain and slid down the street would have produced visual, auditory, and sensory effects. In this way, the Nymphaeum Traiani was a locus for the intersection of the built environment, water and people.

This interplay between architecture, water, and people was not the result of natural phenomena, but rather the conscious product of human engineering. The popularity of monumental *nymphaea* in the Roman world attests to a deliberate play with ideas of water and movement within the cityscape (Longfellow 2005). Prominently located on the Embolos, one of the major thoroughfares in Ephesus, Trajan's Fountain was a conspicuous monument in the urban landscape. Its position was made even more noticeable by its interruption of the colonnade that ran along the street. As people moved along the Embolos they would have been confronted by this imposing fountain with its gushing water. During their circuit of the city, the participants in the civic procession outlined in the Salutaris dedication also moved past the Nymphaeum Traiani.

The Salutaris dedication was bestowed on the people of Ephesus by C. Vibius Salutaris in the year 104 C.E. (Rogers 1991; Wankel *Inschriften von Ephesos* ("*IE*" below) 27.1–568). Both the Salutaris dedication and the Nymphaeum Traiani were bequeathed to the Ephesians during the reign of the emperor Trajan, at a time when there was a considerable upsurge in building projects and civic benefaction (Scherrer 2001; Kalinowski 2002). The dedication itself consisted of the distribution of money given to various Ephesian civic and religious bodies. In addition to the allocation of money, a procession – the movement of people and statues through the city – was to be carried out according to Salutaris' specifications. As they processed through the city with, among others, a silver statue of the emperor Trajan, the water from the Nymphaeum Traiani may have played with his image, reflecting it back.

The Salutaris dedication clearly outlined the route to be followed by the procession (*IE* 27.48–52) (Fig. 2). Travelling along the major thoroughfares, the path taken by the procession made a complete circuit within which the urban centre was circumscribed. Beginning at the Temple of Artemis, the participants crossed the *temenos* of the sacred precinct and followed the Sacred Way to the Magnesian Gate. The Sacred Way skirted the east side of the *Panayir-daği* (the hill of ancient Pion) and led from the Artemision to the sacred Ortygian groves, the mythological birthplace of Artemis. Incidentally, the path from the Artemision along the Sacred Way was also the beginning of the route used for the sacred procession on the annual celebration of Artemis' birthday, and therefore was surely an integral part of the urban civic and religious landscape.

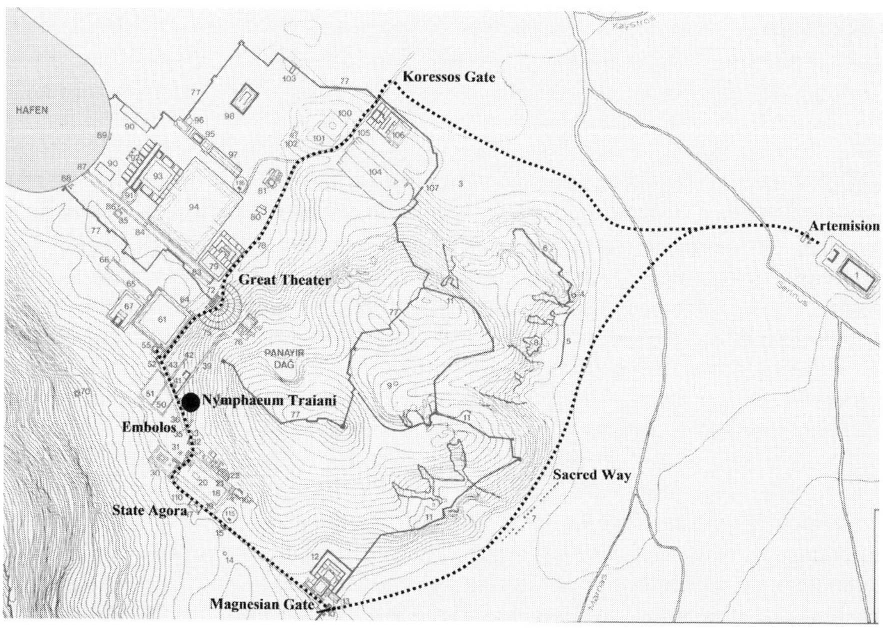

Figure 2: Route outlined in the Salutaris dedication (after Scherrer 2006: Fig. 1, with modifications).

At the Magnesian Gate, Ephesus' main southern entrance, the procession crossed into the heart of the city. The gathering of people would have passed through the State Agora (where the Prytaneion, Bouleterion and other governmental buildings were housed) and then down the Embolos, a busy commercial district and the street along which the Nymphaeum Traiani stands. The procession would then have turned a right angle to travel along the so-called Marble Street, the longest artery in the city. Approximately mid-way down the Marble Street stood the Great Theatre, where the procession made its only stop during its route around the city. After the pause for ceremonies in the Great Theatre, the procession would have continued down the street leading to the Stadium, then out of the Koressos Gate and back to the Artemision. By means of this path the procession circumambulated the city centre, passing several of the major public, civic, and religious centres along the way.

The Salutaris procession played into the architectural and topographical setting of Ephesus. William MacDonald's concept of urban armatures provides a framework within which to understand the processional route as taking advantage of the directional and spatial cues embedded in Ephesus' urban fabric (MacDonald 1986). Transitional moments during the procession were punctuated by transitions within the urban space. For example, the Magnesian Gate was both the point at which the procession entered the city and where the statues were handed over to the *ephebes* (young males about to enter full citizenship) (*IE* 27.49–50). Moreover, Rogers (1991) suggests that the route taken by the procession traced the history of Ephesus from the Imperial present to its foundation, by means of the mythological and historical associations attached to the built environment and the surrounding landscape. Whether or not this was a conscious choice, the procession nevertheless moved through the core of the city which was laden with history and meaning.

The procession also worked with the topographical setting of the city. The processional route wound through the low valley between the Artemision and the urban centre to the east of *Panayir-daği*. Once within the city limits the performers would have moved through the State Agora with buildings towering overhead on both sides. Then, processing down the Embolos, the participants would have descended down a relatively steep slope toward the harbour, visible at the base of the hill (Yegül 1994). As the procession wound its way back to the Artemision it moved through the relatively flat valley to the west and north of *Panayir-daği*. Just as the undulating terrain was utilized in water use and management at Ephesus, so too did the procession play into the landscape as it travelled downhill with the flow of water.

Also incorporated into the ritual were twenty statues representing notable individuals, groups, and topographical features that played a central role in Ephesian civic identity. More than simply visual representations, these statues were also participants in this urban spectacle. The statues dedicated by Salutaris were as follows: a likeness of the Imperial couple, Trajan and his wife Plotina; an image of the Roman senate, the Ephesian *boule* (council), the equestrian order, and the *ephebes*; a silver image of the deified Augustus accompanied by a silver representation of the Sebaste (the Ephesian tribe named in his honour); a silver depiction of 'the loyal demos of the Ephesians' and a silver image of the tribe of the Ephesians; a silver image of Androklos, the mythological founder of the city, and a silver image of Lysimachos, a Hellenistic king and (re)founder of the city in the third century B.C. There were statues representing the other Ephesian tribes and an image of Pion, the god associated with the mountain around which the city of Ephesus was built (*IE* 27.148– 197). As participants in the procession, these statues moved through the city along with the people carrying them.

Based on the occurrences outlined in the dedication, Rogers (1991: 83) estimates that this procession may have occurred as often as once every two weeks. Although the actual frequency is ultimately unknowable, the dedication indicates that this performance occurred regularly over the course of the year. Indeed, if we assume that the procession generally happened in practice in the way it is outlined in the text – relatively frequently, through the major roads in the city, and during the principle civic and religious occasions – it is fair to conclude that the majority of the inhabitants of Ephesus would have, at some point, either participated in or been witness to the procession. We cannot be sure for how long the performance was carried out. Yet, in its Imperial setting in the second century C.E., this performance was probably a regular part of urban rhythms in Ephesus.

The performance must have engendered an entanglement between the performers, the built environment and extra-urban landscape in a manner similar to which the Nymphaeum Traiani created an interplay between water, people and architecture (Casey 2001). The processional route literally tied the urban space to the extra-urban landscape, with the movement of people along this path activating it through their action. I suggest that through the frequent enactment of the performance, and the participants' continued engagement with the urban and extra-urban environment, the procession itself became part of the urban landscape. In contrast to the varied, every-day movements that happen within a city, the choreographed performance provides a clear framework within which to consider specific actions in a specific place. Through its staging and participants (human, architectural, topographic, statuary) the performance moved through and enlivened the urban landscape, and by means of its repeated enactment it continued to engage with the place.

Conclusion

From these two examples – the Nymphaeum Triani and the Salutaris Procession – the centrality of movement within the urban environment is brought into sharper focus. From the aqueduct water flowed into the city and out of both monumental and utilitarian fountains. By closely examining the interrelationship between the water itself, the architecture of buildings constructed to dispense it, and the means by which people accessed it, we get a better sense of the way water was incorporated into the urban landscape. Looking closer at the ways in which water figured in the cityscape highlights the centrality of this resource for urban design, public consumption and civic benefaction; melding together the natural and the cultural (if such a distinction can even be made) within the urban matrix.

Another way to conceptualize movement within the city is to think about civic ritual performance. Movement of people and things within urban environments was obviously a condition of life in antiquity but, in this case, the preservation of both the epigraphic document and the spaces in which the performance took place allow us to re-imagine (with some degree of accuracy) this movement in the city. As outlined in the dedication, the procession was probably carried out relatively frequently, contributing to the cadence of urban life in Ephesus.

Both water and the civic ritual performance flowed through the city. In both cases the flow of movement played into the architectural and topographic setting of Ephesus, with the performativity of water, people and things intimately tied to the broader landscape. Examining the flow of water, people, and things through urban space has been demonstrated to provide a strong case study for Ephesus, and this endeavour could well be expanded to other cities of the Roman Empire. Further, it is feasible to make a general case for the importance of performance in the flows of goods, building materials, light and even, potentially, waste and decay as the result of weathering and erosion. Whether further investigation of movement of a single element in a different context, or of the multiplicity of things flowing through a single city, the potential for further study demonstrated within this paper shows how much the consideration of movement has to offer Roman archaeology. In thinking about what makes a city a 'place', I argue that the movement of both things and people are integral to the process. Both flow through the city, activating the landscape and, in so doing, becoming a part of the place.

Joukowsky Institute for Archaeology and the Ancient World, Brown University

Bibliography

Appadurai, A. 1986. *The Social life of things: commodities in cultural perspective.* Cambridge: Cambridge University Press.

Appadurai, A. 1994. Disjuncture and Difference in the Global Cultural Economy. In P. Williams and L. Chrisman (eds.) *Colonial discourse and post-colonial theory: a reader.* New York: Columbia University Press: 324–339.

Bergmann, B. and Konodleon, C. (eds.). 1999. *The art of ancient spectacle.* New Haven, CT: Yale University Press.

Bourdieu, P. 1977 (Translated by R. Nice 1990). *The logic of practice.* Stanford: Stanford University Press.

Butler, J. 1990. *Gender Trouble: Feminism and the Subversion of Identity.* New York and London: Routledge.

Butler, J. 1993. *Bodies that Matter: On the Discursive Limits of "Sex".* New York and London: Routledge.

Casey, E. 1996. How to get from space to place in a fairly short stretch of time: phenomenological prolegomena. In S. Feld and K. Basso (eds.) *Senses of place.* Santa Fe: School of American Research Press: 13–52.

Casey, E. 2001.Body, self, and landscape: A geophilosophical Inquiry into the place-world. In P.C. Adams, S. Hoelscher and K. Till (eds.) *Textures of place: exploring humanist geographies.* Minneapolis: University of Minnesota Press: 403–25.

Connerton, P. 1989. *How societies remember.* Cambridge: Cambridge University Press.

Hodder, I. 2006. The spectacle of daily performance at Çatalhöyük. In T. Inomata and L.S. Coben (eds.) *Archaeology of performance: theaters of power, community, and politics.* Lanham, MD: AltaMira Press: 81–102.

Ingold, T. 2000. *The Perception of the environment. Essays in livelihood, dwelling and skill.* New York and London: Routledge.

Inomata, T. and Coben, L. (eds.). 2006. *Archaeology of performance: theaters of power, community, and politics.* Lanham, MD: Altamira Press.

Kalinowski, A. 2002. The Vedii Antonini: Aspects of patronage and benefaction in second-century Ephesos. *Phoenix* 56 (1/2): 109–49.

Karwiese, S. 2006. *ΠΟΛΙΣ ΠΟΤΑΜΩΝ* – Stadt der Flüsse. Die Gewässer auf den Ephesischen Münzen. In G. Wiplinger (ed.) *Cura Aquarum in Ephesus: Proceedings of the Twelfth International Congress on the History of Water Management and Hydraulic Engineering in the Mediterranean Region, Ephesus/Selçuk, Turkey, October 2–10, 2004.* Dudley, MA: Peeters: 17–22

Koester, H. (ed.) 1995. *Ephesos metropolis of Asia: an interdisciplinary approach to its archaeology, religion, and culture.* Cambridge: Harvard Theological Studies.

Latour, B. and Yaneva, A. 2008. Give me a Gun and I Will Make All Buildings Move: An ANT's View of Architecture. In R. Geiser (ed.) *Explorations in Architecture: Teaching, Design, Research.* Basel: Swiss Federal Office of Culture: 80–89

Longfellow, B. 2005. *Imperial patronage and urban display of Roman monumental fountains and nymphaea.* PhD.: University of Michigan.

MacDonald, W. L. 1986. *The architecture of the Roman Empire.* Yale Publications in the History of Art. New Haven: Yale University Press.

Ng, D. 2007. Ephesos: The significance of the legendary founder to an internal audience. In D. Ng *Manipulation of memory: Public buildings and decorative programs in Roman cities of Asia Minor.* PhD: University of Michigan: 183–233.

Quatember, U. 2006. The water management and delivery system of the Nymphaeum Traiani at Ephesus. In G. Wiplinger (ed.) *Cura Aquarum in Ephesus: Proceedings of the Twelfth International Congress on the History of Water Management and Hydraulic Engineering in the Mediterranean Region, Ephesus/Selçuk, Turkey, October 2–10, 2004.* Dudley, MA: Peeters: 73–78.

Rogers, G. 1991. *The Sacred Identity of Ephesus.* New York and London: Routledge.

Scherrer, P. 2001. The historical topography of Ephesos. In D. Parrish (ed.) *Urbanism in western Asia Minor.* JRA Supplement 45. Portsmouth, RI: Journal of Roman Archaeology: 57–95.

Scherrer, P. 2006. Die Fernwasserversorgung von Ephesos in der Romischen Kaiserzeit. Synopse der epigraphischen Quellen. In G. Wiplinger (ed.) *Cura Aquarum in Ephesus: Proceedings of the Twelfth International Congress on the History of Water Management and Hydraulic Engineering in the Mediterranean Region, Ephesus/Selçuk, Turkey, October 2–10, 2004.* Dudley, MA: Peeters: 45–58

Sherwood, A. 2000. *Roman architectural influence in provincial Asia: Augustus to Severus Alexander.* PhD.: Princeton University.

Smith, J.Z. 1987. *To take place: Toward a theory in ritual.* Chicago: University of Chicago Press.

Thür, H. 1995. The processional way in Ephesos as a place of cult and burial. In H. Koester (ed.) *Ephesos metropolis of Asia: an interdisciplinary approach to its archaeology, religion, and culture.* Cambridge: Harvard Theological Studies: 157–200.

Tuan, Y.-F. 1977. *Space and place: The perspectives of experience.* Minneapolis: University of Minnesota Press.

Wiplinger, G. 2006. "Wasser für Ephesos. Stand der Erforschug der Wasserversorgung. In G. Wiplinger (ed.) *Cura Aquarum in Ephesus: Proceedings of the Twelfth International Congress on the History of Water Management and Hydraulic Engineering in the Mediterranean Region, Ephesus/Selçuk, Turkey, October 2–10, 2004.* Dudley, MA: Peeters: 23–37.

Yegül, F. 1994. Ephesus: The street experience in ancient Ephesus. In Z. Çelik, D. Favro and R. Ingersoll (eds.) *Streets: Critical perspectives on public space.* Berkeley: University of California Press: 95–110.

Wankel, H (ed.). 1979–84. *Die Inschriften von Ephesos I – VIII.* Bonn: Habelt.

Horti in the City of Rome: Emulation and Transcendence in the Late Republic and Early Empire

Simon Wood

Introduction

Suetonius states that the emperor Otho expended some 50,000,000 sesterces in attempting to complete the *Domus Aurea* (*Oth*.7). Unfinished on Nero's death, its huge scale provoked a literary invective condemning Nero's posthumous reputation, Pliny the Elder suggesting that Nero's palace encircled Rome (*HN*.36.111), and Martial that 'a single house stood in all the city' (*Spect*.2.4). The emphasis placed on the vastness of the *Domus Aurea* is significant, drawing our attention to the real reason for opposition; not the palace itself, but its sprawling grounds which climbed Rome's hills and dominated the heart of the city. One need only consider the actions of Vespasian in founding the Flavian dynasty to confirm this assertion; replacing Nero's expansive estate and enclosed lake with the Colosseum (Suet.*Vesp*.9.1), whilst the palace itself survived until the reign of Trajan before its destruction by fire. More pertinently for this paper, the grounds of the *Domus Aurea* reveal what *horti* had become by A.D. 68, evolving from their early Republican kitchen-garden origins to expansive green areas for public benefit under the Julio-Claudians.

This paper intends to tackle one aspect of this diverse subject, namely the manner in which Rome's late Republican elite and Julio-Claudian emperors exploited *horti* as an influential (propaganda) medium, seeking to emulate and transcend the models of their predecessors in an attempt to validate their positions of authority. In an effort to highlight this trend succinctly, four case studies of *horti* in the city of Rome will receive analysis: the *Horti Luculliani*, the first great set of *horti* to grace the capital, the competing *horti* of Pompey and Julius Caesar, the Augustan *Campus Martius*, and Nero's *Domus Aurea*. Although this makes it necessary to omit detailed discussion of private *horti* such as the *Horti Maecenatiani* on the *Esquiline*, it was through **public** *horti* that Rome's aristocrats and emperors were able to embrace and truly influence a diverse city-populace, fulfilling their political objectives and cultivating their self-styled public images in the process.

The Horti Luculliani

In his discussion of *horti* in the city of Rome, Pliny the Elder (*HN*.19.50) comments that 'Nowadays indeed even under the name of gardens people possess the luxury of regular farms and country houses actually within the city'. While it would take the destruction wrought by the A.D. 64 fire under Nero to make the creation of *horti* 'within the city' a reality, his description highlights the significant transformation *horti* underwent in little more than a century; introducing Rome's poorest to a level of luxury previously reserved for the aristocratic elite. During the mid-late Republic, the fortunes amassed by Roman generals saw them construct palatial villas and vast estates (*horti*) away from the city of Rome in Roman Campania, cluttering the shoreline along the Bay of Naples and conveying the 'impression of cities' (Plin.*Ep*.2.17.27; Strab.5.4.8). Providing the Roman elite with an alternative life of *luxuria* away from Rome, such an existence was nonetheless incompatible with their political responsibilities in the *Forum Romanum* (D'Arms 1970: passim). The general Lucullus was the first to bring luxury *horti* to Rome in the late 60's B.C. (Jolivet 1987: 875-904; Troester

2008: esp. 49–76). Overlooking the *Campus Martius* from their elevated position on the *Pincian*, they were renowned for their lavishness even during the Empire when they became an Imperial holding (Plut.*Luc*.39.2), a fate that befell many of Rome's most prominent estates. Unlike later *horti*, these were a private domain, allowing Lucullus to retire from political life, entertain his aristocratic peers in his famed dining rooms, and mingle with Greek intellectuals in his libraries (Plut.*Luc*.42.1-2). However, their proximity to Rome kept him close enough to the political centre to interfere in the affairs of his great rival, Pompey (Plut.*Luc*.35.7). Indeed, it was the topography of Lucullus' *horti* that was especially significant; close enough to Rome for ease of access, yet outside the city walls, enabling him to withdraw himself from the chaotic activity of the urban centre. Surrounding himself with 'his costly edifices, his ambulatories and baths, and still more his paintings and statues' (Plut.*Luc*.39.2), it was here on the outskirts of Rome that Lucullus could submerge himself in a life of Hellenistic *luxuria*, not dissimilar to his existence on the Bay of Naples (Plut.*Luc*.1.4, 38.2-4). In this respect, the *Horti Luculliani* set a crucial precedent, leading to the transformation of Rome's urban periphery into an opulent cultural retreat for the wealthy minority (Zanker 1996: 204–05; Champlin 1982: 99–101). Furthermore, it highlighted the potential of *horti* as a method of self-display to rival architectural ventures, a concept both Pompey and Julius Caesar would exploit to great effect in the coming decades.

The grandeur of the *Horti Luculliani* was not typical of the numerous villas and adjacent gardens/allotments lining Rome's many access roads. In fact, it is likely that only the *Horti Sallustiani* could have rivalled the size and sumptuousness of Lucullus' estate. As Nicholas Purcell (2001: 548–49) has rightly suggested, the exact composition of Rome's *fascia verde* – the 'green belt' that enveloped the capital from the late Republic onwards – is difficult, if not impossible to quantify (Fig. 1). Nonetheless, his terming of Rome's peripheral *horti* as 'peri-urban' is more than plausible, assuming a position on the outskirts of the city and so separate from Rome's densely packed urban sprawl, yet free from the true *suburbium* beyond. Edward Champlin provides further clarification, classifying Rome's peripheral *horti* as 'sub-urban' (suburb-*horti*-city), that is, as the inner ring of the *suburbium* (Champlin 1982: 98–9). What can be said is that luxury *horti* served as archetypal venues for self-display, a categorical statement of the proprietor's wealth and social standing. *Horti* owners embellished their estates with abundant Greek artworks for aesthetic pleasure (*amoenitas*) (Stewart 2003: 250), along with water features, baths, libraries, galleries and aviaries. This was not only intended to impress a visiting audience, namely aristocratic peers visiting on business (*negotium*) or leisure (*otium*), but the *horti* proprietor too, serving as a pivotal means of self-affirmation in the promotion of his self-image (Beard 1998: 31–2; Champlin 1982: 104–05). Cicero's writings (Cic.*Att*.4.10.1; *Brut*.24; *Orat*.110) reveal how the Roman elite immersed themselves in a private world of leisure within their *horti*, mingling with their senatorial colleagues and sharing in rhetoric, philosophy and other intellectual pursuits. In an effort to provide inspirational backdrops for their activities, they surrounded themselves with statues of renowned Greek thinkers from the distant past such as Plato, Socrates and Aristotle (Zanker 1996: 201, 206–08). As Seneca would later write,

> 'One must acknowledge one's spiritual ancestors and honour them as gods. Why should I not possess the images of great men to inspire my mind and celebrate their birthdays? I worship them and model myself after these great names' (*Ep*.64.9–10).

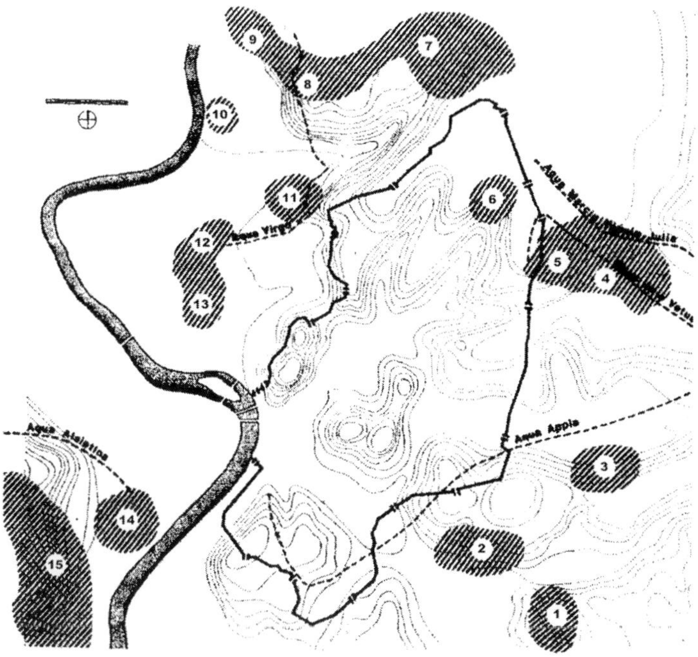

Figure 1: Aqueducts and gardens (horti) of Augustan Rome. 1. Horti Asinii; 2. Nemus Camenae; 3. Horti Vectilii (date uncertain); 4. Horti Maecenati; 5. Horti Lamiani and Maiani; 6. Horti Lolliani; 7. Horti Sallustiani; 8. Horti Luculliani; 9. Horti Aciliorum; 10. Mausoleum of Augustus funerary gardens; 11. Campus Agrippae; 12. Stagnum and Horti Agrippae; 13. Horti Pompeiani; 14. Nemus Caesarum; 15. Horti Caesaris.(Richard H. Abramson, from Favro 1996: Fig. 81).

The Horti Pompeiani and Horti Caesaris Trans Tiberim

Of course, statuary was but one component of luxury *horti*, a combination of art, architecture, water features and landscaping leading to the creation of ornate, highly contrived settings. They remained, to all intents and purposes, the preserve of the Roman elite until the advent of the Augustan Age at least, and so of no tangible benefit to the wider city populace. Nevertheless, it would be wrong to assume that Augustus' opening up of *horti* was without precedent. This was first evident during the political turmoil of the late Republic as Pompey and Julius Caesar vied for supremacy. Their battle for dominance manifested itself throughout Rome's urban fabric and the neighbouring *Campus Martius* as they sought to outmanoeuvre each other via publicly orientated projects, Pompey's stone theatre and enclosed temple of *Venus Victrix* being countered by Caesar's Forum and temple of *Venus Genetrix*. Both men conceived lavish *horti*, Pompey's in the *Campus Martius* adjacent to his portico and stone theatre, Caesar's on the right bank of the Tiber overlooking the *Campus*. The issue of public access is of particular significance here, since they were the first to appreciate the influential potential of green spaces, opening up their *horti* to the *plebs urbana* in order to fulfil their personal objectives. It is nonetheless true that Pompey's stone theatre, portico and surrounding *horti* signified an area which, for the first time, was conceived with the pleasure of the plebs in mind (Patterson 1992: 197). Plutarch writes of the masses going down to Pompey's gardens, probably to a public banquet, as part of Pompey's efforts to secure the election of Afranius as consul (*Pomp.*44.3–4). It seems likely that with the theatre and portico permitting admission to all citizens, his *horti* would have allowed public access also, or at the very least to specially designated areas (see Boatwright 1998: 74). Lying next to his theatre, the *Porticus Pompeii* contained enclosed gardens and accompanying fountains (Prop.2.32.11–16) in the form of a central grove, or *nemus*, 'interiorised *horti*' which complemented the lavish green areas outside (Gleason 1990: 10–11). Typical of other porticoes and religious sanctuaries, Pliny records that it incorporated numerous famous artworks (*HN.*35.59, 114, 126, 132), many of which would have been positioned within the central *nemus* in accordance with the character of exterior *horti* (Gleason 1994: 19). A famed location for social gatherings (Catull.55.6; Mart.11.1.11, 11.47.3; Prop.2.32.20), it afforded some of the most popular walks in the Augustan Age according to both Ovid (*Ars am.*1.67–8, 3.387–8) and Propertius (4.8.75). Collectively, Pompey's *horti* were an area for leisure, offering entertainments, relaxing walks and decorative artworks within fertile grounds. Their location in the *Campus Martius* was hugely significant in this respect, since they provided a sense of escapism from Rome's crowded, dirty cityscape thus far denied to the urban poor. Unquestionably, the *Horti Pompeiani* signified a considerable advance on the *Horti Luculliani*, underlining the untapped potential of green space as public space, and affording an unprecedented level of public *luxuria* to the *plebs urbana*. In addition, Pompey's estate set a valuable precedent for Augustus, revealing the influential potential of the relatively unexploited *Campus* in the dissemination of Augustan ideology.

The *Horti Caesaris trans Tiberim* should be seen as a direct challenge to the *Horti Pompeiani*. Positioned on the river's right bank along with a series of other aristocratic holdings, it was essentially a private estate and the venue where Caesar hosted Cleopatra in 45 B.C. (Cic.*Att.*15.15.2). However, in attempting to outmanoeuvre Pompey, Caesar is known to have hosted a grand public banquet in his *horti trans Tiberim* also in 45 B.C. (Val. Max.9.15.1), where according to Dio (43.42.1) he feasted the entire populace. The true extent of Dio's assertion may be questionable, but it certainly exemplified Caesar's exploitation of the communal meal as a popular measure (Plut.*Caes.*5.5, 55.2, 57.5; Suet.*Iul.*26.2). Additionally, it underlines the extent of Caesar's *horti* in that it was capable of hosting such a grand, large scale spectacle. As with Pompey's *horti*, Caesar's expansive gardens would have afforded Rome's poorest citizens a visual treat, surrounded by numerous statues, paintings and other works of art within verdant grounds on the banks of the Tiber, allowing them to bask in the ambience of their surroundings away from the chaos of Rome beyond. It is significant that while Pompey's *horti* passed on to Mark Antony and in turn Agrippa, Caesar chose to will his estate and all its enclosed artworks to the Roman people on his death (Cic.*Phil.*2.109; Dio Cass.44.35.3; Suet.*Iul.* 83.2). This would have been a conscious ploy, intended to counter the daily access offered by the *Horti Pompeiani* in Caesar's lifetime. It is possible that Caesar could have announced his intentions to the people at the banquet in 45 B.C; it would have been a particularly astute case of political opportunism (D'Arms 1998: 42). It is evident that Caesar's generous benefaction to the masses set a valuable precedent for Agrippa, who would likewise will his *horti* to the Roman people (Dio Cass.54.29.4). In a broader sense, it reinforced the concept of *horti* as public space in the Roman psyche, providing Augustus with the impetus to transform the *Campus Martius* into a luscious communal region of colossal proportions.

The Augustan Campus Martius

The emperor Augustus possessed the authority, the resources, and the time to implement *horti* at Rome on a more comprehensive scale than his predecessors. The Augustan Age witnessed Rome's transformation into a city of greenery, improving the city's physical appearance in the manner of great cities of the Hellenistic east. Cleopatra's Alexandria was characterized by tree-lined streets and lavish gardens (Strab.17.1.8), whilst Antioch had its expansive Daphne Park (Strab.16.2.6), establishing the perception that a great city required ornamental foliage and public green spaces (Favro 1996: 178–79). In emulating and ultimately transcending these models, Augustan Rome became a city of greenery as well as marble (Suet.*Aug*.28.3), reiterating its status as an imperial capital. Landscaping and topiary, relatively quick to implement and a cheaper alternative to grand-scale architectural projects, gave Augustan Rome a more vibrant appearance (Plin.*HN*.12.12; 16.140). Rome's crowded, ill-planned cityscape (Livy.5.55.2–5, 6.4.6) could not accommodate green areas of considerable size – this would not be possible until after the Great Fire of A.D. 64. Although *horti* moved closer to the city and began to subvert Rome's city walls in the form of the *Horti Maecenatiani* and *Horti Lamiani* on the *Esquiline* (Purcell, 2001: 556), it was in the *Campus Martius* to the north of Rome (Fig. 2) that Augustus could implement *horti* on a truly unprecedented scale. As part of Rome's broader topographical expansion during the Augustan Age, the transformation of the *Campus* would have had a centralising effect on formerly peripheral *horti*. As a result, the aforementioned *Horti Caesaris*, *Horti Luculliani* and neighbouring *Horti Sallustiani* would have assumed an enhanced visual and topographical importance (Purcell 2007: 368). These estates had the benefit of overlooking the *Campus* from their respective positions on the *Pincian* and *trans tiberim*; public access to the *Horti Caesaris* affording visitors panoramic views back across the Tiber over the now unrecognisable Field of Mars. Conversely, a greater number of people could survey these *horti* in closer proximity from within the *Campus* itself; the *Horti Caesaris* viewable alongside a whole host of lesser gardens on the Tiber's right bank, whilst the prestigious estates of Lucullus and Sallust towered imposingly above the plain.

The region's susceptibility to flooding from the Tiber River meant that prior to the advent of the *Principate*, Pompey's theatre and adjacent *horti*/portico was the only monumental project to adorn the *Campus Martius*. Recognising the untapped potential of Rome's northern flood plain, Augustus commissioned Agrippa to drain the *Campus* as part of his overhaul of Rome's sewage system during his *aedileship* of 33 B.C. (Dio Cass.49.43). As a result, by the time Augustus ascended to power, he was able to transform the *Campus Martius* into a planned, monumental district during the 20s B.C. (Strab.5.3.8), an area where *horti* would play an ideologically significant role. In doing so, it is not unreasonable to assume that the identity of the *Campus* as a public area was transformed via *horti*. Despite being categorised as public land (*ager publicus*) since the advent of the Republic, the region's function as a public pasture and area for military training (Dion. Hal. 5.13.2; Hor. *Carm. saec*.3.7.25–28) was far removed from the defined, communal pleasure zone it would become at the advent of the *Principate*. Although remaining *ager publicus* during the turmoil of the Late Republic, the sale of areas near the *Capitoline* into private ownership in the time of Sulla (Oros.5.18.27), coupled with the construction of numerous temples as victory monuments, assuredly detracted from its' long-term public identity. Whilst Pompey went some way to reversing this trend with his theatre, portico and *horti*, it was Augustus' extensive implementation of *horti* and leisure facilities which transformed the *Campus* into a unique area for public recreation and relaxation. Porticoes, baths, theatres, and water features set within expansive *horti* – all would contribute to the fulfilment of this unprecedented public ideology. This was a hugely significant achievement for Augustus, underlined by his treatment of the *Theatrum/Porticus Pompeii*; ensuring that Pompey's leisure complex did not retain its status as a garden-theatre and, crucially, its associated ideological connotations (Gleason 1994: 24–6). Clearly, Pompey's successful benefaction to the Roman people could not be allowed to endure in its original form – such a powerful statement of public munificence provided by the transformed *Campus Martius* had to be interpreted as an *Augustan* achievement alone.

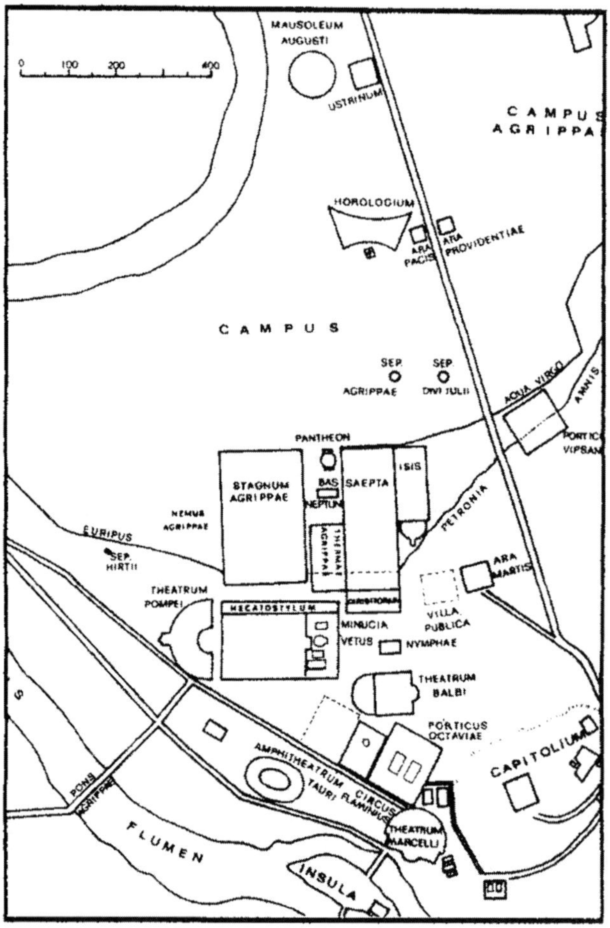

Figure 2: Plan of the Campus Martius, Rome, in the Augustan period. (Davies 2000: Fig. 93).

Many famous structures and monuments adorned the *Campus Martius* at this time. To the north, the *Mausoleum Augusti* dominated the region, whilst further south the *Pantheon*, *Saepta Julia*, and *Diribitorium* reiterated the monumental character of the *Campus*. However, it was as a recreational area set within expansive public *horti* that best defines the ethos of the Augustan *Campus*, when the northern and central sections remained largely open prior to the additions of later emperors. Writing in the Augustan Age, Strabo's description of the northern/central *Campus* (5.3.8) captures its quintessential character;

> 'the works of art situated around the *Campus Martius*, and the ground, which is covered in grass throughout the year, and the crowns of those hills that are above the river and extend as far as its bed, which present to the eye the appearance of a stage-painting – all this, I say, affords a spectacle that one can hardly draw away from.'

The description of the *Campus* as a 'stage-painting' is particularly relevant, a pointed reference to the many public *horti* either bounded by or adjacent to the *Campus*. Incorporating a combination of large scale water features and leisure facilities, it also provided an idyllic setting where Romans could enjoy walks and a variety of recreational pursuits, Strabo (5.3.8) speaking of a 'multitude of people who exercise themselves by ball-playing, hoop-trundling and wrestling.' To the north, visitors to the region could stroll in the lavish funerary gardens of the Augustan Mausoleum (Strab.5.3.8; Suet.*Aug*.100.4), whilst on the other side of the *Via Flaminia* dissecting the Field of Mars, the *Campus Agrippae* was set out as a public park (Gell.14.5.1). It was here that a huge map of the world was housed in the *Porticus Vipsania* (Mart.4.18.1–2; 1.108.3), a powerful statement of the *Pax Romana* and Rome's mastery over the known world. As the capital's main access road from the north, the *Via Flaminia* afforded the huge crowds entering and leaving the city an impressive view of the *Campus Martius* in its entirety. Elevated above the low-lying *Campus*, it would have highlighted the region's status as a monumental forecourt to Rome beyond (Favro 1993: 237–50; Zanker 1990: 139–43), its open, green northern/central portions countered by the already built-up area to the south. As a consequence, it was especially important for those structures punctuating the open areas of the *Campus* to offset its *horti*. To this end, the gleaming white marble of the *Pantheon*, the *Mausoleum Augusti* and *Ara Pacis* counterbalanced the region's abundant greenery, presenting a powerful visual reference to the Augustan Golden Age (*aureum saeculum*) which Rome basked in after 17 B.C. The Mausoleum is an especially relevant example. Strabo (5.3.8) mentions that its towering marble walls were crowned by an earthen tumulus and poplar trees, rising imposingly above the *Campus* to provide a physical extension of the surrounding funerary gardens. It would have provided a commanding sight for viewers both within the gardens and those looking north from the central *Campus*, a towering bronze statue of the *Princeps* at the summit (Strab.5.3.8) reiterating the status of the *Campus Martius* as a truly *Augustan* region.

At the heart of the *Campus Martius* were the *Thermae Agrippae*, a complex that allowed for bathing, rigorous exercise and walks within a public park (Yegul, 1992: 133–37; Ball, 2003: 232–38). As the first of the great imperial bath buildings, it was a venue which combined leisure facilities and abundant works of art within the tranquil surroundings of public *horti*. Agrippa located the renowned *Apoxyomenos* statue (the Body-scraper) before the baths, one of 300 statues to grace the public sanctuaries and green spaces of the *Campus Martius* (*HN*. 34.62, 35.26, 36.121). Together, the facilities and green spaces of the *Thermae Agrippae* would have afforded visitors a diverse recreational experience, but on an altogether grander, more comprehensive scale than Pompey's *horti* and portico. By this stage, Pompey's *horti* had in all likelihood passed to Agrippa, retaining their status as a public area. However, it was Agrippa's creation of large-scale water features that particularly separated the Augustan *Campus* from the exploits of Pompey and Caesar. Lakes and artificial watercourses permeated the region, the *Stagnum Agrippae* assuming a dominant presence at the heart of the *Campus*. Rectangular in form and lined with porticoes, it complemented the adjacent baths by providing a venue for swimming and large scale festivities, the famed Banquet of Tigellinus in the reign of Nero a notorious later example (Tac.*Ann*.15.37). Ovid speaks of plural *euripi* (watercourses) as one of the beauties of the *Campus* (*Pont*.1.8.37–8), a reference to the man-made canal which drained Agrippa's lake to the Tiber and to a channel which is thought to have taken water from the *Aqua Virgo* (Lloyd 1979: 193–204). Speaking of the latter channel, both Ovid (*Pont*.1.8.37f) and Seneca (*Ep*.83.5) confirm that it functioned as a bathing facility for the baths. Across the Tiber to the west, Augustus also constructed a vast body of water called the *Naumachia Augusti*. Some 1,800 feet long and 1,200 wide, it was the venue for a mock naval battle commemorating the dedication of the Temple of *Mars Ultor* in 2 B.C. (Vell. Pat.2.100.1; Suet.*Aug*.43.1; Dio Cass.66.25.3). Being worthy of mention in the *Res Gestae* (*RG*. 23), it too was adjacent to yet another public park (Tac.*Ann*.14.15; Suet.*Tib*.72.1).

The theatre of Pompey was the first permanent theatre to grace Rome. While the city would have to wait until the reign of Vespasian for the Colosseum, the Augustan Age saw the construction of three smaller entertainment structures in the south of the *Campus*; the *Theatrum Marcelli*, the *Theatrum Balbi*, and the *Amphitheatrum Tauri*. As with the projects of Agrippa, these buildings had the collective effect of celebrating the munificence of Augustus as city father (*pater urbis*), since it was his mandate as emperor that permitted the construction of such structures (Suet.*Aug*.29.5). Complementing the theatre of Pompey, they allowed for an unprecedented number of people to be entertained at any one time, promoting the ethic of unabated leisure during the Augustan *aureum saeculum*. Radiating the sun from their marble exteriors, the visual effect would have been striking; towering above the many *horti* of the region, and highlighting the comparative openness of the *Campus* to the north. Collectively, it confirmed the Augustan *Campus* as a defined leisure zone, the Field of the war god Mars transformed into a field of greenery where *horti* flourished. Ultimately, the Augustan *Campus* was a groundbreaking addition to Ancient Rome, advancing on preceding *horti* in scale, diversity, and level of public access. Likewise, it signified a unique blending of public green space and monumental buildings, a balance which would be lost forever with the structural additions of Nero, Domitian, and later emperors.

The Domus Aurea

Undoubtedly, the *Domus Aurea* represented the pinnacle of *horti* at Rome (Fig. 3). The accounts of Suetonius (*Ner*.31.1) and Tacitus (*Ann*.15.39) confirm that Nero's first palace, the *Domus Transitoria*, sought to link imperial residences on the *Palatine* with the *Horti Maecenatiani* on the *Esquiline*, allowing the youthful *Princeps* to pass freely between them at his leisure (Ball 2003: 2). It is safe to say that the *Domus Aurea* would have fulfilled a similar role, but on a wholly more comprehensive, grandiose scale to its predecessor. Exploiting the destruction of the Great Fire (Tac.*Ann*.15.42), its expansive grounds assumed an overwhelming presence in the heart of the city, embracing an area of between 100–200 acres (see the competing accounts of Van Essen (1954) and Warden (1981)). Climbing Rome's hills and dominating the would-be Colosseum valley, it dared to challenge 'the veto of nature' according to Tacitus (*Ann*. 15.42) by transferring the countryside to the centre of Rome (*rus in urbe*), refuting Roman morality and turning the natural order of things upside down (Champlin 1998: 340–42). Contrary to popular opinion which perceives Nero as a madman, his actions need to be considered as those of a youthful emperor aiming to legitimize his rule (Elsner 1994: 112). Egotistical, yes, artistically vain certainly, but such criticisms do not mean the *Domus Aurea* and its lavish *horti* were unplanned. Rather, Nero's actions need to be interpreted as a direct challenge to the urban/horticultural legacy set by Augustus some half a century before, aiming to emulate and ultimately transcend the efforts of the first *Princeps* in the *Campus Martius*, but doing so in the heart of Rome.

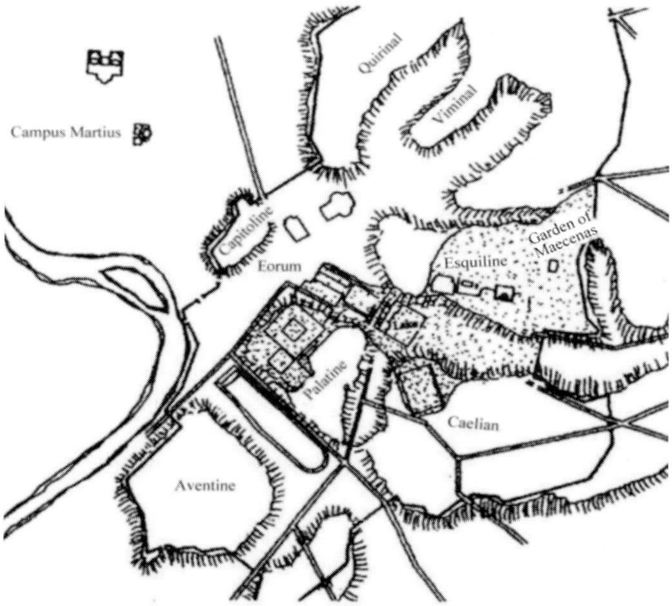

Figure 3: Schematic map of Rome in Neronian times, with the Domus Aurea area stippled. (Ball 2003: Fig. 1).

In the same way that Nero's palace would mark the advent of the Roman architectural revolution, so the *Domus Aurea* estate gave *horti* a new, innovative guise completely alien to Rome. Suetonius (*Ner*.31.2) states that they incorporated 'tracts of country, varied by tilled fields, vineyards, pastures and woods, with great numbers of wild and domesticated animals', whilst Tacitus (*Ann*.15.42) places emphasis on the 'fields and lakes and the air of solitude given by wooded ground alternating with clear tracts and open landscapes'. Embracing nature in both its wild and domesticated forms (Purcell 1987: 199), it is plausible that these varied settings offered a visual allusion to the many lands Rome held sway over, one where the Roman Empire was, metaphorically speaking, transferred to the imperial centre. To this end, viewers could ascend the straightened *Sacra Via* leading to the palace's vestibule and look down on a microcosm of the known world, a highly contrived setting that was intended to amaze and overwhelm viewers (Champlin 1998: 339–40). The *Stagnum Neronis*, a huge lake around which these diverse landscapes were gathered, formed the centrepiece of the estate. It must have been of considerable size, Suetonius stating it was, 'like a sea, surrounded with buildings to represent cities' (*Ner*.31.2). It is possible that the giant lake could have symbolised the Mediterranean as the centre of the Roman world, though this remains open to debate. Contrary to the long held belief that the lake was of irregular form, recent excavations have shown it to have been rectangular and surrounded by porticoes (Panella 1995: 51–5; 1996).

This is especially significant in the context of the Augustan *Campus Martius*, for it can be seen as a deliberate attempt to emulate the *Stagnum Agrippae*. Nero would embellish the *Campus* himself, his baths and adjacent gymnasium notable additions (Suet.*Ner*.12.3; Tac.*Ann*.14.47; Dio Cass.61.21.1). However, it is Nero's imitation of Agrippa's *stagnum* which emerges as a definitive attempt to transcend Augustus; emulating the *Stagnum Agrippae*, but transcending it by locating the *Stagnum Neronis* in the heart of a new Neronian Rome.

Public access to Nero's sprawling *horti* is a hugely important issue, and it is intriguing that there is no definitive answer. The aforementioned references of Pliny the Elder (*HN*.36.111) and Martial (*Spect*.2.4) accuse Nero of dominating Rome by treating the city as his house, further supported by a contemporary epigram recorded in Suetonius (*Ner*.39); 'Rome has become a house; citizens, emigrate to Veii; but watch out that the house does not extend that far too'. Such an invective would suggest that in taking over the city, Nero denied the populace access to his luscious *horti*. In reality, this could not be further from the truth. Various pieces of evidence can be cited to suggest the youthful *Princeps* needed, and in fact wanted, to invite the people into his vast grounds. First, Nero chose to straighten the *Sacra Via* which linked the *Forum Romanum* to the giant vestibule of the *Domus Aurea*, an act which encouraged people to ascend the *Velia* to his front door (Griffin 1985: 140). Also, Nero's construction of the *Porticus Miliariae* nearby (Suet.*Ner*.31.1) would have made this already thriving commercial zone all the busier with additional shops/markets. Interestingly, there is no archaeological evidence to support the presence of boundary walls/gates around the *Domus Aurea* estate, indicating that Nero did not hinder access to his *horti* or to the roads which inevitably crossed the grounds (Champlin 1998: 334-35). Besides, it would have been politically dangerous for Nero to alienate the masses by forcing them to circumnavigate his estate to traverse Rome. Then there is Pliny the Elder's account (*HN*.36.163) of Nero rebuilding the temple of *Fortuna Seiani* in a translucent marble, and 'including it in the Golden House'. In replacing a building destroyed in the A.D. 64 fire, it seems unlikely that Nero would have denied the populace access to the temple on the premise that it fell within his *horti*. The same can be said of another rebuilt temple, *Jupiter Stator*, situated just south of the *Domus Aurea's* vestibule. As Miriam Griffin (1985: 140) has pointed out, Nero would have been seeking an audience, not privacy, with the temple located so close to his palace.

As with the Augustan *Campus Martius*, it is important to consider the character of Nero's expansive *horti* as a public venue. There can be little doubting that, compared to the *horti* of the Augustan *Campus*, Nero's contribution in bringing about *rus in urbe* provided a more spectacular venue. Whereas Augustus consciously embraced existing Republican structures in his creation of an Augustan region, the *Domus Aurea* signified a far more individualistic, emphatic statement of the Emperor's majesty, reaffirmed by its location in the heart of the city rather than on the outskirts. The topographical character of the *Domus Aurea* estate is especially relevant in this context, being usefully interpreted as a bowl incorporating the valley and hillsides, but excluding the summits (Champlin 1998: 343). Whatever the vantage point, looking down from the *Velia* on the colossal *stagnum* or up from the luscious *horti* at the shining façade of the *Oppian* residence, the *Domus Aurea* would have functioned as an amphitheatre, enveloping viewers and compelling them to survey their surroundings. It is unquestionable that this was a consciously staged, public venue where Nero sought to propagate his self-image to a captivated audience. As Edward Champlin (1998: 343) aptly states, 'People are meant to look. Privacy is not an issue'.

As Nero's coinage testifies, the Great Fire of A.D. 64 marked the advent of his self-proclaimed 'solar ideology', with the youthful *Princeps* actively promoting his association with the sun god, Sol. The *Colossus Neronis*, a 120 foot bronze statue of Nero cast in the guise of Sol, was intended to stand in the giant vestibule of the palace (Suet.*Ner*.31.2). Although it is doubtful whether the *colossus* was erected during Nero's lifetime, it would have glorified Nero in the manner of a Hellenistic king; gazing out over a new Neronian Rome from its elevated position on the *Velia* (see Smith (2000: 536–38), who plausibly suggests that the *Colossus Neronis* never actually stood in the vestibule of the *Domus Aurea*, further supported by Champlin (2003: 304)). Likewise, it is probable the exterior of the palace was coated in gold (Suet.*Ner*.31.2; Mart.*Spect*.2). Radiating the sun and creating dazzling light effects, it would have provided a visually potent reminder of Nero's associated deity to viewers both within the *Domus Aurea's* luscious *horti* and beyond in other parts of the city (Hemsoll 1990: 29; Champlin 1998: 338–40). While the solar ideology of Nero's palace has received widespread debate (see L'Orange 1942: 68–100; Boethius 1960; Griffin 1985; Hemsoll 1990; Champlin 1998), the expansive estate within which it was set must have been equally significant in promoting a Neronian *aureum saeculum*. This was an age where a Rome of 'measured lines of streets, with broad thoroughfares, buildings of restricted height, and open spaces' (Tac.*Ann*.15.43) would rise from the ashes, the *Domus Aurea* with its palatial, emblematic *horti* the focal point of a new Neronian Rome. Reference has already been made to Nero's riotous banquet in the *Campus Martius* in A.D 65, an occasion of unrestrained excess altogether untypical of Roman society;

> 'He constructed, then, a raft on the Pool of Agrippa, and superimposed a banquet, to be set in motion by other craft acting as tugs. The vessels were gay with gold and ivory, and the oarsmen were catamites marshalled according to their ages and their libidinous attainments. He had collected birds and wild beasts from the ends of the earth, and marine animals from the ocean itself. On the quays of the lake stood brothels, filled with women of high rank; and opposite, naked harlots met the view' (Tac.*Ann*.15.37)

Utilizing the *Stagnum Agrippae* and its surrounding *horti*, it signified a reversal of societal norms, introducing the Roman plebs to a level of lavishness previously reserved to the elite at Baiae on the Bay of Naples (Cic.*Cael*.35; Sen.*Ep*.51.1-4; D'Arms 1970: passim). This was not a one-off event. Similar revelries had concluded the *Juvenalia* in A.D. 59 (Tac.*Ann*.14.15; Dio Cass.61.20.5), and Nero was renowned for banqueting in public in a variety of venues both within Rome and further afield at Ostia and Baiae (Suet.*Ner*.27; Tac.*Ann*.15.37). Uninhibited behaviour of this nature recalled the *Saturnalia*, a temporary state of affairs in Roman society where drinking and gambling replaced business throughout the city; masters served their slaves, and slaves might act as judges (Macrob.*Sat*.1.7.6; Sen.*Ep*.47.14). It has been plausibly suggested that Nero intended to introduce a perpetual *Saturnalia* at Rome, casting himself in the guise of *Princeps Saturnalicius* (Champlin 1998: 340). Recreating the pleasures of Baiae in the heart of Rome, the Roman poor would have been Nero's closest friends, the *Domus Aurea* an impressive venue for such audacious festivities; a literal stage for theatrical display, with Nero assuming the lead role. Crucially, it should be remembered that Nero was 'carried away by a craze for popularity' in the words of Suetonius (*Ner*.53), one factor which explains why the youthful *Princeps* would have welcomed the Roman plebs into the grounds of the *Domus Aurea*: he was an emperor who wanted to be seen! In addition, it is worth noting that Nero's embracing of the lower orders in such revelries would have served a dual purpose. Hated by the aristocratic elite for his actions after A.D. 64, they would have provided Nero with the popular support necessary to counter his aristocratic enemies. It would also have allowed Nero to satisfy his own base instincts, legitimising his behaviours by sharing them with the ill-educated, immoral masses. Contrasting with the more typically Roman leisure pursuits of the Augustan *Campus*, the *Domus Aurea* intended to offer the Roman people something wholly different and more outrageous, its luscious *horti* and giant lake providing an iconic venue for unrestrained excess in the centre of Rome. Crucially perhaps, it mirrored Nero's eccentric character, a statement of his own sense of self worth (Suet.*Ner*.31.2), and a categorical attempt to cement his place in history. In this, Nero certainly succeeded.

Conclusion

The *Domus Aurea* marked the zenith of luxury *horti* in the city of Rome, culminating an evolutionary process that had begun with the *Horti Luculliani* over a century earlier. The Neronian experiment of *rus in urbe* was an unequivocal failure, compelling Domitian and Hadrian to confine their lavish estates beyond the capital at Alba and Tivoli respectively. One may question whether this would have been the case had Nero ruled for as long as Augustus or Hadrian; had he done so, the topography of the city of Rome would certainly have been very different (Elsner 1994: 123). As has been shown, the development of *horti* in this period saw green spaces assume an ever-increasing public identity and function, a fundamental shift which correlated with the progressive transferral of *horti* from the urban periphery to the centre of Rome. The growing public character of *horti* from Republic to Empire can likewise be linked with the evolving aims and objectives of *horti* proprietors, the blatant self-display of the Republican elite being replaced by the Emperor's use of mass persuasion as *pater urbis*. Whereas self-display served the needs of the individual exclusively, mass persuasion brought reciprocal gain to the *horti* proprietor as well as his public audience (see Jowett and O'Donnell 1999: 1). Evidently, the transition from self-display to mass persuasion should be directly associated with the increasing level of public access to *horti* across the period. For example, whilst the private *Horti Luculliani* functioned as a venue for self-display alone, the estates of Pompey and Caesar were something entirely different; celebrating the power and wealth of their owners, but affording the *plebs urbana* reciprocal benefit in the form of ornate artworks, recreational pursuits, and temporary escapism from Rome's crowded cityscape. Indeed, it is highly plausible that the public green spaces of the ensuing Julio-Claudian era were motivated by mass persuasion, the transformed *Campus Martius* and expansive *Domus Aurea* estate providing all Romans with colossal green spaces and leisure pursuits on an unprecedented level. Yet simultaneously, the magnificence and benevolence of the Emperor remained an all-pervasive message, ensuring these areas would be perceived as definitive Augustan and Neronian regions respectively. Such powerful statements of grandeur and munificence were intended to endure beyond the *horti* proprietor's lifetime, with the result that Republican and Imperial *horti* alike would continue to influence the urban/horticultural strategies of successors (Elsner 1994: 113–16). Therefore, it is evident that the Augustan *Campus Martius* drew inspiration from Pompey's *horti* and associated leisure facilities, whilst similarly, the expansive grounds of the *Domus Aurea* and its enclosed lake were strongly influenced by the open green spaces of the *Campus Martius* and the central *Stagnum Agippae*. Furthermore, it should be remembered that in spite of his demise, Nero's radical reinterpretation of *horti* created a major dilemma for the Flavians, one that would influence and severely test their use of, and attitude towards, green space in the city of Rome in the wake of *rus in urbe*.

Epilogue

As has been stated, the *Domus Aurea* provided an enduring legacy for the succeeding Flavian dynasty (Darwall-Smith 1996: 35–41). Their destruction of the *Domus Aurea* estate denoted a conscious attempt to banish the memory of Nero, the construction of the Colosseum on the site of the *Stagnum Neronis* a forceful statement of their right to rule. Likewise, the Flavians can be seen to have redefined *horti* as public areas, refuting the Neronian model and seeking a return to the propriety of the Augustan Age. According to Dio (66.10), Vespasian is known to have 'dwelt little in the *Palatium*, but for the most part lived in the *Horti Sallustiani*, and there received anyone who wished it, not just the senators, but also of the others'. Whereas Nero utilized the *Horti Serviliani* as a private residence after the Great Fire (Tac.*Ann*.15.55), it was in all probability set up as a public park under the Flavians. A venue rich in Greek works of art, including marble statues of Praxiteles and Scopas (Plin.*HN*.36.23, 25), it would have compared to the many *horti* of the Augustan *Campus Martius* decades earlier where statues proliferated. The construction of the *Templum Pacis* can be seen to have paralleled the many porticoes of the Augustan Age, the likely incorporation of green spaces creating a form of 'interiorised *horti*' in the centre of Rome. It is perhaps fitting that many of the numerous artworks on display within the *Templum Pacis* were seized from the private reception rooms of the *Domus Aurea* (Plin.*HN*.34.84); Vespasian returning art to the Roman people as Augustus had done nearly a century earlier. Green spaces in the city of Rome regained a sense of propriety under the Flavians, but one aspect remains true of all periods from the *Horti Luculliani*, through the horticultural revolution of the Augustan Age, to Nero's *Domus Aurea* and beyond; it was crucial to emulate and transcend preceding models, *horti* functioning as a powerful means of self-display and mass persuasion not unlike Rome's urban landscape. In spite of his downfall and unfulfilled plans, it may be that Nero was more acutely aware of this potential than any of his predecessors.

Institute of Archaeology and Antiquity, University of Birmingham

Bibliography

Ancient Sources

Catullus (Translated by F.W. Cornish 1913). *Catullus*. Cambridge, Mass: Harvard University Press.
Cicero (Translated by R. Gardner 1958). *Pro Caelio*. Cambridge, Mass: Harvard University Press.
Cicero (Translated by D.R. Shackleton Bailey 1999). *Letters to Atticus I*. Cambridge, Mass: Harvard University Press.
Cicero (Translated by D.R. Shackleton Bailey 1999). *Letters to Atticus IV*. Cambridge, Mass: Harvard University Press.
Cicero (Translated by D.R. Shackleton Bailey 2002). *Letters to Quintus and Brutus*. Cambridge, Mass: Harvard University Press.
Cicero (Translated by C.A. Ker 1926). *Philippics*. Cambridge, Mass: Harvard University Press.
Dio (Translated by E. Carey & H.B. Foster 1916). *Roman History IV*. Cambridge, Mass: Harvard University Press.
Dio (Translated by E. Carey & H.B. Foster 1917). *Roman History V*. Cambridge, Mass: Harvard University Press.
Dio (Translated by E. Carey & H.B. Foster 1917). *Roman History VI*. Cambridge, Mass: Harvard University Press.

Dio (Translated by E. Carey & H.B. Foster 1925). *Roman History VIII.* Cambridge, Mass: Harvard University Press.
Gellius (Translated by J.C. Rolfe 1917). *Attic Nights III.* Cambridge, Mass: Harvard University Press.
Livy (Translated by B.O. Foster 1924). *History of Rome III.* Cambridge, Mass: Harvard University Press.
Macrobius (Translated by P.V. Davies 1969). *The Saturnalia.* New York: Colombia University Press.
Martial (Translated by D.R. Shackleton Bailey 1993). *Epigrams I.* Cambridge, Mass: Harvard University Press.
Martial (Translated by D.R. Shackleton Bailey 1993). *Epigrams III.* Cambridge, Mass: Harvard University Press.
Ovid (Translated by L. Wheeler 1924). *Ex Ponto.* Cambridge, Mass: Harvard University Press.
Ovid (Translated by J.H. Mozley 1929). *Art of Love.* Cambridge, Mass: Harvard University Press.
Pliny the Elder (Translated by H. Rackham 2006). *Natural History III.* Cambridge, Mass: Harvard University Press.
Pliny the Elder (Translated by H. Rackham 2005). *Natural History IV.* Cambridge, Mass: Harvard University Press.
Pliny the Elder (Translated by H. Rackham 2004). *Natural History V.* Cambridge, Mass: Harvard University Press.
Pliny the Elder (Translated by H. Rackham 2003). *Natural History IX.* Cambridge, Mass: Harvard University Press.
Pliny the Elder (Translated by D.E. Eichholz 2006). *Natural History X.* Cambridge, Mass: Harvard University Press.
Pliny the Younger (Translated by B. Radice 1969). *Letters I.* Cambridge, Mass: Harvard University Press.
Plutarch (Translated by B. Perrin 2001). *Lives II.* Cambridge, Mass: Harvard University Press.
Plutarch (Translated by B. Perrin 2004). *Lives V.* Cambridge, Mass: Harvard University Press.
Plutarch (Translated by B. Perrin 2004). *Lives VII.* Cambridge, Mass: Harvard University Press.
Propertius (Translated by G.P. Goold 1990). *Elegies.* Cambridge, Mass: Harvard University Press.
Seneca (Translated by R.M. Gummere 1917). *Epistles I.* Cambridge, Mass: Harvard University Press.
Seneca (Translated by R.M. Gummere 1920). *Epistles II.* Cambridge, Mass: Harvard University Press.
Strabo (Translated by H.L. Jones 2006). *Geography II.* Cambridge, Mass: Harvard University Press.
Strabo (Translated by H.L. Jones 2006). *Geography VII.* Cambridge, Mass: Harvard University Press.
Strabo (Translated by H.L. Jones 2001). *Geography VIII.* Cambridge, Mass: Harvard University Press.
Suetonius (Translated by J.C. Rolfe 1998). *Lives of the Caesars I.* Cambridge, Mass: Harvard University Press.
Suetonius (Translated by J.C. Rolfe 1997). *Lives of the Caesars II.* Cambridge, Mass: Harvard University Press.
Tacitus (Translated by J. Jackson 1999). *The Annals XIII–XVI.* Cambridge, Mass: Harvard University Press.
Valerius Maximus (Translated by D.R. Shackleton Bailey 2000). *Memorable Doings and Sayings II.* Cambridge, Mass: Harvard University Press.
Velleius Paterculus (Translated by F.W. Shipley). *Compendium of Roman History. Res Gestae Divi Augusti.* Cambridge, Mass: Harvard University Press.

Modern Sources

Ball, L. 2003. *The Domus Aurea and the Roman Architectural Revolution.* Cambridge: Cambridge University Press.
Beard, M. 1998. Imaginary *Horti* or up the Garden Path. In M. Cima and E. La Rocca (eds.) *Horti Romani. Atti del convegno internazionale: Roma, 4–6 maggio 1995.* Rome: "L'Erma" di Bretschneider: 23–32.
Boatwright, M. 1998. Luxuriant *Horti* and Extravagant Women: the *Horti* of Rome between Republic and Empire. In M. Cima and E. La Rocca, E (eds.) *Horti Romani. Atti del convegno internazionale: Roma, 4–6 maggio 1995.* Rome: "L'Erma" di Bretschneider: 71–82.

Boethius, A. 1960. *The Golden House of Nero: Some Aspects of Roman Architecture.* Ann Arbor: University of Michigan Press.
Champlin, E. 1982. The Suburbium of Ancient Rome. *American Journal of Ancient History* 7: 99–117.
Champlin, E. 1998. God and Man in the Golden House. In M. Cima and E. La Rocca, E (eds.) *Horti Romani. Atti del convegno internazionale: Roma, 4–6 maggio 1995.* Rome: "L'Erma" di Bretschneider: 333–44.
Champlin, E. 2003. *Nero.* Cambridge, Mass: Harvard University Press.
D'Arms, J. 1970. *Romans on the Bay of Naples: A Social and Cultural Study of Villas and Their Owners from 150 B.C to A.D 400.* Cambridge, Mass: Harvard University Press.
D'Arms, J. 1998. Between Public and Private: The *Epulum Publicum* and Caesar's *Horti Trans Tiberim.* In M. Cima and E. La Rocca, E (eds.) *Horti Romani. Atti del convegno internazionale: Roma, 4–6 maggio 1995.* Rome: "L'Erma" di Bretschneider: 33–44.
Darwall-Smith, R. 1996. *Emperors and Architecture: A Study of Flavian Rome.* Brussels: Collection Latomus.
Davies, P. 2000. *Death and the Emperor: Roman Funerary Monuments from Augustus to Marcus Aurelius.* New York: Cambridge University Press.
Elsner, J. 1994. Constructing decadence: the representation of Nero as imperial builder. In J. Elsner, and J. Masters (eds.) *Reflections of Nero: Culture, History, and Representation.* Chapel Hill: The University of North Carolina: 112–27.
Favro, D. 1993. Reading the Augustan City. In P. Holliday (ed.) *Narrative and Event in Ancient Art.* New York: Cambridge University Press: 230–57.
Favro, D. 1996. *The Urban Image of Augustan Rome.* New York: Cambridge University Press.
Gleason, K. 1990. The Garden Portico of Pompey the Great: An Ancient Park Preserved in the Layers of Rome. *Expedition* 32.2: 3–13.
Gleason, K. 1994. Porticus Pompeiana: A New Perspective on the First Public Park of Ancient Rome. *Journal of Garden History* 14.1 (January–March): 13–27.
Griffin, M. 1985. *Nero: The End of a Dynasty.* New Haven: Yale University Press.
Hemsoll, D. 1990. The Architecture of Nero's Golden House. In M. Henig (ed.) *Architecture and Architectural Sculpture in the Roman Empire.* Oxford: Oxford University Press: 10–38.
Jolivet, V. 1987. Xerxes Togatus: Lucullus en Campanie. *Mélanges d'archéologie et d'histoire de l'École française de Rome* 99: 875–904.
Jowett, G and O'Donnell, V. 1999. *Propaganda and Persuasion.* Sage Publications.
Lloyd, R. 1979. The *Aqua Virgo*, *Euripus*, and *Pons Agripppae. American Journal of Archaeology* 83: 193–204.
L'Orange, H. 1942. Domus Aurea, der Sonnenpalast. *Symbolae Osloenses* 11: 68–100.
Panella, C. 1995. *Domus Aurea*: Area dello *Stagnum*. In. E.Steinby (ed.) *Lexicon Topographicum Urbis Romae II.* Rome: Quasar: 51–5.
Panella, C (ed). 1996. *Meta Sudans, I: Un area sacra in Palatio et la valle del Colosseo prima e dopo Nerone.* Rome: Istituto Poligrafico e Zecca dello Stato, Libreria dello Stato
Patterson, J. 1992. Review Article. The City of Rome: From Republic to Empire. *Journal of Roman Studies* 82: 186–215.
Purcell, N. 1987. Town in Country and Country in Town. In E. Macdougall (ed.) *Ancient Roman Villa Gardens.* Dumbarton Oaks colloquium on the history of landscape architecture 10. Washington: D.C, Harvard University Press: 187–203.
Purcell, N. 2001. Dialectical Gardening. *Journal of Roman Archaeology* 14: 546–56.
Purcell, N. 2007. The *horti* of Rome and the landscape of property. In A. Leone, D. Palombi and S. Walker (eds) *Res Bene Gestae: ricerche di storia urbana su Roma antica in onore di Eva Margareta Steinby.* Rome: Quasar: 361–77.
Smith, R. 2000. Nero and the Sun-god: divine accessories and political symbols in Roman imperial images. *Journal of Roman Archaeology* 13: 532–42.
Stewart, P. 2003. *Statues in Roman Society: Representation and Response.* Oxford: Oxford University Press.

Tröester, M. 2008. *Themes, Character, and Politics in Plutarch's Life of Lucullus: The Construction of a Roman Aristocrat. Historia Einzelschriften 201*. Stuttgart: Franz Steiner.

Van Essen, C. 1954. La topographie de la *Domus Aurea Neronis*. *Mededelingen der Koniglijjke Nederlandse Akademie van Wetenschappen Afd Letterkunde. NS 17.12*: 371–98.

Warden, P. 1981. The *Domus Aurea* reconsidered. *Journal for the Society of Architectural Historians* 40.1 (March): 271–78.

Yegul, F. 1992. *Baths and Bathing in Classical Antiquity*. New York and Cambridge: MIT Press.

Zanker, P. 1990. *The Power of Images in the Age of Augustus*. Ann Arbor: University of Michigan Press.

Zanker, P. 1996. *The Mask of Socrates: The Image of the Intellectual in Antiquity*. Berkeley: University of California Press.

Did Cadastres Exist in the Roman Northwest?

Rick Bonnie

Introduction

> 'As far as centuriation is concerned, aerial photographs have formed the basis for some scholars to suggest that many hitherto unsuspected areas in Gaul were regularly laid out. The [native] land allotments were apparently swept away in favour of a new, regulated Roman system. However, [...] many of the proposed centuriations seem to owe more to faith than reality.'(King 1990: 99)

It was with these words that Anthony King began his argument for the absence of centuriation, also known as cadastres, in the north-western Roman provinces. He was not alone in stressing this, since other scholars in the last two decades have argued the same (Willems 1987: 50; Jones 1989: 129; Hart 1998: 112–113; Heimberg 2003: 127; van Enckevort *et al.* 2005: 3). Apart from a tendency to question the use of aerial photographs, the absence of centuriation in these areas also conforms to the evidence of 'continuity' since, in the Roman Northwest, life appeared in many ways to be a continuation of earlier times (see Millett 1990; Slofstra 1991; Roymans 1996; Woolf 1998). These arguments have given scholars a reason to doubt the existence of centuriation in the Roman Northwest.

It was not only the aforementioned arguments which contributed to the dismissal of proposals in favour of Roman cadastres in the north-western provinces, but also the pre-existing ideas of scholars (most notably archaeologists) about 'static' cadastres. Their convictions led to the interpretation of cadastres as a visible colonial symbol of Rome's power over natives (e.g. Alcock 2002: 40–50; Ando 2006), an interpretation that appears to conflict with evidence of 'continuity'.

I argue here that scholars have rejected the existence of Roman cadastres in the north-western provinces too rapidly and on the basis of unsound assumptions. This paper aims to evaluate and deconstruct the arguments used by scholars to reject their existence. Firstly, although aerial photography had its limitations in the past, it is actually a valid study tool. Secondly, the argument in favour of 'continuity' by which scholars have rejected the existence of Roman cadastres in the Northwest will be deconstructed. Finally, the idea of a 'static' cadastre will be questioned. The result and implications of my arguments will be shown by a case study from the region around the Roman provincial city of Tongres (Belgium). However, I will start by giving a brief overview of the history of research on Roman cadastres.

Roman Cadastre Studies

It was a Danish naval captain who, in 1833, identified the chequered landscape around Carthage as a Roman cadastre (see Dilke 1971; Chouquer and Favory 2001). In the following years, other scholars recognised ancient cadastres in such countries as Italy, Croatia and Tunisia. Such discoveries raised the question of why the Romans introduced such a system. It was also around this time that the *Corpus Agrimensorum,* a now fragmentary collection of Roman land-surveyor manuals which described the laws, techniques and methods involved in the implementation and maintenance of cadastres, was first being published (Blume *et al.* 1848; see also Campbell 2000). From this *Corpus*, it was clear that the implementation of the system related to strategies of defence and taxation (Dilke 1971: 178–181; Broadhead 2007: 160–161).

During the early-20th century, Roman cadastre studies were expanded by the introduction of aerial photography into archaeology. This technology was primarily used within cadastre studies to identify remains of linear features which may have related to a cadastre (e.g. Bradford 1957; Chevallier 1957). However, the argument that these linear features were indeed the remains of a former Roman cadastre was often rather subjective, non-verifiable and not related to any Roman context (e.g. King 1990: 99; Quilici 1994: 130–131).

Questioning the use of aerial photographs

In the 1950s a possible cadastre was identified in Belgium centred on the Roman road between Tongres, the capital city of the *civitas Tungrorum*, and the small military settlement at Maastricht (Mertens 1958). Several roads, land boundaries and agricultural fields ran parallel to and diagonally from the Roman road on the same orientation, creating a grid pattern (Fig. 1).

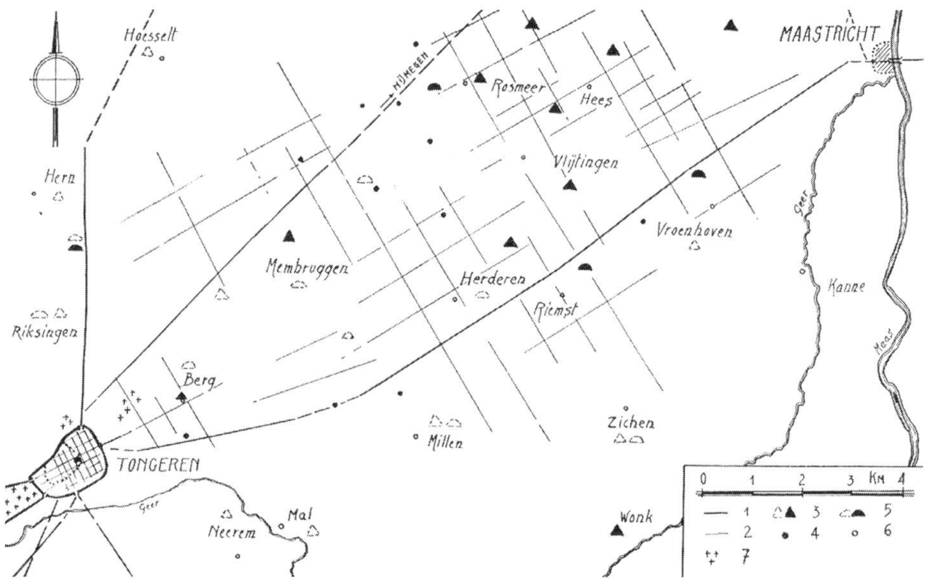

Figure 1: The proposed cadastre to the east of Tongres (Mertens 1958: 258). Legend description: 1) Roman roads; 2) Limites; 3) Villae; 4) Roman finds; 5) Tumuli; 6) Present village; 7) Grave fields.

However, this interpretation was problematic. The lines in the modern landscape that were argued to be Roman cadastre boundaries appeared to be randomly selected and there were no reasons given why certain modern linear features with the same orientation as the road, as well as those with a different orientation, were not taken into account. Furthermore, the proposed cadastre did not correspond with any Roman measurement unit used in land-surveying (such as the *pes* or *actus*). In Mertens' study the historical and spatial association of modern linear features like roads, ditches and boundaries with Roman cadastres was assumed.

The reliance on this assumption in other cadastre studies (e.g. Klinkenberg 1936; Chevallier 1957; Edelman and Eeuwens 1959; Ulrix 1959) led to two main points of criticism regarding the use of aerial photography. First, there was no consistency in the analysis, as the inclusion or exclusion of certain linear features seemed to have been assessed on an intuitive, arbitrary basis rather than on substantial, verifiable evidence. Secondly, scholars often dated their proposed cadastres by a circular reasoning. If a 'recognized' cadastre corresponded to a particular size that was used in Roman land-surveying, then the cadastre had to be of Roman date, if it did not correspond, it was not Roman. Other archaeological evidence rarely corroborated this circular dating argument.

The assumed clash between 'continuity' and Roman cadastres

Apart from their concerns over the use of aerial photography, scholars also question the existence of Roman cadastres in the north-western provinces because of their assumed clash with the archaeological evidence of continuity. As cadastres would transform the landscape, scholars assume that Roman cadastres imply a major break with the past. The implementation of Roman cadastres implied that not only were the native land boundaries swept away (e.g. King 1990), but that cadastres also brought socio-political and cultural change (see Alcock 2002: 40–50; Ando 2006). However, it has been demonstrated that such a major break did not occur in the north-western provinces; rather, changes happened more gradually (Millett 1990; Slofstra 1991; Roymans 1996; Woolf 1998). Hence, the implementation of cadastres is dismissed, and any evidence for the existence of cadastres in the region is overlooked (e.g. Willems 1987: 50; Fulford 1990: 26).

This is, of course, a circular argument. Because it has been argued that the indigenous peoples during the Roman period lived in essentially the same manner as they had prior to the Romans, there seems to be a fear of acknowledging any Roman influence on the landscape. However, there seems to be no direct causality between a decline in the continuity of indigenous ways of life and the implementation of a Roman cadastre. Native land-holdings, as well as the landscape, were not diminished by the establishment of a Roman cadastre. As texts and official tablets relating to the Orange cadastre in France and to other cadastres across the Empire show, the indigenous people were assigned land plots within the newly implemented cadastres (see Piganiol 1962; Dilke 1971; Peterson 1993; Chouquer 1996).

Pre-existing concepts of a 'static' Roman cadastre

A further academic argument employed to deny the existence of Roman cadastres in the north-western provinces concerns their visibility, based on pre-existing concepts of a 'static' cadastre. Often, this has led to an immediate rejection of proposals.

Scholars have equated Roman cadastres with a visible and obvious chequerboard of lines in the landscape, an equation supported by aerial photography, where the clearest examples tend to make the strongest impression. Yet the presumption that cadastres are visible as a chequerboard of lines is not true in all cases, and has led scholars to ignore the less obvious, but perhaps more typical, evidence for Roman cadastres. For example, the cadastres identified around Orange, Lacimurga and in Tunisia did not have linear features that could be detected by aerial photography. At first, the existence of these cadastres was only known through inscribed official tablets (Fig. 2) and, in the case of Tunisia, by boundary stones that were placed on each corner of the cadastre grid (Anon. 1954; Dilke 1971).

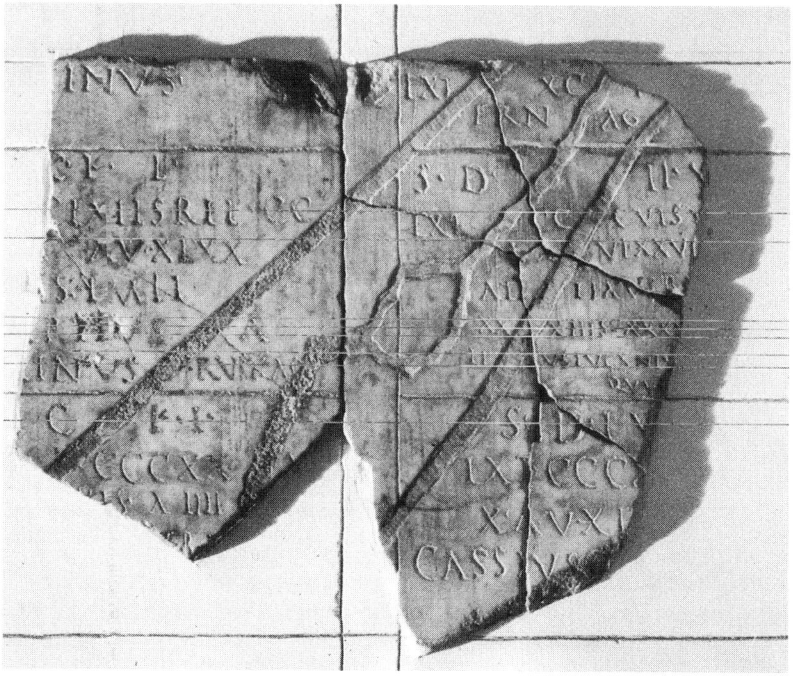

Figure 2: Fragment no. 7 of the Orange tablet of cadastre A, exhibited in the Musée d'Orange (Anon. 1983: Fig. 237).

The idea that Roman cadastres needed to be visible and obvious may have been caused by an oversimplification of the Latin word for 'boundary' (*limes*) as 'road' or 'path'. However, as has been shown, there are only two different meanings for *limes*, i.e. 'military road' or 'boundary' (Isaac 1988: 128). The latter meaning derived from the vocabulary of land-surveyors and was used in the majority of cases as a purely *conceptual* line; it did not necessarily have to be associated with visible roads or paths. Also, the *Corpus Agrimensorum* suggests that a boundary did not necessarily have to be visible. The land-surveyor Siculus Flaccus, for example, mentions cases in which villas could be placed right on top of boundaries (Blume *et al.* 1848: 153.7), which could not happen were these boundaries visible and physical features in the landscape. Therefore, a *limes* was primarily a conceptual boundary, which was made visible in some cases by the construction of a wall or road, but could equally remain invisible (see Terrenato 2007: 153).

The similarity of Roman cadastres

Associated with the concept of the visibility of cadastres is the assumption that Roman cadastres were all quite similar in respect to size, orientation and location (e.g. Rackham 1986: 159; Heimberg 2003: 127; Ando 2006: 127; Mattingly 2006: 288; Van Londen 2006: 188). The 'typical' cadastre was orientated exactly north-south and east-west, was implemented only around Roman *coloniae*, and one square of a cadastre was always 20 by 20 actus (around 708 by 708 metres).

The idea that cadastres were similar in size may be a result of equating the Latin term *centuriatio* with regular Roman land planning. In theory, a *centuriatio* had squares sized at 20 by 20 Roman *actus*, parcelled out to people as 1 *heredium* (5000 m^2) of land. However, over time the size of the plots of land given to people changed. Written sources indicated that, in certain regions and during certain periods, people could receive allotment sizes such as 10, 30, 50 or even 100 *heredia* (Dilke 1971: 179, 184; Broadhead 2007: 155). Consequently, differences may also be expected in regard to the size of squares and, indeed, archaeological studies have found evidence for divergent sizes (e.g. Legros 1970; Chouquer and Favory 1980; Peterson 1993; Chouquer 1996). The problem, however, is that the conclusions reached in these archaeological studies are often rejected for the reason that they do not conform to the theoretical model in the historical sources.

The idea that the cadastres had a static orientation may have been influenced by cadastral drawings in the *Corpus Agrimensorum* and on official tablets. These drawings always appear as straight horizontal and vertical lines, easily relating to north-south and east-west (Peterson 1993: 8–9). Yet, in reality, most of the north-south and east-west orientations were depicted for purposes of legibility. For instance, the cadastres at Orange had, in reality, a different orientation to the north-south east-west direction portrayed on the official tablets on display at the museum in Orange (Piganiol 1962; Peterson 1993: 9). The *Corpus Agrimensorum* contains nine different factors which could determine the orientation of a cadastre (Le Gall 1975), and the factor(s) which Roman surveyors used would vary from case to case and over time.

Similarly, the idea that cadastres were only associated with *coloniae* may have been a misunderstanding of the written source. The *Corpus Agrimensorum* states that 'if the land is divided and assigned [e.g. centuriated], it is the land of a *colonia*' (Blume *et al.* 1848: 2.1). However, historians have argued that this phrase may have a more complex meaning, since the more elementary texts in the *Corpus Agrimensorum* seem to have been simplified (Dilke 1971: 88, 178; Peterson 1993: 7–8). Detail was only added in later passages of the book by the inclusion of examples from real life, which could introduce apparent contradictions (Hinrichs 1974: 172–173). For example, a Roman land-surveyor records one such contradiction in regards to centuriated, but *non-colonial*, land in the province of Pannonia (*c.f.* Favory 1983: 126). Therefore, as Dilke (1971: 178) states, 'the territory centuriated could [...] also be that of a *municipium*'.

Case study: a Roman cadastre around Tongres

Above, I have evaluated and criticized the arguments on which scholars have rejected the presence of cadastres in the Roman Northwest. The implication of this critique is to open up the possibility of cadastres in the north-western provinces of the Roman Empire. This will be illustrated by a case study from the region around the Roman provincial city of Tongres (see also Bonnie 2009); the same region covered by Mertens (1958) fifty years ago (see above). Of course, one cannot compare a Roman cadastre from the Roman Northwest with one from Tunisia or Italy. While cadastres from the latter region can be reconstructed on the basis of boundary stones, inscriptions and literary sources, such evidence is lacking for cadastres from the Roman Northwest so that a different approach is needed. However, this case study shows that through a consistent and critical analysis of archaeological remains, together with historical-geographical evidence, a reconstruction of a cadastre is possible.

Typically, the landscape around Tongres is sloping and is covered with loess soil, which although very fertile is also susceptible to erosion. The fertility of the soil made it an ideal region for the Romans to settle. This is attested by archaeological evidence of their occupation and influence in this area from the late first century A.D. The provincial capital of Tongres, the military presence at Maastricht, Roman *villae*, burial mounds and artefacts show a strongly Roman element (see Vanvinckenroye 1985; Panhuysen 1996; Vanderhoeven 1996). Considering this powerful Roman influence at the periphery of the Empire, a Roman cadastre may have been implemented here. To examine this hypothesis, I have focused on a phenomenon relating to the sloping, loess-covered landscape around Tongres: the escarpment.

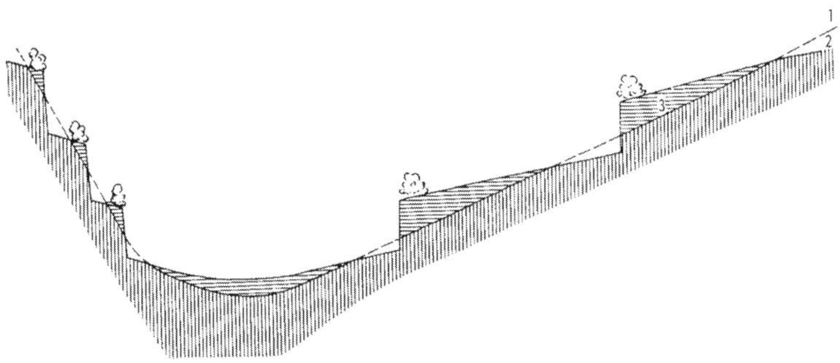

*Figure 3: Schematic representation of the formation of an escarpment (Breteler and van den Broek 1968: Fig. 1). Legend description: 1) Original slope; 2) Slope affected by erosion; 3) Overgrown escarpment, sedimentation (*colluvia*) on the valley side of the slope*

An escarpment is a long steep slope or cliff at the edge of a ridge, which was originally formed by erosion (Fig. 3). As escarpments prevent further erosion, and protect against flooding of valley settlements and decreasing fertility of agricultural soils, they were (and are) important linear features in the landscape, with a high economic and social value to the community in the region (see Breteler and van den Broek 1968).

In order to detect distinct orientation clusters, the orientation of each escarpment was classified into eight groups between 0° and 90° from north, i.e. covering 180° (see also Vermeulen and Antrop 2001: 117–118). Normally, an orientation can vary through 360°, but this would involve double counting as each escarpment clearly points in two directions. For example, a north-east escarpment also points to the south-west. Since Roman cadastres were always square or rectangular, the existence of cadastres requires evidence of linear features at right angles.

In the region around Tongres, the largest group of escarpments are oriented between 45° and 56° from north (Fig. 4), caused in part by the north-easterly inclination of the loess plateau around Tongres. However, assuming that the escarpments are directly related to the boundaries of a cadastre, escarpments perpendicular to the inclination of the loess plateau would also be expected. Of all the escarpments belonging to the group of 45° to 56° from north, 69 escarpments are running north-east, while 52 are actually running perpendicular in a north-westerly direction. This suggests that these escarpments formed part of land plots running along the loess plateau, representing fields whose orientation was shaped by the plateau's north-easterly inclination (see Le Gall 1975).

This raises the question whether these escarpments are related to the Roman period? In order to answer this question, the orientation of the archaeological features was examined. Additionally, the archaeological features were dated and classified into four consecutive periods: Late Iron Age (250–50 B.C.), Early Roman (50 B.C.–A.D. 70), Middle Roman (A.D. 70–270) and Late Roman (A.D. 270–450).

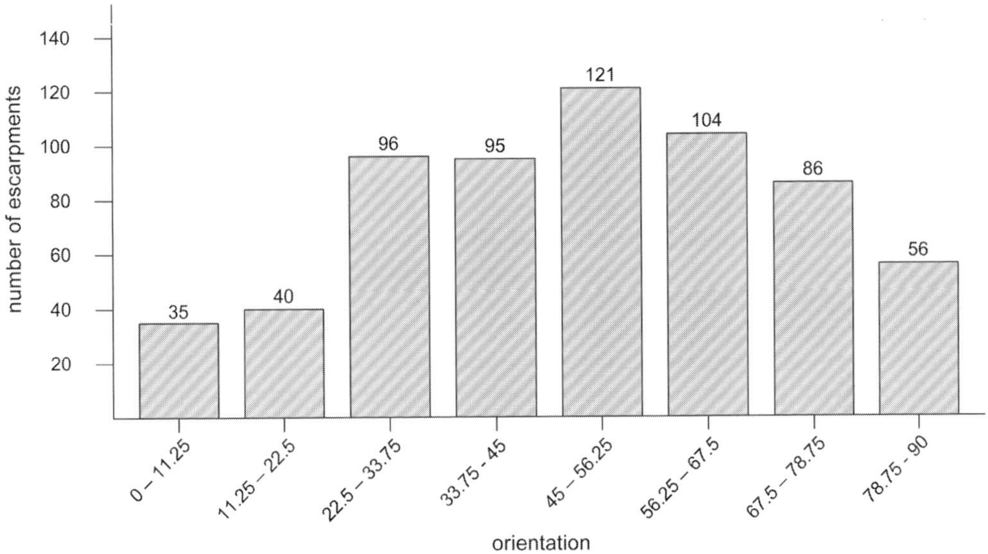

Figure 4: Chart of the orientation of the escarpments in the region around Tongres (Total escarpments=633).

This was done because, as Peterson (1993: 67) has stated, 'there is no doubt that features of all periods, starting from the period when a [Roman] cadastre is first established, tend to be influenced by […] its *limites*'. In the ancient and modern world it is common for features like buildings, burials, fences and ditches to be aligned to boundary features like roads, field boundaries and hedges. This also applies to Roman cadastres. One of the clearest examples to illustrate this is from the countryside around the Roman town of Collatia, close to Rome. Here the central part of the *ager collatinus* shows that the orientation of the individual Roman houses conforms to the orientation of the 15 *actus* Roman cadastre that has been identified there (Fig. 5) (Chouquer *et al.* 1987: 286–288).

Dating and studying the orientation of the archaeological features in the region around Tongres showed a remarkable change in the orientation of the features from the Late Iron Age to the Late Roman period, and there appears to be a correlation between the orientation of an archaeological feature and its date. When the general orientation of the archaeological features is related to that of the escarpments, the Middle Roman period stands out (Table 1). During this period, 46% of all the archaeological features had an orientation between 45° and 56° from north.

There also appears to be discontinuity between the Early and Middle Roman period. While it has been shown that Early Roman sites tended to remain occupied during the Middle Roman period (see Slofstra 1991; Roymans 1996), the archaeological features found around Tongres show a major break in occupation during this transition, with only 6% of the Early Roman features continuing to be used. Furthermore, the features orientated between 45° and 56° show even less continuity. From the 17 Middle Roman features, from eight different sites, only one had been in use during the Early Roman period.

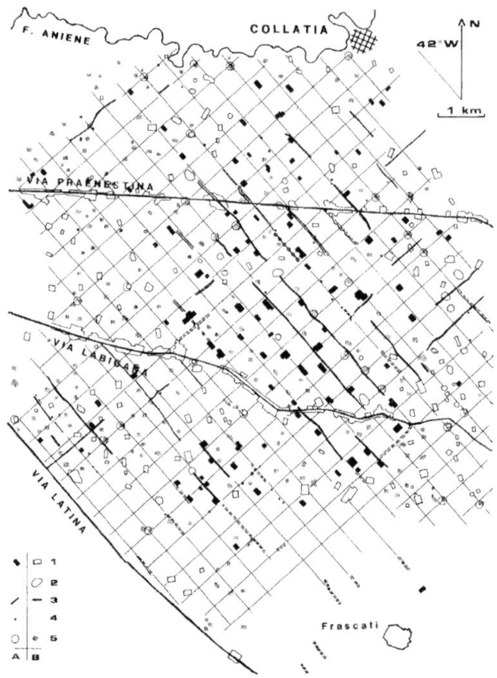

Figure 5: The ager collatinus *at Collatia (Chouquer* et al. *1987: Fig. 104). Legend description: 1) Sites whose boundary is known; 2) Sites whose boundary is unknown; 3) Ancient roads and lines; 4) Burial; 5) Small rural deposit; A) Sites orientated according to the cadastre; B) sites not orientated according to the cadastre.*

	0°–11.25°	**11.25°–22.5°**	**22.5°–33.75°**	**33.75°–45°**	**45°–56.25°**	**56.25°–67.5°**	**67.5°–78.75°**	**78.75°–90°**
Late Iron Age (n=19 s=3)	7 (36.8%)	4 (21.1%)	3 (15.8%)	1 (5.3%)	0 (0%)	0 (0%)	1 (5.3%)	3 (15.8%)
Early Roman (n=52 s=10)	9 (17.3%)	5 (9.6%)	9 (17.3%)	12 (23.1%)	2 (3.8%)	10 (19.2%)	2 (3.8%)	3 (5.8%)
Middle Roman (n=37 s=12)	5 (13.5%)	4 (10.8%)	6 (16.2%)	1 (2.7%)	17 (46%)	3 (8.1%)	0 (0%)	1 (2.7%)
Late Roman (n=32 s=5)	2 (6.3%)	0 (0%)	5 (15.6%)	0 (0%)	2 (6.3%)	0 (0%)	2 (6.3%)	21 (65.6%)

Table 1: The orientation of archaeological features (incl. houses, ditches, fences etc) from the region around Tongres ('n' is the number of archaeological features, while 's' is the number of different sites from which these archaeological features were taken). Note that the Late Roman period is overrepresented by one site, Neerharen-Rekem (see De Boe 1983).

In addition, Tongres' 60° north-east oriented Augustan city plan does not fit with an Early Roman date for an assumed cadastre. If there had been an Early Roman cadastre, it is probable that it would have had the same orientation as Tongres' city plan. A cadastre established contemporaneously with its associated city or military camp would follow the same orientation, as shown by examples at Lugo, Orange, Corinth and Nicopolis (Dilke 1971; Rizakis 1996; Romano 2006).

Therefore it may be argued that, for the landscape around Tongres, the orientation of 45° to 56° from north was introduced during the Middle Roman period. In light of these observations, it seems reasonable to consider that the aftermath of the Batavian Revolt (A.D. 69–70) may have acted as a context for the cadastre's implementation. It has been argued that the Batavian Revolt had a large impact upon the Roman town of Tongres and its hinterland (Vanvinckenroye 1985: 40). Its aftermath was a period of rapid socio-cultural change with the emergence of reinforced hierarchical relationships between the people, demonstrated by the stone-built Roman *villae*, burial mounds and Roman artefacts. As Dyson (1975: 161) stated,

> 'With the Flavian period, the evidence for major social discontent in Gaul disappears […]. The Flavians seem to have perceived the problems of Gaul and taken long range steps to improve conditions. Considerable investment was made in the Gallic countryside […]. These actions laid the foundations of the new prosperity in Gaul.'

In the light of this it must also be noted that, during the Flavian period, many Roman cadastres were either re-surveyed (and re-established) or newly founded, as has been attested for Corinth, Orange, Béziers and North Africa (Piganiol 1962: 77–90; Clavel-Lévêque 1989: 276–278; Peterson 1993: 239; Romano 2006: 71–81). The implementation of a Roman cadastre in the region around Tongres thus coincides with these other cadastres, and may represent Roman interference in local affairs to re-establish order, loyalty and economic activity in the region after the Batavian revolt.

To reconstruct the Middle Roman period cadastre, the premise was that Roman sites, whether cemeteries or settlement sites (and even post-Roman churches), tend to be located near a cadastre boundary (Fig. 6 for a modern example of this premise). This was a result of the religious and symbolic continuity which followed the demarcation of social space through the implementation of cadastres (see Peterson 1993). The distribution of Middle Roman sites in the region around Tongres was tested by using cadastres with different sizes ranging from 15 *actus* (531 meters) to 22 *actus* (780 meters), within the 45° to 56° orientations above.

The result showed that 65% of all the Middle Roman sites sited on the loess soil were distributed closely to the boundaries of an 18 *actus* cadastre. This percentage is the highest of all the tests with cadastres of different sizes, and is even higher than, for instance, for the cadastre around Collatia in Italy (see Chouquer *et al.* 1987: 286–288). The study also showed that the Middle Roman sites were not distributed randomly, and that even the Medieval churches in the region tended to be located near to the boundaries of the cadastre. From all the churches located on the loess soil that date before A.D. 1050, 77% were distributed adjacent to the cadastre boundaries. It appears that 18 *actus* is the most plausible size for the Middle Roman cadastre around Tongres (Fig. 7).

However, the results for Middle Roman sites not sited on the loess, but on the sand in the north of the study area, were remarkably different. First, the percentage of sites distributed closely to the boundaries of an 18 *actus* cadastre was only 45%. Second, in contrast to those on the loess, the Middle Roman sites sited on the sand seem to have been distributed randomly. Thus, it seems that the region covered with sand in the north of the study area was not part of the Roman cadastre around Tongres (Fig. 7). This regional difference between the loess and sand region ties in with the other evidence of socio-cultural and economic differences between these regions (Slofstra 1991; Roymans 1996).

Figure 6: An aerial photograph from the region around Venice, Italy, in which the lines of a Roman cadastre are still visible. Although not easily visible, the original photograph shows that large numbers of modern houses are near cadastre boundaries (Anon. 1984: Fig. 136).

Conclusion

The aim of this paper was to evaluate and deconstruct the arguments by which scholars have rejected the existence of Roman cadastres in the north-western Roman provinces of *Gallia Belgica* and *Germania Inferior*. Scholars have doubted the existence of cadastres based on three arguments, i.e. concerns with the subjective nature of aerial photographic studies, the theoretical contradiction of cadastres with evidence for archaeological continuity, and the assumption that cadastres would be highly visible and unchanging over time. However, as this paper shows, these arguments can be deconstructed. Aerial photography remains a valid method of study if interpreted objectively and within historical and archaeological frameworks. The argument of 'continuity' does not take into account the measured pace of change in the north-western provinces, whilst the implementation of a Roman cadastre may not have substantially altered indigenous habits. Finally, Roman cadastres may have been more flexible and dynamic in layout and size than has been assumed.

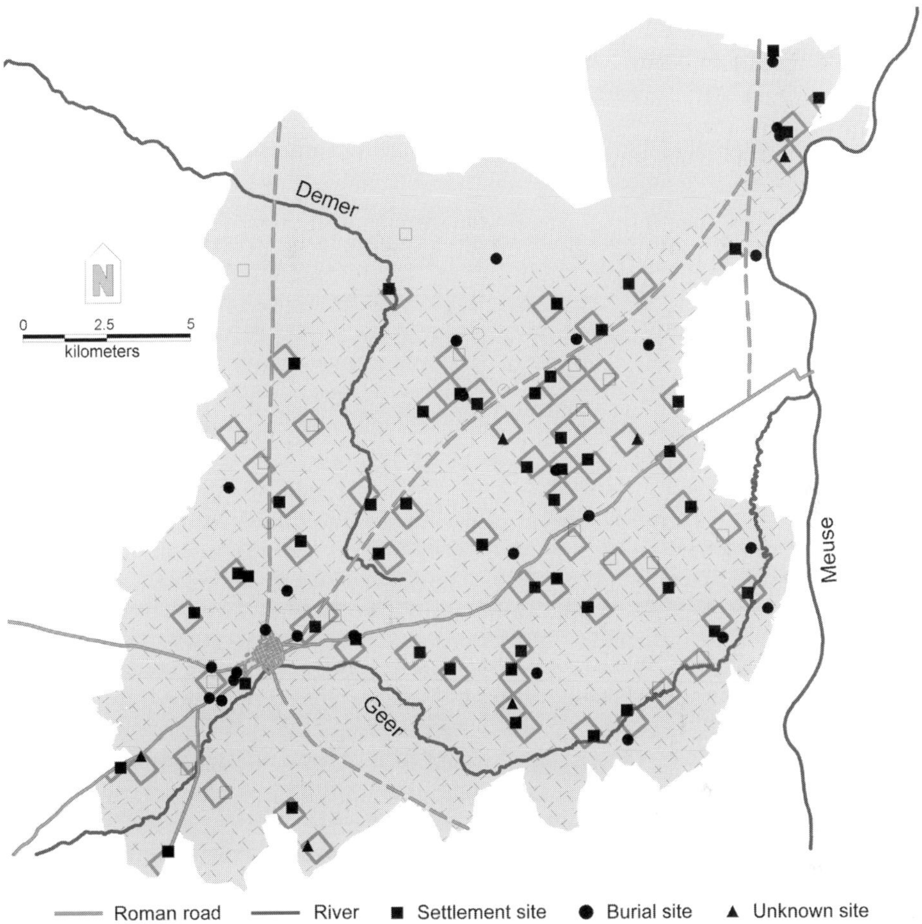

Figure 7: A schematic reconstruction of the Roman cadastre of 18 by 18 actus *around Tongres.*

However, the problems with Roman cadastre studies have not been created solely by those who have been critical of its results; the discipline of Roman cadastre studies has itself played a role. For too long, this has remained an introspective discipline, rarely interacting with other fields of study in Roman archaeology. Therefore, specific knowledge of the historical and archaeological data relating to Roman cadastres and land-surveying has remained outside of mainstream discourse. Recently, however, the discussion has begun to open out and, consequently, is becoming more fruitful. It is to be hoped that the next few years will see a more positive consideration of the existence and role of cadastres in the north-western Roman provinces.

Department of Archaeology, Katholieke Universiteit Leuven

Acknowledgements

This paper is based on my master's thesis at Leiden University and presentations held at Leiden, Ann Arbor (Michigan) and Brussels. The final editing was done under a Ph.D. fellowship of the Research Foundation – Flanders (FWO) at the Katholieke Universiteit Leuven (Belgium). I especially want to thank Miguel John Versluys, John Bintliff, Jasper de Bruin, Harry Pape and Sander van der End, for commenting on earlier drafts of this paper. Furthermore, I would like to thank the two anonymous reviewers, as well as the editors for their helpful comments.

Bibliography

Alcock, S.E. 2002. *Archaeologies of the Greek Past. Landscape, Monuments, and Memories*. Cambridge: Cambridge University Press.

Ando, C. 2006. The Administration of the Provinces. In D.S. Potter (ed.) *A Companion to the Roman Empire*. Oxford: Blackwell: 177–192.

Anonymous 1954. *Atlas des centuriations romaines de Tunisie*. Paris: Institut Geographique National.

Anonymous 1983. *Misurare la terra: centuriazione e coloni nel mondo romano*. Modena: Edizioni Panini.

Anonymous 1984. *Misurare la terra: centuriazione e coloni nel mondo romano. Il caso veneto*. Modena. Edizioni Panini.

Blume, F., Lachmann, K.K.F.W. and Rudorf, A. 1848. *Die Schriften der römischen Feldmesser*. Berlin: Reimer.

Bonnie, R. 2009. *Cadastres, Misconceptions and Northern Gaul. A case study from the Belgian Hesbaye region*. Leiden: Sidestone Press.

Bradford, J.D. 1957. *Ancient Landscapes. Studies in Field Archaeology*. London: Bell.

Breteler, H.G.M. and van den Broek, J.M.M. 1968. Graften in Zuid-Limburg. *Boor en spade* 16: 119–130.

Broadhead, W. 2007. Colonization, Land Distribution and Veteran Settlement. In P. Erdkamp (ed.) *A Companion to the Roman Army*. Malden: Blackwell: 148–163.

Campbell, B. 2000. *The writings of the Roman Land Surveyors. Introduction, Text, Translation and Commentary*. London: Society for the Promotion of Roman Studies.

Chevallier, R. 1957. *Bibliographie des applications archéologiques de la photographie aérienne*. Milano: Fondazione Lerici.

Chouquer, G., Clavel-Léveque, M., Favory, F. and Vallat, J.P. 1987. *Structures agraires en Italie centro-méridionale: cadastres et paysages ruraux*. Rome: École française de Rome.

Chouquer, G. (ed.). 1996. *Les formes du paysage. Tome 1 – Etudes sur les parcellaires*. Paris: Éditions Errance.

Chouquer, G. and Favory, F. 1980. *Contribution à la recherche des cadastres antiques*. Paris: Les belles lettres.

Chouquer, G. and Favory, F. 2001. *L'arpentage romain histoire des textes, droit, techniques*. Paris: Éditions Errance.

Clavel-Lévêque, M. 1989. *Puzzle gaulois: les Gaules en mémoire*. Paris: Les belles lettres.

De Boe, G. 1983. De Laat-Romeinse "Germaanse" nederzetting te Neerharen-Rekem. In *Conspectus MCMLXXXII*. Brussel: Nationale Dienst voor Opgravingen: 70–73.

Dilke, O.A.W. 1971. *The Roman Land Surveyors. An Introduction to the Agrimensores*. London: Newton Abbot.

Dyson, S.L. 1975. Native revolt patterns in the western Empire. In H. Temporini and W. Haase (eds.) *Aufstieg und Niedergang der römischen Welt II.3*. Berlin: Walter de Gruyter: 138–175.

Edelman, C.H. and Eeuwens, B.E.P. 1959. Sporen van een Romeinse landindeling in Zuid-Limburg. *Berichten van de Rijksdienst voor het Oudheidkundig Bodemonderzoek* 9: 49–56.
Enckevort, H. van, de Groot, T., Hiddink, H.A. and Vos, W. 2005. *De Romeinse tijd in het Midden-Nederlandse rivierengebied en het Zuid-Nederlands dekzand- en lössgebied.* NOaA hoofdstuk 18 (versie 1.0). Amersfoort: RACM.
Favory, F. 1983. Propositions pour une modélisation des cadastres ruraux antiques. In M. Clavel-Lévêque (ed.) *Cadastres et Espace Rural Approches et réalités antiques (table ronde de Besançon mai 1980).* Paris: CNRS Éditions: 51–135.
Fulford, M.G. 1990. The Landscape of Roman Britain: A Review. *Landscape History* 12: 25–31.
Hart, J.F. 1998. *The Rural Landscape.* Baltimore: John Hopkins University Press.
Heimberg, U. 2003. Römische Villen an Rhein und Maas. *Bonner Jahrbücher* 203: 57–148.
Hinrichs, F.T. 1974. *Die Geschichte der gromatischen Institutionen.* Wiesbaden: Steiner.
Isaac, B. 1988. The meaning of the Terms Limes and Limitanei. *Journal of Roman Studies* 78: 125–147.
Jones, M. 1989. Agriculture in Roman Britain: The Dynamics of Change. In M. Todd (ed.) *Research on Roman Britain: 1960-89.* Britannia Monograph Series 11. London: Society for the Promotion of Roman Studies: 127–134.
King, A. 1990. *Roman Gaul and Germany.* London, British Museum Publications.
Klinkenberg, J. 1936. Die Stadtanlage der römischen Köln und die Limitation des Ubierlandes. *Bonner Jahrbücher* 140/141: 259–298.
Le Gall, J. 1975. Les Romains et l'orientation solaire. *Mélanges de l'École Française de Rome Antiquité* 87: 287–320.
Legros, R. 1970. Structures agraires gallo-romaines près de Reims. *Photo-Interpretation* 2: 38–42.
Mattingly, D.J. 2006. The Imperial Economy. In D.S. Potter (ed.) *A Companion to the Roman World.* Oxford: Blackwell: 283–297.
Mertens, J.R. 1958. Sporen van een Romeins kadaster in Limburg? *Limburg* 37: 253–260.
Millett, M. 1990. *The Romanization of Britain: an essay in archaeological interpretation.* Cambridge: Cambridge University Press.
Panhuysen, T.A.S.M. 1996. *Romeins Maastricht en zijn beelden.* Assen/Maastricht: Van Gorcum.
Peterson, J.W.M. 1993. *Computer-aided investigation of ancient cadastres.* Unpublished PhD thesis. Norwich: University of East Anglia.
Piganiol, A. 1962. *Les documents cadastraux de la colonie romaine d'Orange.* Paris: CNRS Éditions.
Quilici, L. 1994. Centuriazione e paesaggio agrario nell'Italia centrale. In J. Carlsen *et al.* (eds.) *Landuse in the Roman Empire.* Rome: "L' Erma" di Bretschneider: 127–133.
Rackham, O. 1986. *The history of the countryside.* London: Dent.
Rizakis, A. 1996. Les colonies Romaines des côtes occidentales Grecques. Populations et territories. *Dialogues d'Histoire Ancienne* 22: 255–324.
Romano, D.G. 2006. Roman Surveyors in Corinth. *Proceedings of the American Philosophical Society* 150: 62–85.
Roymans, N. 1996. The sword or the plough. Regional dynamics in the romanisation of Belgic Gaul and the Rhineland area. In N. Roymans (ed.) *From the Sword to the Plough. Three studies on the earliest Romanisation of Northern Gaul.* Amsterdam Archaeological Studies 1. Amsterdam: Amsterdam University Press: 9–126.
Slofstra, J. 1991. Changing settlement systems in the Meuse-Demer-Scheldt area during the Early Roman period. In N. Roymans and F. Theuws (eds.) *Images of the past. Studies on ancient societies in Northwestern Europe.* Studies in Pre- en Protohistorie 7. Amsterdam: Amsterdam University Press: 131–200.
Terrenato, N. 2007. The Essential Countryside: The Roman World. In S.E. Alcock and R. Osborne (eds.) *Classical Archaeology.* Oxford: Blackwell: 139–161.
Ulrix, F. 1959. Centuriatio in de omstreken van Tongeren. *Limburg* 38: 34–44.
Van Londen, H. 2006. *Midden-Delfland. The Roman Native Landscape, Past and Present.* Unpublished PhD thesis. Amsterdam: University of Amsterdam.
Vanderhoeven, A. 1996. The earliest urbanisation in Northern Gaul. Some implications of recent research in Tongres. In N. Roymans (ed.) *From the Sword to the Plough. Three studies on the earliest*

romanisation of Northern Gaul. Amsterdam Archaeological Studies 1. Amsterdam: Amsterdam University Press: 189–260.

Vanvinckenroye, W. 1985. *Tongeren. Romeinse stad.* Tielt: Lanoo.

Vermeulen, F. and Antrop, M. (eds.). 2001. *Ancient Lines in the Landscape. A Geo-Archaeological Study of Protohistoric and Roman Roads and Field Systems in Northwestern Gaul.* Leuven: Peeters.

Willems, W.J.H. 1987. De grote villa van Voerendaal. In P. Stuart and M.E.T. De Grooth (eds.) *Langs de Weg. De Romeinse weg van Boulogne-sur-Mer naar Keulen.* Heerlen: Thermenmuseum: 46–51.

Woolf, G.D. 1998. *Becoming Roman. The origins of provincial civilization in Gaul.* Cambridge: Cambridge University Press.

Age and Identity in Funerary Contexts: The Elderly in Southern Roman Britain

Alison Moore

Introduction

The old in the Roman world remain the invisible social demographic. In contrast to recent archaeological interest in children and childhood, the old are often subsumed within the general category of adulthood in both funerary analyses and in commentaries on the social organisation of the Roman provinces. Currently within western societies there is an increased awareness of the social impact of an increasingly ageing population. Modern medical techniques, coupled with the post-war 'baby boom' generation now reaching the age of retirement, means that those aged over 60 years now form an increasing percentage of modern western European populations, with far-reaching socio-economic implications. This new awareness of the elderly and ageing makes it an appropriate time to examine the elderly in the Roman world. Within the framework of a life course methodology, this paper utilises two aspect of funerary evidence – that of the material culture and grave treatment – to identify whether the elderly were visible as a distinct age group in one region of southern Roman Britain, and to explore whether a gendered identity played a role in elderly burial.

Old Age in Roman Thought

In the Roman period, as much as now, old age and the elderly were regarded with a degree of ambivalence. The textual sources which refer to old age – written primarily by, and for, the benefit of elite Roman males – reflected both a positive and negative attitude towards ageing (Parkin 2003: 57–89). To some, old age could be seen as a good period of life, one associated with wisdom, which could be harnessed to remain a 'useful' member of society (Harlow and Laurence 2002: 111–127; Cokayne 2003: 94–104). The ideal was to be old but not decrepit, an aspiration summarised by Seneca (*Epistles*: 12.4) who wrote that 'life is most delightful when it is on the downward slope, but has not yet reached the abrupt decline.' Similarly, in his treatise on old age, Cicero summarised his attitude towards growing old as 'age will only be respected if it fights for itself, maintains its own rights, avoids dependence and asserts control over its own sphere as long as life lasts' (*De Senectute*: 11.38). A 'good' old age depended upon living a 'correct' life, practicing the philosophical virtues and maintaining physical and mental health (Cokayne 2003: 92–3).

In contrast, the physical decay and mental senility of old age formed the butt of jokes in comedies and satires. The stereotypical portrayal of the elderly was as physically and mentally decrepit, deaf, parsimonious, irascible and sexually impotent (Harlow and Laurence 2002: 129–130). Elderly women were a particular target, often portrayed as drunken, sexually voracious or as evil witches (Esler 1989: Janowitz 2001: 88–9; Cokayne 2003: 150). Parkin (1997) argues that the elderly, as a group, could be portrayed in literature as conduits for excessive or liminal behaviours, as they stood in opposition to the social ideal of the freeborn young adult male. Grotesque characterisations of the elderly also acted as a means of dispelling social fears (Cokayne 2003: 152–3), particularly suggesting an underlying fear of a helpless and hopeless old age. With little or no state provision for elderly welfare, the responsibility for maintaining elderly relatives was the duty of the family (Finley 1989: 6; Parkin 1997: 125–9). For those without family, income or other forms of support, becoming old would be something to fear.

Whilst these positive and negative attitudes towards the elderly tell us how old age was viewed in Rome itself, how being old was experienced at a provincial level remains virtually unexplored. Whilst it is problematic to establish the number of elderly people within the Roman Empire, due to provincial patterns of age commemoration (Revell 2005) and 'age-rounding' (Scheidel 2001: 11), estimates have been attempted using life tables. Parkin (2003: 50), for example, proposes that around 4 million people (or 6–8%) of an assumed Empire-wide population of 60 million, may have been elderly, defined by Parkin as being aged over 60 years. However, the epigraphic habit was very limited in Roman Britain, and little has survived, so that inscriptions provide little that helps to understand the numbers of elderly and their position within society. Applying a life course methodology to the funerary evidence can, though, provide a means of recognising the elderly.

A Life Course Approach

Age and gender – along with other concepts including ethnicity, social status and religious affiliation – are two aspects upon which personal identity is formed and social organisation is negotiated. In turn, these aspects of social identity are socially constructed as organisational categories (Lucy 2007). Within past societies the role of age can be explored through life course theory (e.g. Sofaer Derevenski 1997; 2000; Joyce 2000; Meskell 2000; Stoodley 2000; Gowland 2002; 2007), which examines the socio-cultural constructions associated with different age stages. The life course can be defined in three ways: biological (physical), chronological (time) and social (behaviour and attitudes) (Gowland 2006: 143). These three forms of age are intertwined and are not necessarily primarily biological, but also encapsulate the fulfilment of social roles and obligations (Hareven 1978: 1–2; Gowland 2006: 143). Each stage within the life course is often marked by 'rites of passage', which in themselves are socially variable, and participation is often dependent upon the social class or gender of the individual (Ginn and Arber 1995: 2; Sofaer Derevenski 1997: 876; Gilchrist 1999; 2000: 235). For example, an upper-class boy in Rome became an adult male citizen with the donning of the toga and dedication of his bulla to the gods (Wiedemann 1989: 114–7; Fraschetti 1997: 65–9). In contrast, for an upper-class Roman female, the transition to full adulthood came with marriage, signified by a change of dress and the covering of the hair (Harlow and Laurence 2002: 61–2).

Within archaeological contexts, the most visible expression of the social life course is often found within the mortuary record. A society's burial practices often encapsulate the social norms and expectations relating to age and gender, and it is often through the material culture provided at burial – which can have both a functional and symbolic meaning – that these norms were created, expressed and reinforced (Sofaer Derevenski 1994: 8; 1997: 876; Gilchrist 2000: 325). Just as the types of material culture can reflect the social expectations associated with certain age groups, transitions within the composition of the grave goods, and within other aspects of mortuary data, can signal that an individual has undergone a transition from one life course stage to another. Through tracing these age-related changes, cultural attitudes towards age and gender can be explored on a social level.

Identifying the Elderly: Data and Methodology

To explore age construction of the elderly in detail, I applied a life course analysis to urban burials from the colonia site of Gloucester and civitas capital of Cirencester, located in the west of the province, and to rural burials from a sample area of the modern day counties of Gloucestershire, Avon, Somerset, Wiltshire, southern Worcestershire and Oxfordshire. As this paper is concerned with the expression of elderly age identity, I have concentrated on analysing the mature adult sample, i.e. those osteologically aged from 30 years, and this produced a basic sample of 677 burials. A total of 181 of the basic sample were osteologically aged at 50+ years, and this age category is defined as 'elderly' in this paper. Defining the criteria for identifying the 'elderly' in past skeletal samples is problematic. Establishing the osteological age of adult skeletal material becomes progressively more inaccurate with age (Schwartz 1995: 185; Aykroyd *et al.* 1999; Cox 2000: 62–63); a difficulty compounded by many existing archaeological publications pre-dating recent re-evaluations of osteological age distinctions in the mature adult category, such as the analysis of the burials from Spitalfields, London (Molleson and Cox 1993). In the context of the Roman world, with no set age marker or concept of retirement, the point at which old age began was fluid. As early as the sixth century B.C., Servius Tullus apparently set 46 as the age of seniority (Wiedemann 1989: 113); whilst Augustan laws indicated that women after 50 and men after 60 were not expected to remarry and men were free of the possibility of military service from 60 years (Harlow and Laurence 2002: 117–118). In order to account for the methodological, cultural and osteological problems discussed above, all burials aged 50+ years were classed as 'elderly.' Whilst this broad category does lose a degree of detail in differentiating between elderly age stages, it does allow a comparison of elderly burial treatment to be made with that of younger adults aged 30–39 and 40–49 years. The burials within the data-set were predominantly late Roman (third-fourth centuries), when inhumation was the prevalent burial rite. As has been discussed elsewhere (e.g. Davison 2000), adult males predominated across all age groups, particularly in the urban sample.

The 295 burials aged 30–50+ years which comprised the urban sample from Cirencester and Gloucester mainly came from the later Roman inhumation cemeteries situated alongside the main roads into the city. At Cirencester, five cemeteries contained burials of adults aged 30–50+ years. These were Bath Gate/The Querns and Oakley Cottage, to the west of the city, together with Verulamium Gate and Silchester Gate, to the south. The largest of these was Bath Gate/The Querns, which contained more than 400 inhumation burials dating from the third to the early fifth centuries. The burials at Bath Gate were characteristic of fourth century urban managed cemeteries, being predominantly supine in timber coffins, with few grave goods (McWhirr *et al.* 1982). Oakley Cottage, thought be the original core of the Bath Gate cemetery, contained both cremations and inhumations of a second-third century date (Reece 1962; Holbrook 1994: 81). The remaining cemeteries at Cirencester which produced burials used in this analysis have been less comprehensively excavated. These include a cemetery at the Verulamium Gate, attested through occasional excavations of burials, whilst a cemetery at Silchester Gate has produced a mixture of cremations, inhumations and Flavian period military tombstones (McWhirr 1976: 195–7; Holbrook 1994: 82–3). The cemeteries at Cirencester produced 226 burials aged 30–50+ years, 60 of which were aged 50+ years (Appendix). Of the total of 226 burials, 75.2% (170/226) were sexed as male and 24.8% (56/226) as female.

Six cemeteries from Gloucester were included within the urban data-set. Wotton Pitch, aligned to Ermine Street, was originally a second century cremation cemetery later used for inhumations during the third to fourth centuries (Heighway *et al.* 1980: 58). To the south-west of the city a further cemetery lay below the medieval St Oswald's Priory. Although originally examined in the late nineteenth century, excavation during the 1980s found 16 late Roman burials below the medieval cemetery levels (Heighway 1980). A further cemetery was excavated at Barton Street/Brunswick Road to the east of the Roman city wall and included outliers from Wellington Street, St Margaret's (Rhodes 1980: 67). A fourth to early fifth century Roman cemetery was situated at Kingsholm, to the north of the city (Hurst 1975: 291–4), whilst another cemetery was situated alongside the main London Road (Foundations Archaeology 2000). The majority of the cemeteries in Gloucester were heavily excavated in the eighteenth and nineteenth centuries, so that vital ageing and sexing skeletal evidence, as well as secure contextual dating, were not thoroughly recorded. However, a total of 69 burials aged between 30–50+ years from Gloucester were included within the urban data-set, of which 54 were accurately sexed as 59.3% (32/54) male and 40.7% (22/54) as female.

A total of 382 rural burials were aged between 30–50+ years and these came from a variety of contexts including villas, *vici*, rural settlement sites, small towns, isolated farmsteads, religious sites and isolated single burials. With villas, the burials of adults were primarily within small, enclosed cemeteries within the villa environs (e.g. Darvill *et al.* 1993; Masser and McGill 2004: 97–9). Similarly to larger urban centres, burials at *vici* and small towns were located in small cemeteries on the outskirts of the settlement. For example, at Sea Mills cremation and inhumation burials, ranging in date from the late first to fourth centuries, have been excavated from the south of the settlement (Bennett 1985).

Burials associated with small rural settlements and farmsteads were predominantly located adjacent to the settlement, often enclosed within ditches as at Charlton Mackrell, Gloucestershire, where a scatter of five inhumations were situated to the south of the settlement (Leech 1980). The re-use of disused religious sites as cemeteries also occurred within the rural area, and examples which produced burials utilised in this study include Lamyatt Beacon and Yatton, Somerset (Leech 1986; Watts and Leach 1996). Inhumation was the predominant burial rite in the rural area, although mixed rite cemeteries are known, as at Winterbourne, Wiltshire, where a total of 37 cremations and 14 inhumations were recovered (Foster 2001: 165, 171). Burials were predominantly supine single inhumations in coffins or simple rectangular grave cuts with only limited grave goods. Of the total of 382 rural burials, 99 were aged at 50+ years, whilst 54.6% (197/361 sexed burials) were male and 45.4% (164/361 sexed burials) were female.

As a feature of later Roman burials was a limited use of grave goods, the total sample of 677 burials produced a total of only 318 items of material culture which formed the basis of the analysis. Those items which came as pairs, such as shoes or earrings, were counted as one item. Similarly, unless otherwise stated in the site report, beads were treated as a single necklace and counted as one. These items were either placed within the grave as grave goods or were items of apparel worn at burial. In order to identify how being elderly was expressed in burial, two forms of analysis were employed. The first examined the average number of grave goods per burial. The second form of analysis traced changes in the types of material culture provided at burial. The grave goods were divided into type (e.g. coins, pottery and jewellery) and the amount of times each item appeared in each age group was counted. The total amounts of each item were then converted into percentages of the total number of grave goods. The levels of grave good provision and transitions in material culture were then compared by age and gender and the results were compared between the urban and rural data-sets.

Identifying Old Age in Adulthood

Overall, the percentage of burials with grave goods peaked at 32% (72/225 burials) at 40–49 years, before declining to 24.3% (44/181 burials) at 50+ years. When broken down into urban and rural data-sets, there was an increase in the percentage of burials with grave goods between 30–39 years and 40–49 years in urban areas. In contrast, grave goods were concentrated at 30-39 and 40-49 years in rural contexts before declining at 50+ years (Table 1).

Table 1: Percentage of furnished burials with adults aged 30–50+ in urban and rural contexts.

CONTEXT	Age	No. of burials	No. of furnished graves	Percentage
URBAN	30–39	106	24	22.6
	40–49	107	34	31.8
	50+	82	24	29.3
RURAL	30–39	165	49	29.7
	40–49	118	38	32.2
	50+	99	20	20.2
TOTAL		**677**	**189**	

In contrast, the overall use of coffins rose slightly with age, up from 24.2% (63/260 with grave treatment recorded) at 30–39 years to 30.3% (53/175) at 50+ years. Similarly to the analysis of the percentage of furnished burials, the greatest differentiation in the urban sample was between 30–39 years and older adults. Again, the rural elderly showed a separate pattern to younger adults, recording a slight increase in the use of coffins at 50+ years (Table 2).

Table 2: Grave treatment with adults aged 30–50+ in urban and rural contexts.

CONTEXT	Age	No.	Coffin %	RGC* %	Cist %	Pit %	Urn %
URBAN	30–39	101	27.7	62.4	2.0	-	7.9
	40–49	101	38.6	55.4	3.0	-	3.0
	50+	79	32.9	62.0	3.8	-	1.3
RURAL	30–39	159	22.0	72.3	4.4	1.2	-
	40–49	116	22.4	70.7	6.0	0.8	-
	50+	96	28.1	62.5	7.3	2.1	-

*RGC = rectangular grave cut

When the average number of grave goods in each band was examined further, differences in the age patterning between urban and rural burials were visible. Within the urban contexts the levels of grave good provision rose from 0.36 items per burial at 30–39 years to 0.49 items at 50+ years (Table 3). This rise in the number of grave goods at 50+ was recorded at both Cirencester and Gloucester at 0.43 items (26/60 burials) and 0.64 items (14/22 burials) respectively. In contrast, grave goods were concentrated at 40–49 years at 0.61 items per burial (72/118 burials) in rural contexts.

The gendered analysis of the data-sets also recorded some degree of age-based variation, particularly visible amongst elderly rural males and urban females. Elderly rural males showed a decline in the numbers of furnished burials from 32.1% (17/53 sexed burials) at 40–49 years

Table 3: Average number of grave goods with adults aged 30–50+ in urban and rural contexts.

CONTEXT	Age	No. of burials	No. of grave goods	Average
URBAN	30–39	106	38	0.36
	40–49	107	43	0.40
	50+	82	39	0.47
RURAL	30–39	165	76	0.46
	40–49	118	72	0.61
	50+	99	50	0.50
TOTAL		**677**	**318**	

to 16.7% (9/54 burials) at 50+ years in contrast to urban elderly males, whilst the average number of grave goods per burial also declined from 0.74 items at 40–49 years (39 items) to 0.39 (21 items) at 50+ years. Elderly urban males showed a less pronounced decline in the number of furnished burials from 29.5% (23/78 burials) to 22.8% (13/57), whilst the average number of grave goods remained steady at 0.39 and 0.4 items. Elderly urban female burials recorded a rise in the number of furnished burials from 30.8% (8/26) at 40–49 years to 47.6% (10/21) at 50+ years. Elderly urban females also had the highest average number of grave goods at 0.66 items per burial, and this focus on the older female was a feature of both urban sites. Overall rural elderly females showed a similar pattern of decline in the number of furnished burials from 34.5% (20/58 burials) at 40–49 years to 26.3% (10/38 burials) at 50+ years, but the average number of grave goods rose from 0.55 items per burial at 40–49 years to 0.73 items at 50+ years.

The analysis of grave treatment by gender also showed a small increase in the concentration of coffined burials with elderly rural females, from 24.1% at 40–49 years (14/58 burials with grave treatment recorded) to 31.6% (12/38) at 50+ years; there was no corresponding increase in coffin use amongst elderly rural males. In the urban data-set, differentiation was again visible between 30–39 years and older males, with a rise in coffined burial from 23.9% (16/67) at 30–39 years to 36% at 40–49 years (27/75). Amongst elderly urban females, the provision of coffins declined sharply from 42.3% (11/26) at 40–49 years to 23.8% (5/21).

Table 4: Percentage of grave good types with urban and rural burials aged 40–49 and 50+

TYPE	Urban 40–49	No.	Urban 50+	No.	Rural 40–49	No.	Rural 50+	No.
Metalwork	23.3	10	5.1	2	6.9	5	4.0	2
Coins	44.2	19	38.5	15	36.1	26	30.0	15
Jewellery	4.6	2	28.2	11	1.4	1	24.0	12
Utensils	2.3	1	5.1	2	2.8	2	6.0	3
Dress accessories	4.6	2	10.3	4	5.6	4	10.0	5
Hobnail shoes	4.6	2	5.1	2	15.3	11	16.0	8
Glassware	2.3	1	-	-	9.7	7	-	-
Pottery	14.0	6	5.1	2	6.9	5	6.0	3
Caskets	-	-	2.6	1	2.8	2	-	-
Animal bone	-	-	-	-	11.1	8	4.0	2
Amulets	-	-	-	-	1.4	1	-	-
TOTAL		**43**		**39**		**72**		**50**

Whilst the analysis of levels of grave good provision recorded a degree of age and gender patterning, the analysis of the types of material culture recorded a more restricted range of items being placed with the elderly, particularly in rural burials. Whilst coins remained the most common type of grave goods in urban contexts at 40–49 years and 50+ years, the provision of jewellery increased sharply at 50+ years from 4.6% (2/43 items) to 28.2% (11/39 items) (Table 4). This pattern was also mirrored in the rural data-set, where jewellery formed 24.0% (12/50 items) of the grave goods with elderly adults.

Table 5: Percentage of grave good types with male urban and rural burials aged 40–49 years and 50+ years.

TYPE	Urban 40–49	No.	Urban 50+	No.	Rural 40–49	No.	Rural 50+	No.
Metalwork	27.6	8	9.1	2	10.2	4	9.5	2
Coins	44.8	13	54.5	12	38.4	15	52.4	11
Jewellery	6.9	2	13.6	3	2.6	1	-	-
Utensils	3.4	1	4.5	1	2.6	1	14.3	3
Dress accessories	6.9	2	9.1	2	2.6	1	9.5	2
Hobnail shoes	3.4	1	4.5	1	15.4	6	14.3	3
Glassware	-	-	-	-	15.4	6	-	-
Pottery	6.9	2	4.5	1	5.1	2	-	-
Animal bone	-	-	-	-	7.7	3	-	-
TOTAL		**29**		**22**		**39**		**21**

Table 6: Percentage of grave good types with female urban and rural burials aged 40–49 years and 50+ years.

Type	Urban 40–49	No.	Urban 50+	No.	Rural 40–49	No.	Rural 50+	No.
Metalwork	22.2	2	-	-	3.2	1	-	-
Coins	44.4	4	18.8	3	35.5	11	14.3	4
Jewellery	-	-	50.0	8	-	-	39.3	11
Utensils	-	-	-	-	3.2	1	-	-
Dress accessories	-	-	12.5	2	9.7	3	10.7	3
Hobnail shoes	11.1	1	6.2	1	12.9	4	21.4	6
Glassware	11.1	1	-	-	3.2	1	-	-
Pottery	11.1	1	6.2	1	6.5	2	7.1	2
Caskets	-	-	6.2	1	6.5	2	-	-
Animal bone	-	-	-	-	16.1	5	7.1	2
Amulets	-	-	-	-	3.2	1	-	-
Total		**9**		**16**		**31**		**28**

When the material culture types associated with the elderly in both urban and rural contexts were examined by gender, further patterns could be seen. In urban contexts there was no visible difference in the range of material culture types with males aged between 40–49 years and 50+ years, with coins predominating at 44.8% (13/29 items) at 40–49 years and 54.5% (12/22 items) at 50+ years (Table 5). In contrast, elderly rural male burials showed a restricted range of only five types of material culture, with coins predominating at 52.4% (11/21 items) of the total.

Amongst the elderly female sample in both urban and rural contexts an age transition at 50+ years was visible. At 40–49 years coins were the most common form of female grave goods in both contexts at 44.4% (4/9 items) in the urban sample and 35.5% (11/31 items) in the rural group. At 50+ years jewellery predominated, forming 50% (8/16 items) of the grave goods with female urban burials and 39.3% (11/28 items) with elderly females in rural contexts (Table 6).

Contextualising Old Age in Roman Britain

The results outlined above do indicate that the 'elderly' are recognisable in the burial record, primarily through changes in the levels and forms of material culture and, to a lesser extent, through an increased use of coffin burial. However, these variations are embedded within the overall pattern of adult burial in general. The 'elderly' were not differentiated in burial through age alone, but rather through variations which related to environment and gender. Amongst urban males, for example, there was little variation in the burial treatment between those aged 40–49 years and 50+ years; rather, the difference lay between younger males (30–39 years) and the older age groups. In contrast, rural male burial revealed a sharper division between the 50+ age group and younger adults. Although the numbers are small, an increase in the provision of jewellery was seen with females at 50+ years in both urban and rural environments. How, then, to interpret these patterns within the mature and elderly adult burials?

Whilst the elderly remained a part of the wider social group, evidenced by similar types of material culture and burial treatment as younger adults, growing older may have well impacted upon the social roles of males and females. As an individual ages through the life course, how he or she is perceived, their social role and relationship to others within both the familial structure and the wider world, changes. In the Roman world, the idealised social role of males was primarily external, relating to the world beyond the immediate domestic sphere. As such, the impact of the environment in which he moved, whether urban or rural, may have been influential on how the elderly male was perceived. Funerals function as a means of repairing the break in the familial and social fabric caused by the death of an individual (Shaw 1991: 75, 81). Within an urban environment, where people lived and inter-acted closely on a daily basis, the mourners may have included not only children and grandchildren, but also those with whom the elderly male had associated outside of the domestic sphere, such as close neighbours and those with whom he had worked or socialised. It may that the focus on the mature and elderly urban male in burial was an acknowledgement of the value of life experience, learnt knowledge and the social networks which come from living within a tightly knit community.

In contrast, the patterns seen in elderly male burials in rural contexts, with a decline in the range of material culture and levels of provision, may represent a transition in how males in old age were perceived. Whilst the elderly rural male retained knowledge and experience, the ill-health and physical degeneration associated with old age may have precluded him from being able to engage fully with the labour-intensive work required in a predominantly agricultural society such as Roman Britain. Allied to this possible transition, it has been suggested that attitudes and behaviour towards the elderly within agricultural societies is conditioned by the underlying economic and social system (Johnson 1998: 7). For example, in medieval northern Europe, where the nuclear family was the prevalent social structure, the elderly peasant transferred the management and working of the land to his children in return for support in old age (Gaunt 1983: 255, 365–66). Whilst what constituted the prevalent social structure in rural

Roman Britain remains open to debate, Millett (1990: 205–10) argued that by the late Roman period, from where the majority of these burials originated, small nucleated agricultural settlements of *coloni* were closer to the pattern of medieval villages. If this was the case, it may represent a transition towards a more nuclear family structure closer to that of medieval northern Europe. As such, the patterning visible in elderly male rural burials may be representative of the impact of the demands and needs of the rural environment on the perceived value of the elderly male.

Amongst females, the most striking pattern associated with the elderly was a transition in the type of grave goods provided, from coins at 40–49 years to jewellery at 50+ years. This transition, seen in both urban and rural contexts, suggests that the patterning may be related to the social identity of elderly females as a whole in this region. If the male social role was external, the predominant role of the female in antiquity was internal: focussed around the home and the roles of wife and mother (Harlow 2007: 197). It may be that what is visible in burial is a transition in the position of elderly females in relation to these social roles. During her younger adult years, the female would have been constrained by the social norms and expectations inherent within the domestic role and by her relationships to family members: firstly as a daughter, then as a wife and mother (Parkin 2003: 246). In old age, transitions within these social relationships would have impacted upon the female. For example, one possible transition could be widowhood. In particular, the transition to widowhood would have been a reality for many elderly women in the Roman period (McGinn 1999). Studies on age at marriage in Roman contexts show that males tended to marry, on average, a decade later than females (Saller 1987; Shaw 1987). Unless they remarried, this age difference would have led to a high proportion of elderly women outliving their husbands.

A preponderance of older females over older males, due to widowhood, may have moved the older female into a more central familial role. She may have become a focus of the household structure, providing a degree of continuity with the past. It may be that, on being widowed at a relatively young age, females would have taken on economic roles to support themselves and their families. Utilising skeletal data from Poundbury, Dorset, Allason-Jones (2005: 81) estimates that the majority of females had given birth by their late twenties. Hypothetically, if a woman was widowed at 40, she may still have had young children to support. The economic role played by women in Roman Britain remains unknown, but females may have been involved in aspects of, for example, agricultural work. Recent studies on rural land use in southern Roman Britain have suggested that agricultural development strategies were designed to create a surplus for sale or trade, with evidence for the cultivation of marginal land for both arable and animal husbandry (Taylor 2007: 115). Many settlements would have relied upon the labour of the immediate household, particularly at times of intense activity such as harvesting (Scheidel 1995: 207; Erdkamp 1999: 558). The differentiation seen in the burial of elderly women may have been associated with a transition in working patterns. As her children grew and could support themselves, the elderly female entered a new phase in her life course, reflected in changes in grave good provision.

The differentiation in the provision of type of grave goods between younger females and those aged over 50 years may have been related to perceptions of fertility. The menopause – and the biological ending of the primary female role in reproduction – may have impacted upon the perceived social identity of elderly women. It has been suggested that concentrations of grave goods with children and young females in some Romano-British cemeteries may be related to fertility, either in actuality or in potential (Oliver 2002; Puttock 2002: 41–55). Whilst it is problematic to tie the menopause into the elderly female burial record, as the ending of fertility and the physical symptoms associated with the transition may have been essentially a private matter, the 'social' end of fertility may have been recognised. Under the Augustan marriage legislation, women over 50 years were not expected to remarry, tacitly assuming that the ability to bear children had passed (Harlow and Laurence 2002: 127–9). Similarly, physical signs of ageing, or social transitions such as the birth of grandchildren or great grandchildren, may have impacted on the identity of elderly females. This latter milestone may itself have provided elderly females with a continued role in old age, and many elderly women may have been involved in the upbringing of grandchildren. It has been suggested that patterns of epigraphic commemoration from Roman Spain showed a bias towards elderly females (Revell 2005: 53–4; 57), interpreted as an increase in social status due to their roles as grandmothers and great-grandmothers (Nielsen 1989: 79). Such transitions as widowhood, grown children and the arrival of grandchildren may have freed older women from the social constraints of expected behaviour, but may also have provided a continuing social role in both urban and rural contexts. Thus the social identity of the older female – rather than being subsumed within the family – may have become more visible and reflected within the burial record.

However, the change in material culture in burial between younger and older females may have more negative interpretations. The biological ending of fertility, and the arrival of grandchildren, may have removed the elderly female from her position at the centre of the family structure to a more peripheral position (Harlow 2007: 200). This marginal position within the familial structure may have brought a greater level of dependency on economic resources from children or other relatives (Hin 2007: 4). In many traditional societies the social position of elderly females was uncertain. In Roman literature witches were usually portrayed as elderly females; characterised as dabbling in fortune-telling, casting spells and mixing love-potions (Rosivach 1994: 113, 116; Maxwell-Stuart 2000: 28–29; Janowitz 2001: 88–89). In Anglo-Saxon contexts, the *wergild* (social worth of the individual expressed in monetary value) of a post-menopausal female was one third that of a free-born female of child-bearing age (Crawford 1990: 30). It may be that the transition visible in burial at 50+ years reflected a degree of ambiguity in regard to the elderly female.

Conclusion

The elderly in the Roman world were not invisible but remain overlooked in archaeological discourse. A life course approach, when applied to the funerary evidence, can provide a means of exploring the experience of age and ageing in the past. Within this small group of burials the elderly were acknowledged within the adult burial rite through degrees of variation in grave treatment, levels of grave good provision and the range of material culture. However, age alone was not the only factor which influenced how the elderly were buried; the impact of environment and gender were also at work. Whilst possible interpretations as to the meanings behind these variations in the treatment of the elderly are open to debate, they do underline how much remains to be understood about the elderly in the past. This survey utilises only a fraction of the available funerary data relating to the elderly in Roman Britain, and it is likely that these burials represents only one of many ways of expressing 'being old' in the burial record. The results here, coupled with other studies (e.g. Gowland 2002; 2007) on age identity in Roman Britain, hint at a multiplicity of attitudes towards the elderly which need to be explored further to gain a more rounded picture of social organisation in Roman Britain.

Department of Archaeology, University of Southampton

Acknowledgements

I would like to thank Dr Louise Revell for reading and commenting on drafts of this paper, the anonymous reviewers for their advice and Geoff Taylor for his editorial efforts. Thanks also to Alison Brooks at Cirencester Museum and Phil Greatorex at Gloucester Museum for their time while gathering data for the database.

Appendix

Burials with adults aged 50+ years used in this study.

Site Name	Total	M	F	Date (A.D.)	Reference
Abingdon, Oxfordshire	2	1	1	300–400	Parrington 1978
Alcester, Warwickshire	3	2	1	250–400	Cracknell and Mahany 1994
Appleford, Oxfordshire	1	1	-	350–400	Hinchliffe and Thomas 1980
Barton, Gloucester	11	6	3	300–400	Rhodes 1980
Bath Gate/Querns, Cirencester	59	45	14	230–400	McWhirr *et al.* 1982
Bishops Cleeve, Gloucestershire	1	-	1	200–400	Parry 1999
Bristol, Avon	1	-	-	350–400	Rahtz and Clevedon Brown 1958/9
Bradley Hill, Somerset	8	6	2	300–350	Leech 1981
Cassington, Oxfordshire	2	1	1	300–400	Harman *et al.* 1981
Cave's Inn, Warwickshire	3	1	2	300–400	Cameron and Lucas 1973
Charlton Mackrell, Somerset	1	-	1	300–400	Leech 1980
Curbridge, Oxfordshire	1	1	-	350–400	Chambers and Williams 1976
Devizes, Wiltshire	1	1	-	300–400	Annable 1962
Dorchester-on-Thames, Oxfordshire	25	17	6	350–450	Chambers 1988
Frilford, Oxfordshire	1	-	1	300–400	Gosden *et al.* 2004
Frocester, Gloucestershire	4	2	2	300–400	Price 2000
Gatcombe, Somerset	1	1	-	300–350	Brannigan 1977
Hardwick, Oxfordshire	1	1	-	300–400	Chambers and Williams 1976
Henbury, Gloucestershire	1	-	1	300–400	Russell 1983
Hucclecote, Gloucestershire	5	-	5	100–200	Thomas *et al.* 2003
Illchester, Somerset	3	1	2	300–400	Everton and Rogers 1990
Kemble, Gloucestershire	3	-	1	300–400	Timby 1998
Kingsholm, Gloucester	1	-	1	200-300	Atkin 1987
Lamyatt, Somerset	2	-	2	350–450	Leech 1986
London Road, Gloucester	10	6	3	100–400	Foundations Archaeology 2000
Naunton, Gloucestershire	4	3	1	100–200	Mays 1980
Nettleton Shrub, Wiltshire	1	1	-	350–400	Wedlake 1982
Oxford, Oxfordshire	1	-	-	100–200	Hassall 1972
Roden Downs, Oxfordshire	6	2	4	300–425	Philpott 1991
Radley, Oxfordshire	10	8	1	300–400	Atkinson 1952
Stanton Harcourt, Oxfordshire	1	-	1	200–300	McGavin 1980
Tockington, Gloucestershire	2	1	-	350–300	Masser and McGill 2004

Winterbourne, Wiltshire	1	-	1	300–400	Algar 1961
Wyre Piddle, Worcestershire	1	-	1	300–400	Mercian Archaeology 2003
Verulamium Gate, Cirencester	1	1	-	-	McWhirr *et al.* 1982
Yatton, Somerset	2	2	-	270–450	Watts and Leach 1996
Total	**181**	**111**	**59**		

Bibliography

Ancient Sources

Cicero (Translated by W.A. Falconer 1946). *De Senectute, De Amicitia, De Divinatione.* London: Heinemann.

Seneca (Translated by R.M. Gummere 1937). *Epistulae Morales.* London: Heinemann.

Modern Sources

Algar, D.J. 1961. Winterbourne Down: Roman Cemetery. *Wiltshire Archaeology Magazine* 58: 470.

Allason-Jones, L. 2005. *Women in Roman Britain: New Edition.* York: Council for British Archaeology.

Annable, F.K. 1962. *Wiltshire Archaeology Magazine* 58: 222–223.

Atkin, M. 1987. *Found at Richard Cound: The Kingsholm Dig.* Gloucester: Gloucester Excavation Unit and Richard Cound (BMW) Ltd.

Atkinson, R.J.C. 1952. Excavations at Barrow Hills Field, Radley. *Oxoniensia* 17: 32–35.

Aykroyd, R., Lucy, D., Pollard, M.A. and Roberts, C.A. 1999. Nasty, brutish, but not necessarily short: A reconsideration of statistical methods used to calculate age at death from adult human skeletal and dental age indicators. *American Antiquity* 64(1): 55–70.

Bennett, J. 1985. *The Roman Town of Abonae: Excavations at Nazareth House, Sea Mills, Bristol 1972.* Bristol: City of Bristol Museum.

Brannigan, K. 1977. *Gatcombe: The Excavation and Study of a Romano-British villa.* BAR British Series 44. Oxford: British Archaeological Reports.

Cameron, H. and Lucas, J. 1973. Tripontium: Second interim report. *Transactions and Proceedings of the Birmingham Archaeological Society for 1971–1973* 85: 93–144.

Chambers, R.A. 1988. The late and sub-Roman Cemetery at Queensford Farm, Dorchester-on-Thames, Oxon. *Oxoniensia* 52: 35–70.

Chambers, R.A. and Williams, G. 1976. A late Iron Age and Romano-British settlement at Hardwick. *Oxoniensia* 41: 21–35.

Cokayne, K. 2003. *Experiencing Old Age in Ancient Rome.* London: Routledge.

Cox, M. 2000. Ageing adults from the skeleton. In M. Cox and S. Mays (eds.) *Human Osteology in Archaeology and Forensic Science.* London: Greenwich Medical Media Ltd: 61–81.

Cracknell, S. and Mahany, C. 1994. *Roman Alcester: Southern Extra-mural area 1964–1966 excavations. Volume 2: Finds & Discussion.* CBA Report 97. York: Council for British Archaeology.

Crawford, S. 1999. *Childhood in Anglo-Saxon England.* Stroud: Sutton Publishing Ltd.

Darvill, T.C., Green, L.S. and Jones, M.V. 1993. *Excavations at Roughground Farm, Lechlade, Gloucestershire: A Prehistoric and Roman Landscape.* Oxford: Oxford Archaeological Unit.

Davison, C. 2000. Gender imbalances in Romano-British cemetery populations: a re-evaluation of the evidence. In J. Pearce, M. Millett and M. Struck (eds.) *Burial, Society and Context in the Roman World.* Oxford: Oxbow Books: 231–237.

Erdkamp, P. 1999. Agriculture, under-employment and the cost of rural labour in the Roman World. *The Classical Quarterly: New Series* 49(2): 556–572.

Esler, C.C. 1989. Horace's Old Girls: Evolution of a Topos. In T.M. Falkner and J. De Luce (eds.) *Old Age in Greek and Latin Literature.* Albany: State of New York University Press: 172–182.

Everton, R.F. and Rogers, J. 1990. The Human Remains. In P. Leach (ed.) *Ilchester Volume 1: Archaeology, Excavations and Fieldwork 1970–1975.* Sheffield Excavation Report 1. Sheffield: University of Sheffield: 263–267.

Finley, M.I. 1989. The Elderly in Classical Antiquity. In T.M. Falkner and J. De Luce (eds.) *Old Age in Greek and Latin Literature.* Albany: State University of New York Press: 1–20.

Fraschetti, A. 1997. Roman youth. In G. Levi and J.C. Schmitt (eds.) *A History of Young People in the West. Volume One: Ancient and Medieval Rites of Passage.* Cambridge, Mass: Belknap Press: 51–82.

Foster, A. 2001. Romano-British burials in Wiltshire. In P. Ellis (ed.) *Roman Wiltshire and After: Papers in Honour of Ken Annable.* Devizes: Wiltshire Archaeological and Natural History Society: 165–175.

Foundations Archaeology. 2000. *124–130 London Road, Gloucester: Archaeological Excavation Report.* Wiltshire: AMS Ltd.

Gaunt, D. 1983. The property and kin relationships of retired farmers in northern and central Europe. In R. Wall (ed.) *Family Forms in Historic Europe.* Cambridge: Cambridge University Press: 249–281.

Gilchrist, R. 1999. *Gender and Archaeology: Contesting the Past.* London: Routledge.

Gilchrist, R. 2000. Archaeological biographies: realizing human lifecycles, -courses and histories. *World Archaeology* 31(3): 325–328.

Ginn, J. and Arber, S. 1995. 'Only Connect': gender relations and ageing. In S. Arber and J. Ginn (eds.) *Connecting Gender and Ageing: A Sociological Approach.* Buckingham: Open University Press: 1–14.

Gosden, C., Lock, G. and Daly, P. 2004. *The Ridgeway and Vale Project: Excavations at Marcham/Frilford 2004.* *http*://www.arch.ox.ac.uk/_data/assets/pdf-file/1545/Interim_2004.pdf (accessed 23 June 2007).

Gowland, R.L. 2002. *Age as an Aspect of Social Identity in 4th–6th century AD England: The Archaeological Funerary Evidence.* University of Durham: Unpublished PhD Thesis.

Gowland, R. 2006. Ageing the Past: Examining age identity from funerary evidence. In R. Gowland and C. Knusel (eds.) *Social Archaeology of Funerary Remains.* Oxford: Oxbow Books: 143–154.

Gowland, R. 2007. Age, ageism and osteological bias: the evidence from Late Roman Britain. In M. Harlow and R. Laurence (eds.) *Age and Ageing in the Roman Empire.* Journal of Roman Archaeology Supplementary Series No. 65. Ann Arbor, Michigan: Journal of Roman Archaeology: 153–169.

Hareven, T.K. 1978. Introduction: the historical study of the life course. In T.K. Hareven (ed.) *Transitions: The Family and the Life Course in Historical Perspective.* London: Academic Press Inc (London) Ltd: 1–16.

Harlow, M. 2007. Blurred visions: Male perceptions of the female life course – the case of Aemilia Pudentilla. In M. Harlow and R. Laurence (eds.) *Age and Ageing in the Roman Empire.* Journal of Roman Archaeology Supplementary Series No. 65. Ann Arbor, Michigan: Journal of Roman Archaeology: 195–207.

Harlow, M. and Laurence, R. 2002. *Growing Up and Growing Old in Ancient Rome: A Life Course Approach.* London: Routledge.

Harman, M., Molleson, T. and Price, J.L. 1981. Burials, bodies and beheadings in Romano-British and Anglo-Saxon Cemeteries. *Bulletin of the British Museum Natural History Magazine* 35(3): 145–188.

Hassall, T.G. 1972. Roman finds from the Radcliffe Science Library Extension, Oxford, 1970–71. *Oxoniensia* 37: 38–50.

Heighway, C.M. 1980. Excavations at Gloucester: 5th interim report: St Oswalds Priory 1977–8. *Antiquaries Journal* 60: 207–226.

Heighway, C.M., Garrod, A.P., Rhodes, J.F. and Goudge, C.E. 1980. Roman Cemeteries in the Gloucester District. *Transactions of the Bristol and Gloucester Archaeological Society* 60: 57–72.

Hin, S. 2007. *Family Matters: Economy, Culture and Biology: Fertility and its constraints in Roman Italy.* Princeton: Princeton/Stanford Working Papers in Classics.

Hinchliffe, J. and Thomas, R. 1980. Archaeological investigations at Appleford. *Oxoniensia* 45: 9–112.

Holbrook, N. 1994. Corinium Dubunnorum: Roman Civitas Capital and provincial capital. In T. Darvill and C. Gerrard (eds.) *Cirencester: Town and Landscape.* Cirencester: Cotswolds Archaeological Trust Ltd: 57–86.

Hurst, H. 1975. Excavations at Gloucester: Third Interim Report: Kingsholm 1966–75. *Antiquaries Journal* LV: 267–94.

Janowitz, N. 2001. *Magic in the Roman World: Pagans, Jews and Christians.* London: Routledge.

Johnson, P. 1998. Historical readings of old age and ageing. In P. Johnson and P. Thane (eds.) *Old Age from Antiquity to Post-Modernity.* London: Routledge: 1–18.
Joyce, R.A. 2000. Girling the Girl and Boying the Boy: The production of adulthood in Ancient Mesoamerica. *World Archaeology* 31(3): 473–483.
Leech, P. 1986. The Excavation of a Romano-Celtic temple on Lamyatt Beacon. *Britannia* XVII: 259–328.
Leech, R. 1980. Religion and Burials in South Somerset and North Dorset. In W. Rodwell (ed.) *Temples, Churches and Religion: Recent Research in Roman Britain Volumes I and II.* BAR British Series 77. Oxford: British Archaeological Reports: 329–366.
Leech, R. 1981. The excavation of a Romano-British farmstead and cemetery on Bradley Hill, Somerton, Somerset. *Britannia* XII: 177–253.
Lucy, S. 2007. The archaeology of age. In M. Diaz-Andreu, S. Lacy, S. Babic and D.N. Edwards (eds.) *The Archaeology of Identity: Approaches to Gender, Age, Status, Ethnicity and Religion.* London: Routledge: 42–66.
McGavin, 1980. A Roman cemetery and trackway at Stanton Harcourt. *Oxoniensia* 45: 112–123.
McGinn, T.A.J. 1999. Widows, orphans and social history. *Journal of Roman Archaeology* 12: 617–632.
McWhirr, A. 1976. The Roman Town Plan. In A. McWhirr (ed.) *Archaeology and History of Cirencester: Based on papers presented to a research seminar on the post-Roman development of Cirencester held at the Corinium Museum, November 1975.* BAR British Series 30. Oxford: British Archaeological Reports: 5–15.
McWhirr, A., Viner, L. and Wells, C. 1982. *Romano-British Cemeteries at Cirencester.* Cirencester: Cirencester Excavation Committee Report II.
Masser, M. and McGill, B. 2004. Excavations of Romano-British sites at Tockington Park Farm and Westerleigh, South Gloucestershire in 1997. *Transactions of the Bristol and Gloucestershire Archaeological Society* 122: 95–116.
Maxwell-Stuart, P.G. 2000. *Witchcraft: A History.* Stroud: Tempus Publishing Ltd.
Mays, S. 1980. *Romano-British Skeletons from Naunton, Gloucestershire.* AML Report 1980. English Heritage: Unpublished Report.
Mercian Archaeology. 2003. *Osteological Analysis of Human Remains from Upper Moor, near Wyre Piddle, Worcestershire.* Mercian Archaeology Specialist Reports PJ108. Worcester: Mercian Archaeology.
Meskell, L. 2000. Cycles of life and death: narrative homology and archaeological realities. *World Archaeology* 31(3): 324–441.
Millett, M. 1990. *The Romanisation of Britain.* Cambridge: Cambridge University Press.
Molleson, T.I. and Cox, M. 1993. *The Spitalfields Project: Volume 2: The Anthropology – The Middling Sort.* CBA Research Report 86. York: Council for British Archaeology.
Nielsen, M. 1989. Women and family in changing society: a quantitative approach to late Etruscan burials. *Analecta Romana Instituti Danici* 17–18: 53–98.
Oliver, A. 2002. Jewellery for the unmarried. In D. Kleiner and S. Matheson (eds.) *I Claudia II: Women in Roman Art and Society.* Austin: University of Texas Press: 115–124.
Parkin, T.G. 1997. Out of Sight, Out of Mind: Elderly Members of the Roman Family. In B. Rawson and P. Weaver (eds.) *The Roman Family in Italy: Status, Sentiment, Space.* Oxford: Clarendon Press: 123–148.
Parkin, T.G. 2003. *Old Age in the Roman World: A Cultural and Social History.* Baltimore and London: John Hopkins University Press.
Parry, C. 1999. Iron Age, Romano-British and Medieval Occupation at Bishop's Cleeve, Gloucestershire: Excavations at Gilder's Paddock 1989 and 1990–1. *Transactions of the Bristol and Gloucester Archaeological Society* 117: 89–118.
Parrington, M. 1978. *The Excavation of an Iron Age Settlement, Bronze Age Ring-Ditches and Roman Features at Ashville Trading Estate, Abingdon (Oxfordshire) 1974–76.* London: Council for British Archaeology/Oxford Archaeological Unit.
Philpott, R. 1991. *Burial Practices in Roman Britain: A survey of grave treatment and furnishing AD43–410.* BAR British Series 219. Oxford: British Archaeological Reports.

Price, E. 2000. *Frocester: A Romano-British Settlement, its Antecedents and Successors, Volume 2.* Stonehouse: Gloucester and District Archaeological Research Group: 203–210.

Puttock, S. 2002. *Ritual Significance of Personal Ornament in Roman Britain.* BAR British Series 327. Oxford: British Archaeological Reports.

Rahtz, P.A. and Clevedon Brown, J. 1958/9. Blaise Castle Hill, Bristol, 1957. *Proceedings of the University of Bristol Spelaeological Society* 8(3): 147–171.

Reece, R. 1962. The Oakley Cottage Romano-British Cemetery, Cirencester. *Transactions of the Bristol and Gloucestershire Archaeological Society* 81: 51–72.

Revell, L. 2005. The Roman Life Course: A view from the inscriptions. *European Journal of Archaeology* 8(1): 43–63.

Rhodes, J. 1980. College of Art Site. In Heighway, C.M. 1980. Roman Cemeteries in Gloucester District. *Transactions of the Bristol and Gloucester Archaeological Society* 98: 67–68.

Rosivach, V. 1994. *Anus:* Some Older Women in Latin Literature. *Classical World* 88(2): 107–117.

Russell, J. 1983. Romano-British burials at Henbury Comprehensive School, Bristol: A preliminary report. *Bristol & Avon Archaeology* 2: 21–4.

Saller, R. 1987. Men's age at marriage and its consequences for the Roman family. *Classical Philology* 82: 21–34.

Scheidel, W. 1995. The most silent women of Greece and Rome: Rural labour and women's life in the ancient world (II). *Greece and Rome, second series* 43(1): 1–10.

Scheidel, W. 2001. Roman Age Structure: Evidence and Models. *The Journal of Roman Studies* 91: 1–26.

Schwartz, J.H. 1995. *Skeleton Keys: An Introduction to Human Skeletal Morphology, Development and Analysis.* Oxford: Oxford University Press.

Shaw, B. 1987. The age of Roman girls at marriage: some reconsiderations. *Journal of Roman Studies* 77: 30–46.

Shaw, B. 1991. The cultural meaning of death: Age and gender in the Roman family. In D.I. Kertzer and R.P. Saller (eds.) *The Family in Italy from Antiquity to the Present.* New Haven and London: Yale University Press: 66–90.

Sofaer Derevenski, J. 1994. Where are the children? Accessing children in the past. *Archaeological Review from Cambridge* 13(2): 7–20.

Sofaer Derevenski, J. 1997. Age and gender at the site of Tiszapolgar-Basatanya, Hungary. *Antiquity* 71: 875–888.

Sofaer Derevenski, J. 2000. Rings of life: the role of early metalwork in mediating the gendered life course. *World Archaeology* 31(3): 389–406.

Stoodley, N. 2000. From the cradle to the grave: Age organisation and the early Anglo-Saxon burial rite. *World Archaeology* 31(3): 456–472.

Taylor, J. 2007. *An Atlas of Roman Rural Settlement in England.* CBA Research Report 151. York: Council for British Archaeology.

Thomas, A., Holbrook, N. and Bateman, C. 2003. *Later Prehistoric and Romano-British Burial and Settlement at Hucclecote Gloucestershire.* Bristol and Gloucestershire Archaeological Report No. 2. Gloucester: Bristol and Gloucestershire Archaeological Society.

Timby, J.R. 1998. *Excavations at Kingscote and Wycomb, Gloucestershire.* Cirencester: Cotswolds Archaeological Trust.

Watts, L. and Leach, P. 1996. *Henley Wood, Temples & Cemetery Excavations 1962–69 by the late Ernest Greenfield and Others.* CBA Research Report 99. York: Council for British Archaeology.

Wedlake, W.J. 1982. *The Excavation of the Shrine of Apollo at Nettleton, Wiltshire, 1956–1971.* Reports of the Research Committee of the Society of Antiquaries of London No. XL. London: The Society of Antiquaries of London.

Wiedemann, T. 1989. *Adults and Children in the Roman Empire.* London: Routledge.

Beyond the Warlike Samnites: Rethinking Grave Goods, Gender Relations and Social Practice in Ancient Samnium (Italy)

Rafael Scopacasa

Introduction

This paper aims to contribute to the changing image of society and culture in ancient Samnium (central Apennine Italy) by analysing the social practices of men and women expressed through the mortuary evidence. The area of Samnium, which includes present-day Molise, south Abruzzo, north Campania and northwest Puglia (Fig. 1), is described in ancient literary sources as the homeland of the Samnites, who are portrayed in these texts as an enduring warlike people. Ancient authors describe the Samnites as clad in splendid and abundant armour, strongly resisting Roman encroachment during the so-called 'Samnite Wars' of the late fourth and early third centuries B.C., in which the Romans were ultimately victorious (e.g. Diodorus: 19.10.1; Livy: 7.29–33, 10.31; Strabo: 5.4.11, Frontinus: *Strat.* 2.1.8, 2.4.1; Pliny the Elder: 3.106–107; Silius Italicus: 10.309–315). The continued legacy of these literary portrayals is still apparent in many current interpretations of the archaeological evidence from Samnium. One assumed characteristic of communities in the region is the centrality of warfare, with an emphasis on the role of men as warriors while women are consigned to household activities (Parise Badoni and Ruggieri Giove 1980; 1981; Saulnier 1983; Tagliamonte 1996; Bispham 2007). This predominant view is based on generalising interpretations of grave good assemblages, whereby burials containing weapons are assumed to belong to men while those featuring personal ornaments and no weapons are associated with women.

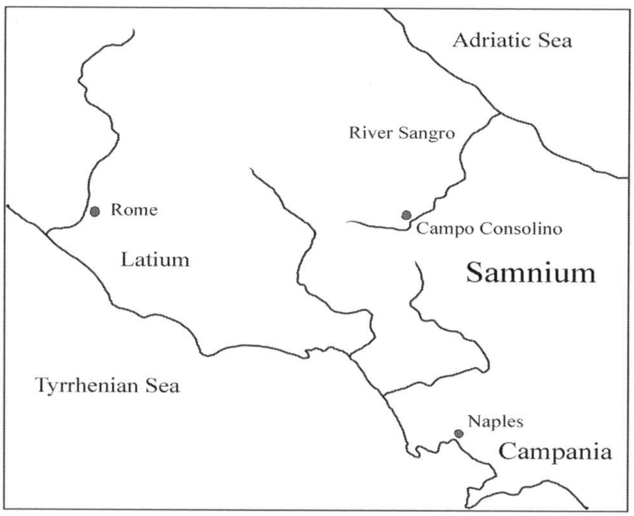

Figure 1: Central Apennine Italy, with Samnium and the funerary site of Campo Consolino.

This traditional view has begun to be challenged by alternative approaches (Suano 1991; 2000), as will be discussed below. Here, I propose to reconsider the traditional assumptions that prevail in the archaeology of Samnium by examining correlations between grave goods and the men and women buried at Campo Consolino, a key funerary site in Samnium. Located in the Apennine hinterland and used between the late sixth and fifth centuries B.C., Campo Consolino provides a strong sample of individuals whose biological sex has been securely determined from skeletal analysis. Chi-square tests are employed to identify correlations between the sex of individuals and their grave goods. This is done in order to assess what the correlations, or their absence, can inform us about social roles and practices associated with men and women in the community – practices which need not be entirely confined to the conventions of mortuary ritual. Before outlining the methodology, a brief overview will be given of the extant scholarly assumptions about grave goods and gendered social practices in Samnium generally, and at Campo Consolino in particular.

The 'sexing' of grave goods in Samnium and its shortcomings

Between the sixth and early third centuries B.C., the main funerary sites in Samnium can be seen to include two different classes of grave good assemblages. Whilst some burials contain weaponry (iron spears, axes, daggers) and armour (bronze helmets and breastplates, belts), other burials include items of personal adornment (bronze and iron rings, glass and amber beads, glass pearls, bronze pendants, arm-rings, bracelets, collars and chains). In the past, archaeologists have tended to assign each of these grave good assemblages to either of the biological sexes, often without the support of skeletal analysis. In broad terms, weapons, razors, belts and, to some extent, knives are considered diagnostic of the masculine sex, whilst personal ornaments unaccompanied by the 'masculine' artefacts are seen as indicative of the feminine sex (e.g. Capini 1980: 117; 1991; Di Niro 1980; 1991).

Most scholars have regarded these supposedly 'masculine' and 'feminine' grave goods as indicative of social activities and identities which characterized the men and women of Samnium before Roman encroachment began in the third century B.C. There has developed a somewhat circular argument whereby the 'sexing' of artefacts supports a preconceived view of gendered social relations in ancient Samnium. Thus, because warfare is assumed to be a 'male' activity, weapon burials are attributed to men, and are interpreted as evidence that men engaged in warfare and emphasised their role as warriors and community leaders (Salmon 1967; Saulnier 1983; Tagliamonte 1996: 116, 121, 123–4). The traditional viewpoint believes that the emphasis on weaponry indicates the centrality of warfare in the communities in Samnium. On the other hand, burials devoid of weapons but featuring personal ornaments (which are assumed to indicate women) tend to be seen as evidence that household activities were the domain of women, who were supposedly in charge of the holding and guarding of family trinkets and heirlooms. There is a general agreement that this strict division of 'masculine' and 'feminine' social roles in Samnium originated in the sixth century and was perpetuated into the fourth and third centuries B.C. (e.g. Tagliamonte 1996: 212).

The interpretative framework outlined above has been applied to the key funerary site of Campo Consolino, which was used during the late sixth and fifth centuries B.C. Although the individuals at the site have been sexed and aged through skeletal analysis, archaeologists have not yet verified whether this data effectively supports the traditional interpretative framework outlined above (Parise Badoni and Ruggieri Giove 1980). In line with the general consensus, weapon burials at Campo Consolino are seen as indicative of men belonging to a 'warrior aristocracy' that headed the community, although warfare is also argued to have been practiced by non-aristocratic men (Parise Badoni and Ruggieri Giove 1981: xxxvi; Bispham 2007: 189*ff.*). On the other hand, the burials without weapons but featuring personal ornaments are argued to indicate women showcasing the finery accumulated by their male counterparts. However, as will be seen below, it has not yet been taken into account that most of the men at Campo Consolino were buried with artefacts other than weapons, and that many of the artefacts buried with men are also found with women.

Before examining such trends in more detail, it should be noted that the traditional interpretations of grave goods in Samnium, and at Campo Consolino in particular, are grounded on assumptions which are problematic. The association of weapons with men, and 'warrior men' in particular, is not peculiar to the archaeology of Samnium, having been common since the early developments of archaeology in Italy (Toms 1998: 157). In the case of Samnium, the association is arguably encouraged by the ancient literary emphasis on Samnite male warriorhood. However, such literary sources are not a reliable guide to the study of the communities of Samnium. The basic problem is that the literary accounts were written several centuries after the events to which they refer, from the point of view of Greek and Roman authors whose representations of the Roman and Italian past were tied to pressing ideological agendas (Scopacasa 2007). It has already been demonstrated that ancient authors conceptualised the relationship between Romans and Samnites in light of the ideologically-laden polarization of Greeks versus Barbarians (Dench 1995: 99–103).

Awareness of such problems has begun to encourage alternative approaches to grave goods and mortuary practice in Samnium, based on a more contextual examination of material culture. In particular, Suano (2000) has shown how the 'sexing' of artefacts can be very problematic in light of cases where assumedly 'masculine' and 'feminine' grave goods are found together in the same burial. For example, instances where bronze belts (supposedly 'masculine' items) appear in graves also containing loom weights and spindle whorls (traditionally regarded as 'feminine'). Suano (2000: 188) argues that such overlaps demonstrate the need to move away from the traditional sexing of grave goods, and to search instead for the social meaning of these artefacts in light of the associations between them.

Much work remains to be done along these lines. In particular, the sexing of artefacts remains to be systematically tested with regard to samples of individuals whose biological sex and age can be confidently determined from skeletal evidence. Otherwise, it remains unclear to what extent the grave goods indicate both the biological sex of the individual and patterns in the social practices of men and women in Samnium.

Evidence and methods

This section contains an explanation of how the present investigation will be carried out, using a controlled and well documented sample of funerary evidence. The sample consists of 134 burials at Campo Consolino, one of the largest and best documented funerary sites in Samnium (Parise Badoni and Ruggieri Giove 1980; 1981). Campo Consolino was part of the much larger necropolis of Alfedena, which lay in the vicinity of roughly contemporaneous funerary sites at Val Fondillo and Barrea. The burials at Campo Consolino are loosely dated to the late sixth and fifth centuries, roughly spanning an interval of 125 years. As the more precise dating of individual graves remains very tentative (Parise Badoni *et al.* 1982), it is preferable to maintain the wider chronological framework in this paper.

The importance of Campo Consolino lies in the fact that it alone encompasses around 25% of the published burials in the entire study area of Samnium, as well as *c.* 50% of the burials in Samnium whose skeletons have been sexed and aged on the basis of anthropological analysis (Parise Badoni and Ruggieri Giove 1981; Parise Badoni *et al.* 1982). The analysis of the skeletons from Campo Consolino adhered to conventional criteria laid out by the *Istituto Italiano di Antropologia*, the *Journal of Human Evolution* and other specialist literature (Ferembach *et al.* 1977–79; Brothwell 1981: 59–70). Such anthropological analysis relies on diagnostic traits in the pelvis, skull and teeth, as well as bone robusticity, to situate individuals within a spectrum ranging from 'male' to 'female', with 'ambiguous' as the middle term. As the biological sexing of skeletons has been argued to be biased towards men by a factor of 12% (Weiss 1972), disputed or ambiguous cases in the present sample will be noted as often as possible.

Of the 134 burials at Campo Consolino, 109 have been securely sexed, of which 60% were men and 40% were women. Only 86 of the 109 sexed individuals (79%) have been aged. These 79% can be classed into two main age sets, those under 45 years old (43%) and over 45 years old (57%) (Table 1). Children, on the other hand, accounted for only 10% of the burials. As their small number is not enough to reveal patterns, they do not form the main focus of the present paper.

Table 1: Numbers of men and women (under and over 45) at Campo Consolino

	all ages	under 45	over 45
men	65	25	30
women	44	12	19
total	109	37	49

Chi-square and Yule's Q tests constitute the statistical methodology for determining which artefacts correlate with men or women at Campo Consolino. These tests are conventional in Prehistoric archaeology (e.g. Clarke 1968; Shennan 1997) and are also used in analyses of mortuary sites in Roman Britain (Cool 2004: 439–442) and, to a lesser extent, in Classical archaeology (Morris 1992: 113*ff.*). Chi-square tests are based on a 'null-hypothesis' that a given grave good is randomly distributed between men and women. The test generates a numerical result called the P value, which expresses the probability that the observed distribution is random (Shennan 1997: 106). In cases where samples are small, *Yates' correction for continuity* is applied to the chi-square tests, to minimize the risk of considering a correlation to be significant when it is not (Weglian 2001).

Whilst chi-square tests reveal the probability that a correlation between an artefact and biological sex exists, they do not indicate how strong the correlation is. The strength is determined by means of the Yule's Q coefficient, which ranges from -1 to 1 (Shennan 1997: 116–117). In the present case, the closer the coefficient is to 1, the stronger the correlation is between an artefact and biological sex. A parallel set of Yule's Q coefficients measures the correlation between the artefacts and the two main age groups (under and over 45 years old), to check whether correlation with age is stronger than with biological sex.

When chi-square tests suggest a correlation and Yule's Q tests confirm its strength, a case can be made that an artefact is related to socio-cultural differentiation of individuals based on their biological sex. This form of differentiation is conceptualised as 'gender', which is a key analytical category in this paper (Claassen 1992; Whitehouse 1998; Gilchrist 1999: xv; Sorensen 2000; Arnold 2002). Although many agree that gender is the socio-cultural interpretation of sexual difference, some argue that sex is also culturally constructed and therefore conflates with gender (Butler 1990: 7). However, the traditional distinction remains valid, as biological sex is less culturally determined than gender (Claassen 1992: 3; Lucy 1997; Carmen Vida 1998: 16–17; Sorensen 2000: 41–59). Given that gender is culturally-specific, it must be investigated in terms of how it is structured or manifested in specific cultural contexts, not in terms of modern preconceptions (Claassen 1992; Hodder 1997; Sorensen 2000; Arnold 2002). The methodology adopted in this paper is most suited to identifying 'two-gender systems', that is, the existence of a masculine and a feminine gender rooted in biological sexual difference (Nanda 2000). However, the statistical methodology also has the potential to reveal more complex gender systems that go beyond such a binary opposition. This is particularly so when individuals of one sex are buried with artefacts that strongly correlate with the opposite sex. Such occurrences remind us that gender is related not simply with biological sex but also with age, class, rank or socio-economic status. This complexity has led some to argue that, instead of searching for 'gender' as a distinct category of social organization, focus should be placed on social relations that are more or less 'gendered'; i.e. that are related to or determined by the socio-cultural interpretation of sexual difference (Sofaer Derevenski 2000).

Analysis of correlations between grave goods and biological sex at Campo Consolino

Table 2 shows the results obtained upon applying the Chi-square and Yule's Q tests to the sample of men and women at Campo Consolino. Artefacts that correlate significantly with men or women (i.e. with a P value of 0.05 or lower) are shown in bold. The first striking point is that the correlation between men and weapons is only valid provided that the total number of weapons is added together, but ceases to be significant if each individual type of weapon is considered separately.

Moreover, the weapon burials are overall quite rare, as they account for a mere 3% of the 134 burials. Some of the weapons are not even exclusive to men. For example, the iron spear – the most common weapon in the cemetery – was buried with a woman in one of five cases (grave 58: Parise Badoni *et al.* 1982). Similar cases of women buried with weapons are known from slightly earlier contexts elsewhere in Italy, particularly Etruria and Picenum in the seventh and sixth centuries B.C. In these contexts, the women buried with weapons also featured exceptionally lavish grave goods, so that the presence of weapons is interpreted as indicating a privileged social status shared by both men and women (Riva 2004; Izzet 2007). However, this does not appear to be the case at Campo Consolino, where weapon burials are not particularly lavish. If future excavation reveals further occurrences of weapons with women in Samnium, serious doubt can be cast on the certainty with which weapon burials are seen as signifiers of male identity.

Aside from the weapons, Table 2 shows that the men at Campo Consolino correlate with a series of other items, none of which seem to point consistently to the sphere of warfare or warriorhood. These artefacts are iron knives, rod-arch brooches, wine jugs (both fine ware *bucchero* imported from Campania and locally made coarse ware), and all other drinking vessels taken together as a single category. The association of men with knives and rod-arch brooches at Campo Consolino has already been noted (Parise Badoni and Ruggieri Giove 1980), and is here confirmed by the chi-square tests. Although knives might function as weapons in certain contexts, there is no good reason to discard their range of domestic and ritual uses, especially as only 6% of the knives were accompanied by weapons. On the other hand, less attention has been given to the correlation between men and drinking vessels in general, and wine jugs in particular. These correlations suggest an association between men and drinking practices, with an emphasis on wine consumption. However, the Yule's Q coefficients show that the drinking vessels correlate more strongly with individuals aged over 45 than with men, which will be discussed in more detail below.

Table 2: Main correlations between grave goods and biological sex at Campo Consolino

ARTEFACTS	ARTEFACT QUANTITY		CORRELATIONS		
	MEN	WOMEN	CHI SQUARE (P value)	YULE'S Q (SEX)	YULE'S Q (over 45)
cooking pots (ollae)	7	5	0.563	--	--
amphorae	17	18	0.865	--	--
drinking vessels (all)	**57**	**35**	**0.021 (men)**	0.06	0.181
wine jugs	**20**	**9**	**0.041 (men)**	0.266	-0.052
jugs	1	0	1	--	--
cups	17	12	0.353	--	--
skyphoi	3	1	0.617	--	--
kylikes	2	0	0.479	--	--
kantharoi	0	1	1	--	--
bowls	14	12	0.694	--	--
bronze basins	2	2	1	--	--
pans	3	2	1	--	--
brooches (all)	82	97	0.262	--	--
brooches (rod-arch)	**39**	**5**	**0.0001 (men)**	0.802	0.068
brooches (band-arch)	**7**	**36**	**0.0001 (women)**	0.846	0.108
rings	**14**	**39**	**0.0006 (women)**	0.703	-0.361
pendants	**51**	**164**	**0.0001 (women)**	0.843	-0.162
bracelet	2	2	1	--	--
chain mail	**9**	**24**	**0.009 (women)**	0.771	0.032
beads	**0**	**52**	**0.0001 (women)**	1	--
glass pearls	**0**	**41**	**0.0001 (women)**	1	--
chains	0	5	0.073	--	--
collars	0	3	0.248	--	--
weapons (all types)	**8**	**1**	**0.045 (men)**	0.476	-0.706
spears	4	1	0.371	--	--
daggers	3	0	0.248	--	--
axes	1	0	1	--	--
knives	**18**	**0**	**0.0001 (men)**	1	--
bronze belts	4	0	0.133	--	--

The women correlate with band-arch brooches and the majority of the personal ornaments; namely bronze and iron rings, chain mail, pendants, glass and amber beads and glass pearls. The Yule's Q coefficients in Table 2 demonstrate that these ornaments correlate much more strongly with female biological sex than with age. Nor do these ornaments seem to be restricted to the more lavish burials. At first sight, such a scenario seems to suggest a strong cultural association between women and personal ornaments, which would confirm the traditional view that personal ornaments indicate a feminine gender in Samnium, characterised by the wearing and custody of finery. However, a set of ambiguous occurrences adds complexity to this observation. Table 3 shows that many of the ornaments correlated with women (pendants, rings, chain mail, band-arch brooches), if all taken together, are also found with 20% of the men, 75% of whom are aged under 45 years. A similar overlap occurs with the rod-arch brooches, which correlate with men but also occur with 9% of the women. Among these women, the only two that can be aged are both over 45 years.

Table 3: percentages of men and women buried with each artefact

ARTEFACTS	BURIALS	
	MEN (65)	WOMEN (44)
cooking pots (ollae)	10%	11%
amphorae	26%	41%
wine jugs	30%	20%
jugs	1%	0%
cups	26%	23%
skyphoi	5%	2%
kylikes	3%	0%
kantharoi	0%	2%
bowls	22%	25%
bronze basins	3%	5%
pans	5%	5%
brooches (all)	75%	91%
brooches (rod-arch)	48%	9%
brooches (band-arch)	8%	50%
rings	11%	41%
pendants	3%	27%
bracelet	1%	5%
chain mail	5%	27%
beads	0%	14%
glass pearls	0%	23%
chains	0%	11%
collars	0%	7%
weapons (all types)	6%	2%
spears	6%	2%
daggers	5%	0%
axes	2%	0%
knives	26%	0%
bronze belts	6%	0%

While the pendants which were buried with men differ in shape and style from those of the women, the same does not hold for rings, chain mail and band-arch brooches, which are found in similar shapes and styles among men and women. Similarly, the rod-arch brooches found with 9% of the women do not show any distinguishing features that set them apart from those buried with men. One possible interpretation is that the personal ornaments and rod-arch brooches may not have carried direct connotations of femininity or masculinity in every context. The personal ornaments that correlate with women may not have been perceived as feminine when deposited with men, as they may have been mortuary offerings made by (possibly female) relations. This seems possible, as some of the men with 'feminine' ornaments also feature items that correlate strongly with men, namely knives, rod-arch brooches and wine jugs. If this was the case, there is also the possibility that the personal ornaments did not bear feminine connotations even when they were worn by or deposited with women. These results confirm Suano's suggestion that artefacts should not be viewed as carrying sex or gender connotations by themselves (Suano 2000: 188). Alternatively, the presence of ornaments in the graves of younger men may suggest that attributes of femininity were viewed as connected with certain younger men by the mourners. This would mean that the community that buried its dead at Campo Consolino regarded femininity as not completely dependent on female sex, but instead as a set of more fluid attributes responding to additional cultural criteria. A similar interpretation can be put forward regarding the rod-arch brooches. Of the women buried with these brooches, the only two whose skeletons could be aged were both found to be over 45 years old. This would suggest that, if the rod-arch brooches were indeed regarded as some type of indicator of masculinity, the very notion of masculinity in the community at Campo Consolino was tied not only to male biological sex but also older age, and possibly other cultural criteria which remain to be determined.

Overall, the ambiguous cases discussed above suggest that, if the correlations between grave goods and biological sex are at all indicative of a gender system at Campo Consolino, there is evidence that this system was complex. This is not surprising, since gender differentiation tends not to be straightforward or to conform to a binary opposition between men and women. The personal ornaments that may have been used to communicate gender at Campo Consolino may also have communicated rank, status or other social identities. It is also necessary to bear in mind that representations of gender roles can differ from the actual social behaviour of men and women. It has been demonstrated that even though working-class women may be aware of feminine gender models which essentially refer to the upper classes, they are obliged to perform social practices at odds with such a model, such as intense farm labour (Stine 1992). However, the ability to perform such activities can be a source of pride for the women in question, even though these are activities primarily associated with men.

Finally, the small proportion of children at Campo Consolino (10%) is not enough to suggest correlations with grave goods. Nevertheless, it is significant that items correlated with men (iron knives) and women (personal ornaments) also occur with children. Although it is impossible to specify the ages of these children, it seems that none of them are infants (i.e. 0–3 years of age) (Scott 1999: 2–4). Therefore it is possible that the children at Campo Consolino received formal burial when reaching an age threshold at which they were perceived as members of the community. Membership status for these children would have been emphasised by burial with artefacts strongly associated with adults.

Communal drinking: crossing gender boundaries?

Alongside the trends discussed above, an interesting case is the distribution of drinking vessels among men and women. At Campo Consolino there is an overall emphasis on drinking vessels, which are mainly represented by cups, beakers, jugs, wine jugs and skyphoi. These vessels are present in almost half (47%) of the burials at the site. Moreover, 36% of the drinking vessels are wine jugs.

Whilst it was noted that wine jugs correlate statistically with men, Table 3 shows that wine jugs also occur with 20% of women, compared to 30% of men. Furthermore, those wine jugs which were made of fine *bucchero* ware, imported from the neighbouring region of Campania, are distributed equally among men and women. Lastly, the Yule's Q coefficients suggest that drinking vessels taken together correlate more strongly with individuals aged over 45 years old than with men. This suggests that, even though most of the men and women may have been classified into 'masculine' and 'feminine' genders at Campo Consolino, they may have shared important spheres of social practice in life, namely social or communal drinking activities, as indicated by the distribution of drinking vessels at the cemetery. In particular, this shared participation may have been more prominent among older individuals of both sexes.

The analysis of drinking equipment as related to commensality and communal drinking has received little attention in studies of the archaeology of Samnium. This is because drinking vessels have usually been viewed as evidence for libations performed as part of the funerary ritual. However, archaeologists working on Iron Age cemeteries of Europe have approached the emphasis on drinking vessels from an anthropological perspective, with the vessels viewed as vehicles for social interaction centred on drinking, which also occurs in funerary contexts (Dietler 1990; 2003). It is useful to view the emphasis on drinking vessels at Campo Consolino in light of these studies, particularly with regard to the probable gender differentiation discussed above.

Drawing on anthropological case studies, archaeologists suggest that drinking practices may serve to strengthen social bonds among community members in pre-industrial societies, usually as a key element in the establishment of reciprocal obligations between host and guest (Dietler 1990). The dispensing of drink can favour social cohesion by promoting solidarity among people who alternate as hosts and guests. However, this mechanism can also create and reinforce social inequality whenever the guests are incapable of reciprocating by hosting drinking events of their own. Thus communal drinking may empower certain individuals and groups at the expense of others (Mauss 1967; Pitts 2005).

The conclusions reached in these case studies can help to formulate new interpretative possibilities for Campo Consolino. If the wine jugs and other drinking vessels at the funerary site are indicative of communal drinking, it remains unclear what may have been the specific social functions of this practice in the community. It is also unclear what form of drink was consumed (although the predominance of wine jugs does suggest that wine was an important component), whether it was acquired through exchange, locally produced or whether it was consumed exclusively at funerals or also in other contexts. The importance of wine might also be reinforced by the equally widespread presence of amphorae in the graves. Anthropological and archaeological case studies demonstrate that, when wine is available exclusively through trade, it is normally employed to symbolically differentiate elite drinking patterns. For example, in Hallstatt Europe Mediterranean wine would have been a 'luxury' item, given its restricted access and complex acquisition (Dietler 1990). Alternatively, it is also possible that the drinking vessels at Campo Consolino, including the wine jugs, were used for the consumption of other types of beverage which may have been locally produced. In that case, the production of the drink may involve an intense mobilization of resources such as a labour force for land cultivation and the production of agricultural implements.

These interpretative possibilities can help to guide future studies on Campo Consolino and other funerary sites in Samnium. The current evidence does suggest an emphasis on drinking equipment, which may be indicative of drinking practices. Such practices may have had an important function in the social, political and economic life of the community that buried its dead at Campo Consolino, possibly acting as a catalyst in the negotiation of power relations. More specific hypotheses on the role of communal drinking at Campo Consolino depend on further excavation of mortuary and non-mortuary sites in the vicinity, to place the practice into a wider context. For the present it is significant that, at Campo Consolino, the evidence suggests that participation in power-related and communal events was not restricted to men. This has an impact on the current idea of contrasting social practices of men and women in communities of Samnium. Further, the emphasis on drinking may indicate that power relations were negotiated not through warfare or the monopoly of violence, but rather through a possibly competitive dispensation of commensality in the form of drinking events.

Conclusion

By examining the correlation between biological sex and grave goods, it has been possible to reconsider aspects of gendered social relations in a community of pre-Roman Samnium. The analysis above demonstrates the possibility that communities in ancient Samnium acknowledged different forms of gender relations than those traditionally credited to them. It is clear that the men at Campo Consolino are not associated primarily with weapons or the sphere of warfare, but instead with activities related to commensality, at the least at household level, which also appear to have been associated with women. This result should be taken into account in future analyses, as a deterrent to a reliance on preconceived gender systems not supported by the evidence.

There is currently no neighbouring and contemporaneous settlement evidence that might be compared with Campo Consolino regarding the emphasis on communal drinking. Nevertheless, on a broader level, contemporaneous settlements in the neighbouring region of Lucania seem to confirm the hypothesis suggested here for Campo Consolino. The Lucanian settlements at Pomarico Vecchio and Civita di Tricarico suggest the practice of public dining, in what have been interpreted as 'public dining rooms', which involved large amounts of fine ware vessels (Isayev 2007: 136). On the other hand, the overlaps between what appear to be 'masculine' and 'feminine' personal ornaments at Campo Consolino support the complexity of gender differentiation as noted by anthropologists.

On the whole, the present suggestions remain to be verified with non-funerary evidence. Although the existing correlations of personal ornaments with women may indicate some form of 'gendered' social distinction in burial, there is no conclusive evidence that these distinctions were regularly observed outside of the funerary context. Future excavation of settlement sites will help to verify whether the distinctions observed in mortuary practice also applied to everyday domestic life.

Department of Classics and Ancient History, University of Exeter

Acknowledgements

This paper is based on a chapter of my PhD thesis. I thank my supervisors, Dr. Elena Isayev and Dr. Martin Pitts, as well as Dr. Marlene Suano (University of Sao Paulo, Brazil) and Dott.ssa Angela Di Niro (Molise, Italy) for their suggestions on the draft. My thanks also go to the two anonymous referees, the TRAC Editorial Committee and all of those who contributed with questions and comments upon the presentation of the paper at TRAC 09, particularly Dr. Louise Revell who chaired the session.

Bibliography

Ancient sources

Diodorus of Sicily (Translated by R.M, Geer, 1947). *Library of History, vol. IX*. London: Heinemann.
Frontinus (Translated by C.E. Bennet, 1925). *Stratagems; Aqueducts of Rome*. London: Heinemann.
Livy (Translated by B.O. Foster, 1919–1929). *Ab Urbe Condita: Books 1–10*. London: Heinemann.
Pliny the Elder (Translated by H. Rackham, 1942). *Natural History, vol. II*. London: Heinemann.
Silius Italicus (Translated by J. Duff, 1934). *Punica, vol.II*. London: Heinemann.
Strabo (Translated by H.L. Jones, 1923). *Geography, vol. II*. London: Heinemann.

Modern sources

Arnold, B. 2002. Sein und werden: Gender as process in mortuary ritual. In S.M. Nelson and M. Rosen-Ayalon (eds.) *In Pursuit of Gender: Worldwide Archaeological Approaches*. Walnut Creek: Rowman Altamira: 239–257.

Bispham, E. 2007. The Samnites. In G. Bradley, E. Isayev and C. Riva (eds.) *Ancient Italy: Regions Without Boundaries*. Exeter: University of Exeter Press: 179–223.

Brothwell, D.R. 1981. *Digging up Bones*. Ithaca: Cornell University Press.

Butler, J. 1990. Gender trouble. In A.J. Cahill and J. Hansen (eds.) *Continental Feminism Reader*. Lanham: Rowman & Littlefield: 29–55.

Capini, S. 1980. La Necropoli di Pozzilli. In *Sannio. Pentri e Frentani dal VI al I sec. a.C.* Roma: De Luca: 112–128.

Capini, S. 1991. L'alta Valle del Volturno: la necropoli di Pozzilli. In S. Capini and A. Di Niro (eds.) *Samnium. Archeologia del Molise*. Roma: Quasar: 57–59.

Carmen Vida, M. 1998. The Italian scene: Approaches to the study of gender. In R.Whitehouse (ed.) *Gender and Italian Archaeology: Challenging the Stereotypes*. London: Accordia Research Institute: 15–22.

Claassen, C. 1992. Questioning gender: An introduction. In C. Claassen (ed.) *Exploring Gender through Archaeology*. Madison: Prehistory Press: 1–10.

Clarke, D.L. 1968. *Analytical Archaeology*. London: Methuen.

Cool, H.E.M. 2004. *The Roman Cemetery at Brougham, Cumbria*. Britannia Monograph Series No. 21. London: Society for the Promotion of Roman Studies.

Dench, E. 1995. *From Barbarians to New Men: Greek, Roman and Modern Perceptions of the Central Appenines*. Oxford: Clarendon.

Dietler, M. 1990. Driven by drink: The role of drinking in the political economy and the case of early Iron Age France. *Journal of Anthropological Archaeology* 9: 352–406.

Dietler, M. 2003. Clearing the table: Some concluding reflections on commensal politics and imperial states. In T. L. Bray (ed.) *The Archaeology and Politics of Food and Feasting in Early States and Empires*. New York, London: Kluwer Academic/Plenum: 271–284.

Di Niro, A. 1980. La necropoli di Termoli. In *Sannio. Pentri e Frentani dal VI al I sec. a.C.* Roma: De Luca: 53–71.

Di Niro, A. 1991. Le necropoli dell'area interna, Le necropoli della zona costiera. In S. Capini and A. Di Niro (eds.) *Samnium. Archeologia del Molise*. Roma: Quasar: 61–71.

Ferembach, D., Schwidetzky, I. and Stloukal, M. 1977–79. Raccomandazioni per la determinazione dell'eta e del sesso sullo scheletro. *Rivista di Antropologia* 60: 5–51.

Gilchrist, R. 1999. *Gender and Archaeology: Contesting the Past*. London: Routledge.

Hodder, I. 1997. Commentary: the gender screen. In J. Moore and E. Scott (eds.) *Invisible People and Processes: Writing Gender and Childhood into European Archaeology*. London: Leicester University Press: 75–78.

Isayev, E. 2007. *Inside Ancient Lucania: Dialogues in History and Archaeology*. BICS Supplement 90. London: Institute of Classical Studies.

Izzet, V. 2007. Etruria and the Etruscans: Recent approaches. In G. Bradley, E. Isayev and C. Riva (eds.) *Ancient Italy: Regions Without Boundaries*. Exeter: Exeter University Press: 114–131.

Lucy, S. 1997. Housewives, warriors and slaves? Sex and gender in Anglo Saxon burial. In J. Moore and E. Scott (eds.) *Invisible People and Processes: Writing Gender and Childhood into European Archaeology*. London: Leicester University Press: 150–68.

Mauss, M. 1967. *The Gift: Forms and Functions of Exchange in Archaic Societies*. New York: Norton.

Morris, I. 1992. *Death Ritual and Social Structure in Classical Antiquity*. Cambridge: Cambridge University Press.

Nanda, S. 2000. *Gender Diversity: Cross-Cultural Variations*. Prospect Heights: Waveland Press.

Parise Badoni, F. and Ruggieri Giove, G. 1980. Alfedena: la necropoli di Campo Consolino. In *Sannio. Pentri e Frentani dal VI al I sec. a.C.*. Roma: De Luca: 84–106.

Parise Badoni, F. and Ruggieri Giove, G. 1981. *Alfedena: la Necropoli di Campo Consolino*. Chieti: Ministerio per i Beni Culturali e Ambientali, Soprintendenza dell'Abruzzo.

Parise Badoni, F., Ruggieri Giove, M., Brambilla, C. and Gherardini, P. 1982. Necropoli di Alfedena (scavi 1974–1979): Proposta di una cronologia relativa. *Annali dell'Istituto Orientale di Napoli Sezione Archeologia e Storia Antica* 4.

Pitts, M. 2005. Pots and pits: drinking and deposition in late Iron Age south Britain. *Oxford Journal of Archaeology* 24(2): 143–161.

Riva, C. 2004. Keeping up with the Etruscans? Picene elites in central Italy during the orientalising period. In E. Herring, R.D. Whitehouse and J.B. Wilkins (eds.) *Accordia Research Papers vol. 9*. London: Accordia Research Institute: 69–91.

Salmon, E.T. 1967. *Samnium and the Samnites*. Cambridge: Cambridge University Press.

Saulnier, C. 1983. *L'Armée et la Guerre Chez les Peuples Samnites (VII-IV s.)*. Paris: Diffusion de Boccard.

Scopacasa, R. 2007. *Essere Sannita: Rappresentazioni d'un Popolo Italico nelle Fonti Letterarie e Storiografiche Antiche*. Campobasso: Istituto Regionale per gli Studi Storici del Molise (Iresmo).

Scott, E. 1999. *The Archaeology of Infancy and Infant Death*. British Archaeological Reports, International Series 819. Oxford: Archaeopress.

Shennan, S. 1997: *Quantifying Archaeology*. Edinburgh: Edinburgh University Press.

Sofaer Derevenski, J. 2000. *Children and Material Culture*. London: Routledge.

Sorensen, M.L.S. 2000. *Gender Archaeology*. Cambridge: Polity Press.

Stine, L. 1992. Social differentiation on the farmstead. In S. Claassen (ed.) *Exploring Gender Through Archaeology*. Madison: Prehistory Press: 103–111.

Suano, M., 1991. Alcune Osservazioni sui Cinturoni di Bronzo di Tipo Sannitico. In S. Capini, A. Di Niro (eds.) *Samnium. Archeologia del Molise*. Roma: Quasar: 135–9.

Suano, M. 2000. Il Cinturone Sabellico-Sannita come abbigliamento sociale. In *Studi sull'Italia dei Sanniti*. Roma: Electa: 183–191.

Tagliamonte, G. 1996. *I Sanniti. Caudini, Irpini, Pentri, Carricini, Frentani*. Milano: Longanesi and Company.

Toms, J. 1998. The construction of gender in early Iron Age Etruria. In R. Whitehouse (ed.) *Gender and Italian Archaeology: Challenging the Stereotypes*. London: Accordia Research Institute: 157–177.

Weglian, E. 2001. Grave goods do not a gender make: A case study from Singen am Hohentwiel, Germany. In B. Arnold and N.L. Wicker (eds.) *Gender and the Archaeology of Death*. Walnut Creek: Rowman Altamira: 137–155.

Weiss, K.M. 1972. On the systematic bias in skeletal sexing. *American Journal of Physical Anthropology* 37: 239–250.

Whitehouse, R. 1998. Introduction. In R. Whitehouse (ed.) *Gender and Italian Archaeology: Challenging the Stereotypes*. London: Accordia Research Institute: 1–8.

Collapse, Change or Continuity? Exploring the three Cs in sub-Roman Baldock

Keith J. Fitzpatrick-Matthews

Introduction

The 'small towns' of Roman Britain are the under-theorised 'Cinderellas' of the province's archaeology yet, at the same time, they should be regarded as the great success story of Roman rule. They were the dominant class of urban settlement, with a huge variety of forms, presumably reflecting different social, economic and political roles. Yet studies of the fifth-century collapse of urban civilisation in Britain focus almost exclusively on the major cities and ignore the 'small towns'. However, because of their diversity, they have the potential to offer unique insights into the processes that operated from the early fifth century on, to transform Roman Britain into the early medieval successor states.

The archaeology of one place, the 'small town' of Baldock in Hertfordshire (Fig. 1) is unusual in that it has produced unequivocal evidence for sub-Roman activity, extending well into the sixth century, before the site was finally abandoned. Because there are so few sites with which it can be compared, it is impossible to know how typical of the 'small town' experience it may have been. If it was atypical, why did it survive the end of imperial control when other places apparently did not? If it was typical, why has the archaeological evidence not been found or recognised for what it is in other places? Is there a general failure of archaeology to deal with data of this type?

This paper will explore these issues by examining the evidence from Baldock, placing it in its local and wider setting. It concludes by proposing models for the way in which 'small towns' experienced the fifth century transformation of Roman Britain and by suggesting avenues for further archaeological research.

Baldock

Baldock developed from a Late Iron Age *oppidum* that had its origins in the early first century B.C., if not earlier (Burleigh 1995a: 112; 1995b: 179; Burleigh & Fitzpatrick-Matthews 2010: 21). After a period of steady growth during the first century A.D., it seems to have reached its largest extent in the second century. After the middle of the second century, though, its story has been seen as one of slow, inexorable decline as the inhabited area shrank and ever fewer new features were created. Ian Stead concluded that, by A.D. 400, a civilisation had ended and that Baldock had ceased to exist, with red deer wandering throughout the abandoned town and occasionally tumbling into wells (Stead & Rigby 1986: 87).

However, Stead's work raised a number of paradoxes that do not fit well with this model and that have not been resolved by later work. The most impressive buildings, with stone foundations and *opus signinum* floors, all date from the fourth century or even later; moreover, there are new buildings that cannot be earlier than A.D. 400. At least one of the late Roman cemeteries has produced hand made sub-Roman pottery. On two sites, there is evidence for the resurfacing of roads during the fifth century. On one of these sites, Jonathan Drake's unpublished analysis identified a minimum of four phases later than A.D. 400.

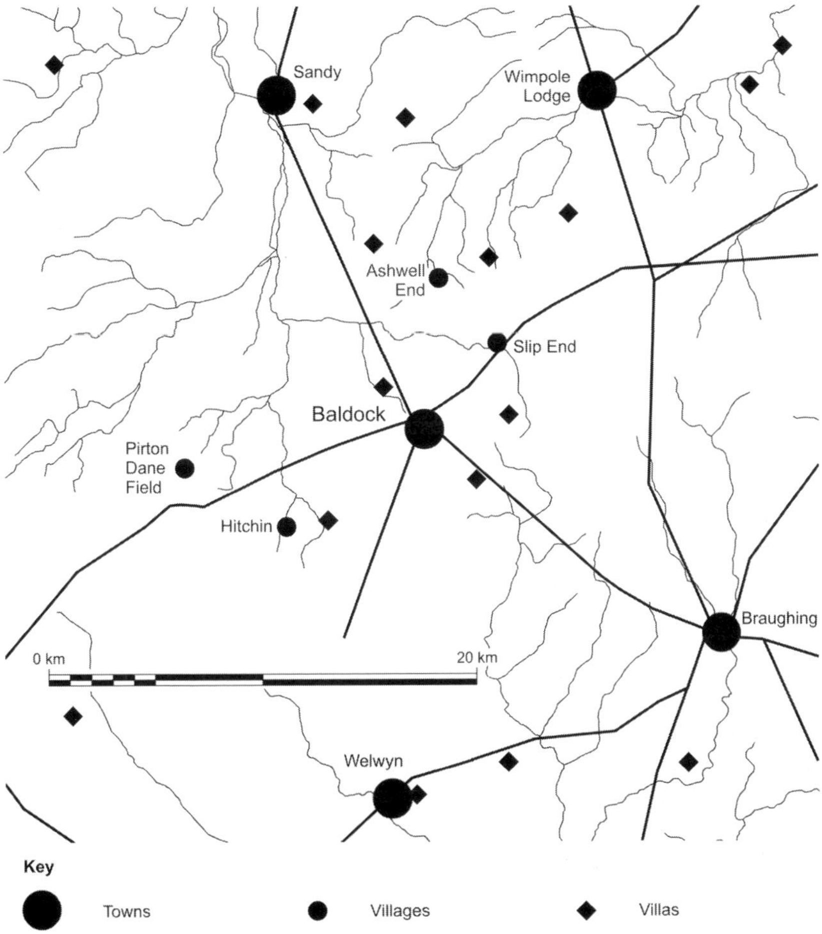

Figure 1: The Baldock area in the fourth century A.D.

These isolated bits of data suggest that Stead's model of fourth-century decline is wrong and that something more complex happened during the fading away of Roman Britain (Burleigh & Fitzpatrick-Matthews 2010: 27). To understand what may have been taking place, it is necessary to look in greater detail at some of the sites in question.

Historical background

It is clear that the town contracted during the fourth century. Areas on Upper Walls Common that had first been used for burial were colonised for domestic purposes by the early second century A.D. at the latest; some reverted to cemetery use by the end of the third century. However, this is a peripheral part of the town and, even here, there are new substantial fourth-century buildings (Stead & Rigby 1986: 86), as at Weaver's Way (BAL-18) (Goodwin 1983). On the northern edge of the town, a building with a corridor over 14 m long was built during the fourth century; it has been conjectured that this was the town's *mansio*, evidently a new facility (Richmond *et al.* 1992: 15).

The centre of the town is one of the least explored elements of the settlement and there have been almost no excavations there. However, there is an undeveloped area on its western edge, at Bakers Close, which has remained open since the Roman period, allowing aerial photography and geophysics to give an idea of what lies beneath it (Hillelson 1986; Burleigh 2008: 191). The area is dominated by a Romano-Celtic temple, set back from but apparently facing a main road. Nearby, there are large walled enclosures containing buildings and a winged corridor house, which, it has been argued, are associated with the temple complex (Burleigh & Stevenson 2000: 51). To the south, a number of substantial fourth-century buildings were found during development work in the 1960s.

The pattern of coin loss is striking. Although late fourth-century losses are generally high in Britain, the Valentinianic and Theodosian losses at Baldock are unusually so and can be compared with Cirencester (small sites), Water Newton and Cow Roast (Northchurch), as well as with the temple sites at Chelmsford and Thistleton Dyer (Duncan *et al.* 2009: 155). These last two suggest that there may be a religious aspect to this pattern, which perhaps relates to other aspects of the town's archaeology, not least the temple complex at Bakers Close.

The sites

In the infelicitously-named sub-Roman period, continuing activity can be demonstrated on stratigraphic and artefactual grounds on a few sites; on others there is none. All of the areas examined by Ian Stead between 1968 and 1972 were in parts of the town that were abandoned by A.D. 400 or shortly thereafter, leading him to propose that the settlement was abandoned by that time. However, it is possible that a re-examination of the data from these sites in light of what was discovered in the 1980s may show that there was activity.

At the excavation of a site towards the east-north-eastern periphery of the town between 1980 and 1985 (BAL-1, California), it was possible to demonstrate that some features could not be earlier than A.D. 400. Analysis of the pottery from these features revealed the presence of several pottery fabrics not found in earlier contexts. They fall into two main types: vegetable tempered wares and hand-made sandy wares. One of the fabrics (Fabric 53, a vegetable-tempered ware (Ashworth 1990: 6)) is identical to Fabric A1 from Bedford (Baker & Hassall 1979: 152), where it is dated to A.D. 600 or later. The hand-made sandy wares are found only in association with the vegetable-tempered wares or in stratigraphically very late contexts in the town.

This was also one of the few sites where a stratigraphic sequence had been preserved in a large doline, a periglacial solution hollow in the chalk bedrock. This had begun to silt up during the Middle Iron Age and was finally completely filled by the early medieval period. A lengthy sequence included closely dated activities such as human burial (in the Middle Iron Age, the late first century B.C. and the third century A.D.), metalling the entire bowl-shaped hollow (late first century A.D.), quarrying (late fourth and fifth centuries A.D.) and the construction of a timber-framed hall-type building (sixth century A.D.).

Cemeteries

Baldock is perhaps best known for the number and variety of its burials (Burleigh 1993: 41-9; Fitzpatrick-Matthews 2007: 150), ranging from an exceptionally early Welwyn-type grave to late Roman inhumation cemeteries. A number of these late cemeteries continued to be used throughout the fourth century (one was probably established only in the middle of the century) and several were clearly still in use well into the fifth century (and in one case, the sixth). Although the numbers of burials known to have been deposited in the fourth century was much lower than at any time since the Roman conquest, it is unclear whether this represents a real drop in population, a change in patterns of burial (it is possible, for instance, that some of those buried in the town's cemeteries during the second century were not urban residents but had been brought in from outside, although this is not likely), or the vagaries of archaeological discovery (none of the cemeteries that presumably existed on the western and north-western sides of the town has ever been located).

Three of the cemeteries with burials later than A.D. 400 lie on the east-north-eastern side of the town, at Icknield Way East (BAL-45), Royston Road (BAL-15) and California (BAL-1), with a fourth on its southern edge, at The Tene (BAL-30, BAL-31 and BAL-48) (Fig. 2). At California, the ceramic evidence shows that burials were made well into the sixth century, while it is unclear when the others fell into disuse, although there are circumstantial reasons for suspecting that, at Icknield Way East and Royston Road, burials were still being deposited in the second half of the fifth century.

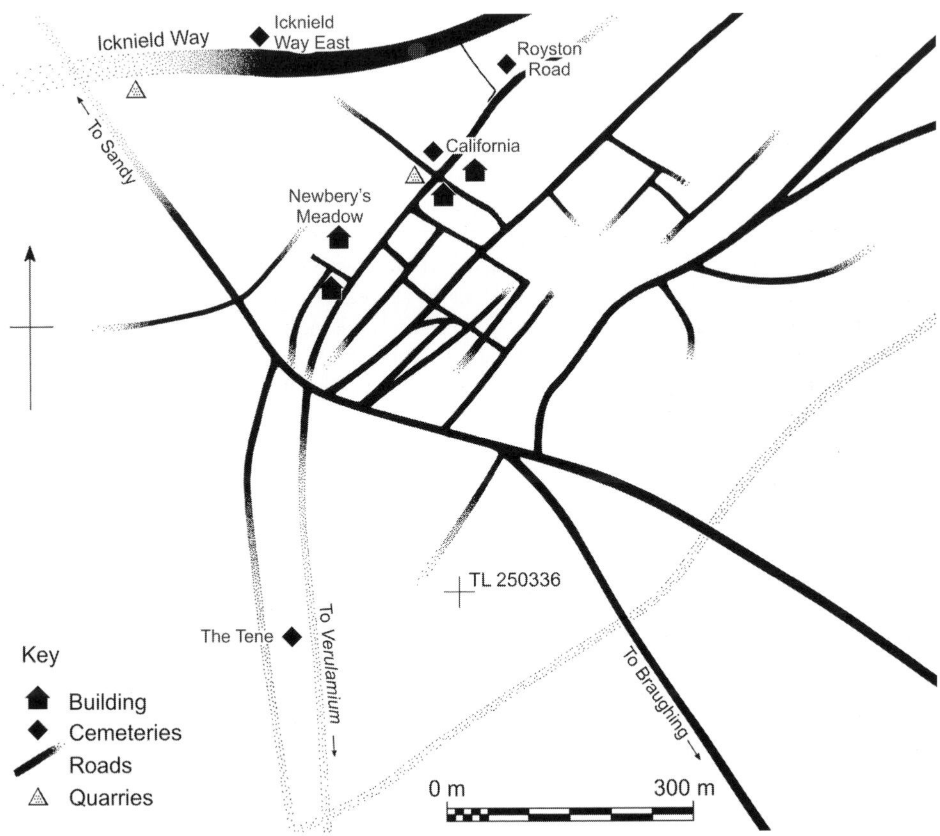

Figure 2: Sites in Baldock with sub-Roman evidence

Although these burial grounds continued to be used, they show a massive decline in the numbers of burials per year. In A.D. 400, the burial rate can be calculated as 1.3 per year, falling to 0.6 per year by A.D. 500 (Fitzpatrick-Matthews 2007; Fig. 4). If the numbers of burials are proportional to the population of the town – which is a problematical assumption – then this suggests that it dropped by more than a half during the fifth century. Although this is a catastrophic decline, it is nevertheless remarkable in that, apparently uniquely among Romano-British 'small towns', people were still living, dying and being buried in organised cemeteries a century after Roman rule had ended. One intriguing feature is that the number of male burials at California almost doubled during the late fifth century.

Figure 3: St Menas ampulla (Letchworth Museum Acc. No. 7421), actual size

One of the challenges of curating a museum collection that has grown over more than a century, partly through private donations, is to understand the provenance of items for which virtually no documentation exists. An excellent example of this is a flask from the shrine of St Menas at Abu Mena, 45 km south-west of Alexandria (Egypt), donated to Letchworth Museum on 15 September 1936 by a Mr Lee of 5a Royston Road, Baldock (Fig. 3). According to the accessions register (Number 7421), it is a '*small Roman pottery flask from Pompeii'*. However, by the time these flasks were being produced, after *c.* A.D. 500 (Griffiths & Bangert 2007: 59), Pompeii had lain under many metres of volcanic ash for more than four centuries. Moreover, southern Italy is outside the distribution of such objects, which are found along Anthea Harris's (2003: 64*ff.*) 'second Byzantine-Western trading axis', operating via northern Italy and the Rhine. It is possible that the provenance was attributed to the object by a museum curator puzzled by the exotic and unfamiliar nature of the flask. More interestingly, it was not the only object donated by Mr Lee: he also deposited a Belgic jar, deriving from a cremation burial found in his garden, on 4 April 1933 (Accession Number 6573) (Applebaum 1932: 257). Mr Lee's garden was located on the site of the Icknield Way East cemetery, which had developed over the site of an early first century A.D. burial enclosure. Mr Lee also found part of the enclosure ditch and late Roman inhumation burials. This St Menas flask may well have been found in one of the late burials on his property, in which case it could push use of the cemetery into the early sixth century, at least.

The cemetery at California (BAL-1) has the best stratigraphic and artefactual evidence for continuity after A.D. 400. Established around A.D. 200, it developed at one corner of a crossroads in a previously domestic enclosure. Altogether, 81 graves were identified, although they held 94 individuals as a number of graves had been re-used, with the bones of former occupants being carefully reinterred, sometimes packed around the outsides of the coffins (Frere *et al.* 1986: 401; Burleigh 1993: 46-8; Fitzpatrick-Matthews 2007: 157). There were also numerous intercutting graves, although this had not occurred through lack of space as there were always empty areas within the cemetery. The earliest burials appear to have been made towards the crossroads, moving towards the back of the plot as time went on. The intercutting and re-use of graves in these circumstances appears deliberate and it has been suggested that some were family groups or other close social groupings (Burleigh 1993: 48).

In a number of instances, the earliest grave in a sequence can be dated no earlier than the end of the fourth century and could be considerably later. Some graves contained sub-Roman pottery fabrics and it is possible that some of the few ceramic grave gifts are of fifth-century date rather than earlier. Although only seventeen graves contained gifts of complete or near-complete pots, most graves had 'residual' pottery in their backfills. The presence of types that post-date the start of use of the site for burial is difficult to explain in terms of residuality, as the sherds or the vessels from which they derive must have been introduced to the site in a cemetery context. This suggests that they may be better regarded as deliberate depositions or as the residue from activities taking place within the cemetery.

Although the boundary ditches of the former domestic enclosure that had occupied the site before it became a cemetery were allowed to silt up and were not recut (indeed, several burials were deposited in their soft fills), the roadside ditches were maintained and recut well into the fifth century. The road on the south-eastern side of the plot was resurfaced in the fifth century, its surface surviving beneath the later ploughsoil where the road ran through the north-western edge of the doline. It is therefore possible that the road on the south-western side, the metalling of which had not survived, was also resurfaced at the same time.

By contrast with the California cemetery, which was excavated completely, the cemetery at The Tene is very poorly known, as it is in a part of Baldock partly overlain by the medieval town. Most discoveries have been made during development in this area, and only a few small sites have seen formal excavation. Some of the discoveries made in the 1960s were inadequately published by Ian Stead (Stead & Rigby 1986: 78), but others await full publication (Burleigh 1980: 35–7; Fenton *et al.* 2003: 10*ff.*). Nevertheless, there is much that can be said about this cemetery.

It is the only cemetery so far discovered in the town to display the type of careful organisation evident in large urban cemeteries such as Poundbury, a type that seems to have become prevalent after A.D. 350 (Petts 1998: 115) and where the likelihood of Christian burial is high. All the burials are arranged in rows, with no sign of intercutting; the bodies are laid supine, with heads to the west, and no grave gifts have been recorded. The cemetery is extensive, with outliers known to the north-west of the core and some distance to the south, and, although its plan is not known in detail, it is evident that there were zones within it that were never used for burial. The possibility that these were areas where structures may have stood should not be dismissed, since they are always difficult to detect in Baldock.

Domestic sites

Although the burial evidence remains the best explored aspect of Roman and sub-Roman Baldock, there are a number of domestic sites that also demonstrate the continuity of occupation well into the fifth century and later. Most of these are concentrated around Upper Walls Common, where extensive excavations during the 1980s and 1990s took place in advance of development (Burleigh & Fitzpatrick-Matthews 2010: 14*ff.*). However, there are hints from other parts of the town that the settlement did not come to a sudden end in the early decades of the fifth century and that survival was not restricted to Upper Walls Common.

The large periglacial hollow, mentioned above as preserving a long stratigraphic sequence, has clearly domestic activity in its upper fills. As well as evidence for quarry pits, roadside ditches and enclosure ditches, a post-built structure has been recognised, cut into the uppermost of the sub-Roman deposits before the development of a ploughsoil above it (Burleigh 1982: 14; Selkirk & Selkirk 1983: 74). A complete plan of the structure was not recovered, although it is evident that it was at least 10 m long and 5 m wide, with an internal partition carried on a ground beam.

This is the only evidently domestic structure in the doline and its location at a crossroads, overlooking a contemporary cemetery, makes it tempting to suggest that this was all that remained of the settlement: a single farmstead and its associated burial ground. However, this is not the complete story on the site, as a sill-beam structure was built over the latest metalling of the road to the south of the doline. Although dated only by stratigraphic association, it is evident that this was also of sub-Roman date (Rankov *et al.* 1982: 369). It demonstrates that, at some point, the west-north-west to east-south-east road had gone out of use, at least to the east of the crossroads. Given the sequence of sub-Roman roadside ditches on the north side of this road, it suggests that its disuse came towards the end of the period rather than earlier on.

Even more intriguing is a ditched enclosure on the south-western side of the crossroads. Only its north-eastern corner lay within the excavation area, but it had been cut through a backfilled quarry of early fifth-century (or later) date. Four massive postholes were found at the entrance, suggesting that there was a potentially defensive gateway. In front of the entrance, and running at an angle of about 40° to the front of the gate, was a line of three further pits or postholes, suggestive of an outwork, allowing the enclosure to be approached only from the south-east. There was no evidence for internal structures or other activity, which probably lay outside the area available for excavation. Unfortunately, when the site immediately to the west was developed in 2001, no archaeological condition was imposed and it is unknown how far in this direction the enclosure extended. The main road running north-north-east to south-south-west was diverted to the east not only by the construction of the enclosure but also by the earlier quarry.

A short distance to the south-west, Shimon Applebaum excavated a substantial house in Newbery's Meadow, now the Grosvenor Road estate, the foundations of which incorporated a coin of Theodosius I (Applebaum 1932: 250). Although not definitely of fifth-century date, Applebaum considered this likely. No other sites in the town have produced definite evidence for such late structures, but it is unclear if sub-Roman activity was confined to this north-eastern part of the settlement or if stratigraphy of this date has not been recognised. Given the probable continuity of use of the cemetery at The Tene into the fifth century, it is possible that there was also domestic activity at the southern end of the town.

Roads

An important element in the sub-Roman sequences in the town is evidence for the continued maintenance of at least elements of the road system. Again, the evidence is restricted to those parts of the town where large-scale excavation has taken place since the first recognition of fifth-century activity by Gil Burleigh in the early 1980s (Fig. 4). Ditches were recut on a number of sites, including on the south side of the road that formed the southern boundary of the cemetery at Royston Road, on both sides of the same road by the cemetery at California and at Hartsfield School. There was also evidence for the resurfacing of the road by the Royston Road cemetery, where it sealed a silted ditch recut containing a slightly worn coin of Arcadius, and by the California cemetery. At a later date, this road was partially blocked by a pair of offset cuts, which would have permitted access by pedestrians but not by wheeled vehicles or large groups of people moving *en masse* (Frere *et al.* 1989: 298).

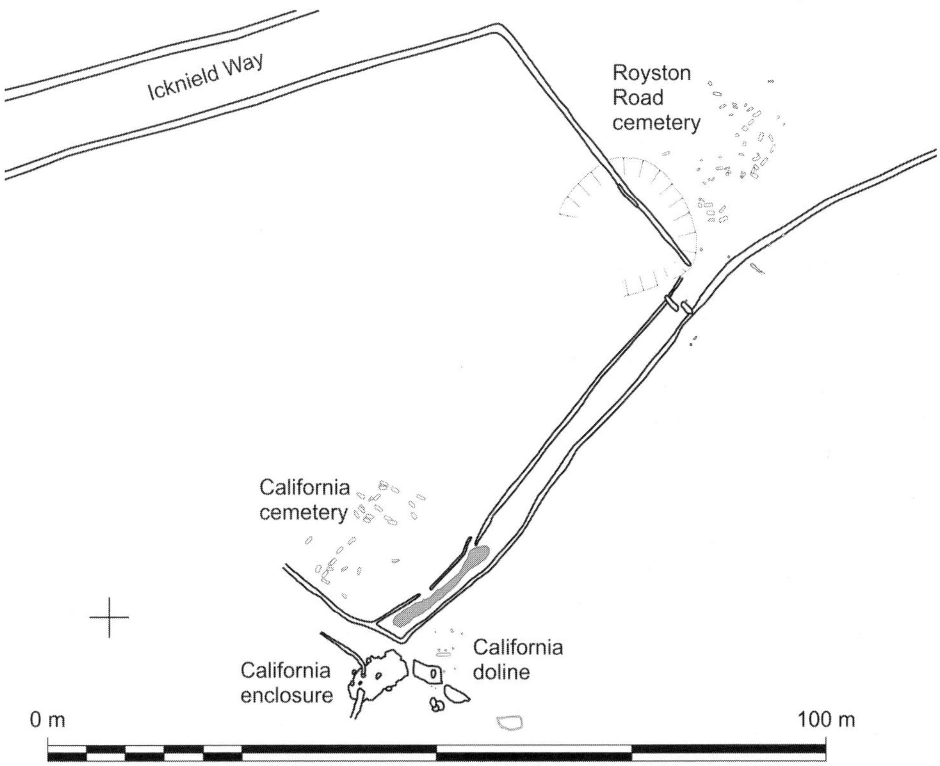

Figure 4: Sub-Roman activity at Clothall Common

To the south, the same road had to be diverted eastwards by the construction of a large quarry pit in the late fourth century (or later) and by a series of similar pits cut into the developing hollow way fills on the slope downhill by Hartsfield School. At some point, the northern ditch of the road running at right angles to this, that formed the crossroads at California, was recut, blocking off the other road.

The urban hinterland

In the *territorium* of Baldock – the edges of which may be defined by a number of important religious sites (Burleigh 2008: 192) – the archaeology of the fifth and sixth centuries is difficult to recognise. Although there are later fifth-century 'pagan Saxon' remains in south Bedfordshire and south-west Cambridgeshire (e.g. a late sixth-century inhumation cemetery near Ashwell Station), there are few in the immediate vicinity of Baldock (Fig. 5). Two probable cemeteries were discovered during the construction of Letchworth Garden City in the early twentieth century (Fitzpatrick-Matthews & Fitzpatrick-Matthews 2009, 26), at least one of which was mixed rite, while another was discovered at Dane Field, Pirton, in the 1790s and further explored in 1834 (Went & Burleigh 1990a: 1). There are some metalwork items, including a fifth-century penannular brooch from Arlesey, and a little pottery, including a late sixth-century jar from Ashwell Springs (Went & Colley (1990: 16), where it is wrongly dated to the early seventh century), but this material lacks proper context. Of course, Germanic material style cannot be equated in any simplistic manner with Germanic settlement, and the complexity of the relationship between the two is made all the more difficult by the nature of this material from the Baldock region.

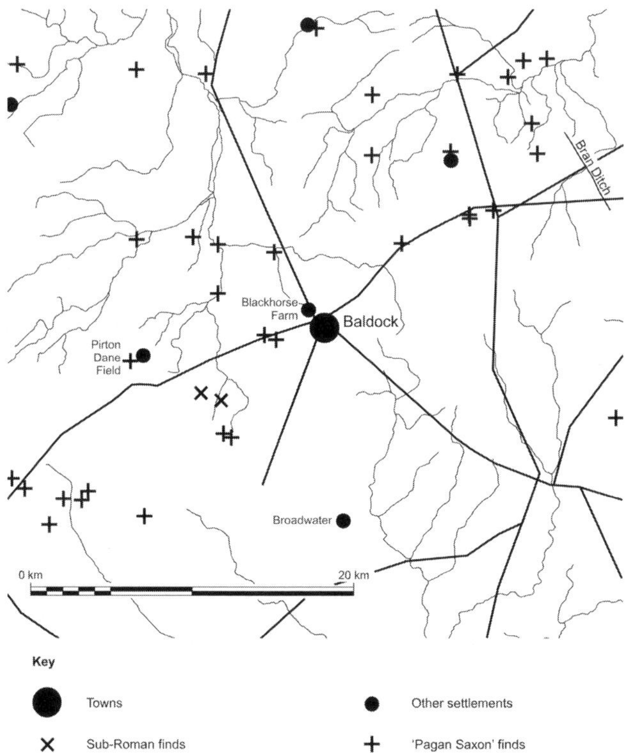

Figure 5: Fifth- to seventh-century sites and finds in the Baldock region

However, there are two sites where small-scale investigation has yielded a few scraps of evidence. The first, at Blackhorse Farm just a kilometre north of Baldock, was evaluated by trial trenching in 1994 as part of proposals for two routes of a new bypass. The site was designated as a Scheduled Ancient Monument in 1975 and trenching was limited to an area south of the main focus of the cropmarks from which the site is best known. In one trench, a *grubenhaus* was identified, 2.4 m wide and 0.13 m deep, with only 1.5 m of its length exposed inside the trench. It had rounded corners and a flat base, with a posthole in the centre of the eastern (short) side and another in the north-eastern corner (Fenton 1994: 15). A posthole a short distance away produced a sherd of early medieval pottery of fifth- or sixth-century date, the only such material from the site. The presence of apparently Germanic settlers a very short distance from what was evidently a still viable sub-Roman settlement raises interesting questions about interaction that cannot be answered with the limited data we currently possess (Phillips & Duncan 2009: 160).

The second site lies some eleven kilometres to the west of Baldock, at Pirton. This is close to the Anglo-Saxon cemetery in Dane Field mentioned previously. In January 1990, preliminary archaeological fieldwork along the proposed route of an oil pipeline from Buncefield to Humberside was followed by larger scale work in May. Although no evidence for the cemetery was found, an extensive and previously unknown Romano-British settlement was located. It was established in the later first century B.C. towards the northern end of Dane Field and expanded through the first and second centuries A.D., reaching its greatest extent during the third century. However, occupation on the site continued into the fifth century, with the formation of an occupation surface and the digging of a pit containing sub-Roman pottery (Went & Burleigh 1990b: 8). Fragments of an unusual sixth- or seventh-century jar, found unstratified on the site, suggest occupation contemporary with the supposed cemetery elsewhere on the field; although the style is reminiscent of Early Saxon pottery, the fabric is one of the sub-Roman sandy wares discussed above (Fig. 6).

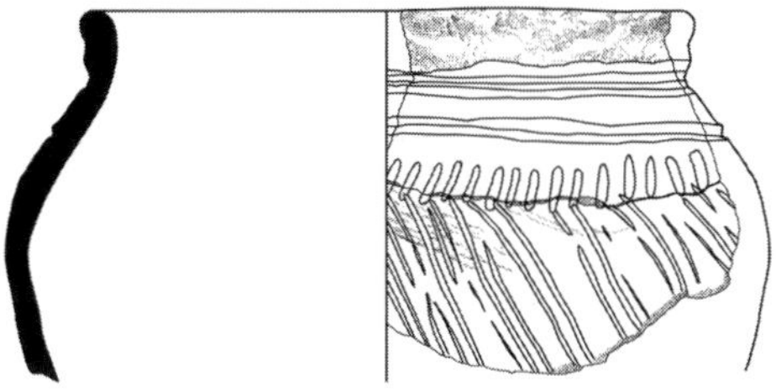

Figure 6: Hybrid sub-Roman/'Pagan Saxon' jar from Dane Field, Pirton (1:4)

As with the settlement at Blackhorse Farm, there are interesting questions of cultural interaction, which in this instance suggest several possible scenarios. Firstly, the sub-Roman settlement may have been abandoned before the development of the nearby cemetery. However, this does not account for the jar of uncertain ceramic tradition. Secondly, a community of Britons may have been taken over, even wiped out, by a group of invading Saxons. Again, this does not explain this discrepancy between the form and fabric of the jar. The third possibility is that the community of Britons slowly became Germanicised through the sixth century, either by intermarriage with settlers or by acculturation. This is the only scenario that accounts for all the archaeological evidence.

Hitchin

A more important early medieval site developed eight kilometres to the south-west of Baldock, becoming the sub-regionally important urban centre at Hitchin. Although nineteenth-century historians sought evidence that it had been a Roman town, archaeology suggests that it was an area of farmsteads and perhaps part of a large villa estate, based at the Ninesprings (or Purwell) Villa just outside the parish boundary (Seebohm 1883: 431). Its name derives from that of a people called *Hicce* in Tribal Hidage, a probably seventh-century list of kingdoms and their subdivisions drawn up as a tax assessment. The name has no plausible Old English etymology and probably derives from Brittonic **siccā*, 'dry', referring to the feeble River Hiz that runs through the town (Fitzpatrick-Matthews & Fitzpatrick-Matthews 2008: 15). By the later tenth century, the settlement had been laid out along a planned grid and was surrounded by a massive bank and ditch. Intriguing discoveries in recent years have enabled a model to be constructed of its development from the late Roman period to the foundation of a *burh* in the early tenth century. Most significant of these have been burials excavated at Queen Street, on the eastern periphery of the medieval town. Reports of burials in this area have been made over many years and have generally been regarded a 'plague victims' (the Great Plague of 1665 is known to have devastated the population of this part of the town), but separate projects uncovered a series of unaccompanied inhumation burials laid with their heads to the west. Originally thought to be pagan Saxon, radiocarbon dates indicate that they are of late to sub-Roman date (Davis 2005: 62), suggesting that the burials are of Christian Britons. This would go some way to explaining why the name of the town is of Brittonic rather than Old English origin and could also be of relevance to the apparently early origins of the church. Attested as a minster church by *c*. 1000 (Whitelock *et al*. 1968: 31), its origins are clearly much earlier and it has been argued that it was the site of *Clofesho*, the location of a series of important synods between the seventh and ninth centuries (Offer 2002: 75).

The regional context

The *Hicce* of Hitchin occupy part of a well-known gap in the distribution of pagan Anglo-Saxon burials. To the north, the *Gifle*, whose name is also Brittonic (from **gablā*, 'forked') and is preserved in the River Ivel, and to the south-west, the *Cilternsœte*, also with a partly Brittonic name (**celternoi*, 'high ones'), are neighbouring peoples named in the Tribal Hidage whose territories also lack such burials. It has long been hypothesised that *Verulamium* was the capital of the sub-Roman state (Wheeler & Wheeler 1936: 34) and its fifth-century archaeology has been known since the 1960s, even if it remains controversial (Niblett & Thompson 2005: 164; Faulkner 2000: 175). Here, the archaeological data is backed up by the documentary evidence of the *Vita Sancti Germani* by Constantius of Lyons, written *c*. 480×90 (Koch 2006: 805). At Baldock, there are no such links, but it may be suggested that the *Hicce* were the people of the *territorium* of Baldock and the *Gifle* of the *territorium* of Sandy and the *Cilternsœte* of *Verulamium* (Fig. 7).

So far, none of the other 'small towns' in the vicinity – Sandy, Braughing and Welwyn – has produced definite evidence for sub-Roman activity, although it has been argued for Sandy and Braughing (Baker 2006: 34; 89). However, Braughing became an important royal estate on the western edge of the kingdom of the East Saxons (Short 1987: 14); like Hitchin, the name of the settlement derives from the name of the people, the *Breahhingas*, whose name is Old English ('Breahha's people'). At both Braughing and Welwyn, there are important early churches (Williamson 2000: 168), which may suggest some continuity of elite function, while the presence of fifth-century Saxon burials at Sandy suggests disruption (Edgeworth & Steadman 2003: 26).

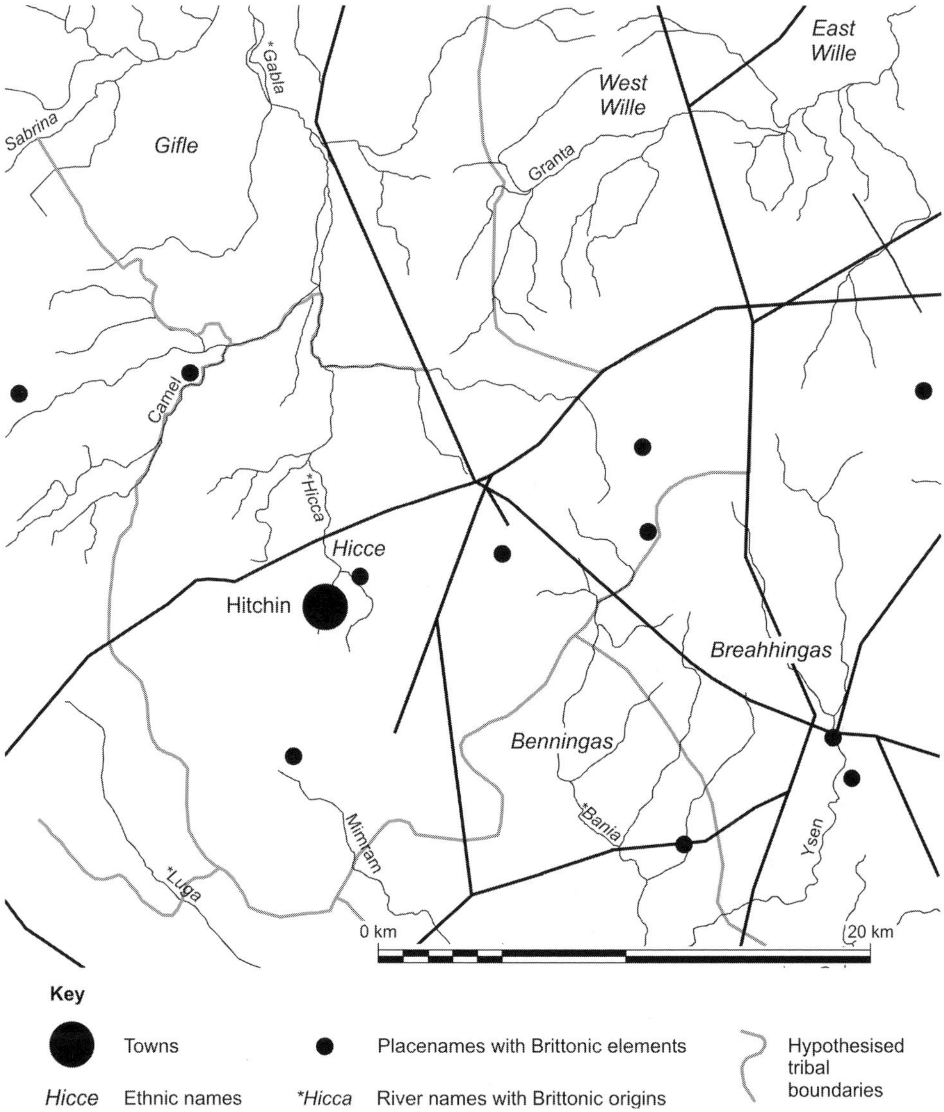

Figure 7: Peoples of the Tribal Hidage in the Baldock region

Modelling the transformation

As already pointed out, there is no such thing as the 'typical small town', as the term encompasses a wide variety of forms and functions. Nevertheless, few have produced any evidence for sub-Roman activity, which may suggest that they were generally unable to survive the economic storms of the early fifth century and were simply abandoned once their *raisons d'être* had ceased to exist. If this be the case, then Baldock is atypical and it is important to understand why it should have survived when most other towns did not.

Is there perhaps a clue in the specialised nature of some 'small towns'? Burnham & Wacher (1990: 5) recognised three classes of specialised 'small towns': industrial, religious and administrative. Baldock appears to have been a religious centre, a type which seems to have been relatively uncommon. It may be suggested that ancient cult centres such as Baldock and Bath (Pearce 2004: 126) formed a focal point for devout pagans at a time of increasing Christianisation. After pagan practices were outlawed by Theodosius I in a series of laws enacted after 391 (although their importance may have been exaggerated (Smith 2008: 186), various types of religious observance were effectively proscribed and pagans were increasingly subject to persecution by Christians. It is possible that the inhabitants of places where pagan cults had long been important resisted moves to outlaw their religions, and they may have driven out the politically dominant Christians who threatened their cherished beliefs.

A transformation of this nature may explain the sudden appearance of a sizeable community of evident Christians in Hitchin at the end of the Roman period: finding life in stubbornly pagan Baldock impossible to tolerate, they perhaps found a sympathetic landowner who gave them space to build a church and establish a burial ground. There are hints in the re-use of Roman brick and tile in St Mary's Church, as well as from finds from nearby, that it lies close to the site of a Roman building (Fitzpatrick-Matthews & Fitzpatrick-Matthews 2008: 13). As pagan belief declined over the next century or more, so Baldock was abandoned and forgotten while the Christian community at Hitchin flourished, especially after the conversion of Mercia in the middle of the seventh century. Conversely, a model involving the continuation of Christian worship in contrast to pagan worship has been used to explain the sub-Roman activities at Wroxeter, Chester and Lincoln (White & Barker 2002: 131; Matthews 2003: 24–5; Jones 1993: 25).

It is unlikely that sub-Roman continuity at either Baldock or *Verulamium* was a consequence of the lack of early Germanic settlement; rather, it is more likely that settlement was controlled by the presence of organised administrative machinery in those places. Indeed, the *grubenhaus* at Blackhorse Farm shows that such settlement did take place. Even in areas where Germanic settlement was early and intense, such as Lindsey, there is nevertheless evidence for the continuation of sub-Roman Christianity, which may indicate the controlled nature of that settlement, at least in its early phases.

It is notable that there is no early medieval (Anglo-Saxon) material from the site of Baldock whatsoever. The site appears to have lain deserted and forgotten from 600 until its re-founding five and a half centuries later, during the 1140s. The Knights Templar appear to have selected the site as it lay at the intersection of a number of important routes and had a prosperous rural hinterland. In creating their new town, they provided competition for the nearby Domesday borough of Ashwell, which declined rapidly and whose status was no more than a village by the later Middle Ages.

An agenda for future research

The archaeology of Baldock demonstrates that sub-Roman features – including structures and more surprising elements such as road metalling – can survive in 'small towns'; the identification of pottery fabrics associated with these features demonstrates that there was also an associated material culture, even if only in small quantities. The survival of this material at Baldock is all the more surprising, given the intensity of medieval ploughing, which has devastated so much of the stratigraphy of the Roman town. This suggests that it ought to be possible to recognise it in other places, if it is there to be recognised.

This can only be achieved through an active research agenda that targets certain aspects of the archaeological record by:

1. analysing the contents of the stratigraphically latest 'Romano-British' features to determine whether or not they are associated with distinctive types of material culture (pottery fabrics, metalwork and so on), which means the excavation of more than small samples from such features and more detailed analysis of the finds than often occurs;

2. targeting areas where there is no early Germanic archaeology but where 'small towns' are present (such as north Essex, northern Hampshire, Dorset and West Sussex) to assess British survival, both in the towns and in the surrounding countryside, by seeking out any distinctive material culture recognised through the work in (1) above;

3. targeting areas where there is early Germanic material and where 'small towns' are also present (such as the Upper Thames valley, Cambridgeshire, north-eastern Leicestershire and Norfolk) to refine the existing models of the interaction between native Britons and incoming Saxons.

In times of economic difficulty, the first step may seem an unnecessary luxury as commercial units pare their costs to a minimum, but without this close analysis, the two remaining questions cannot be attempted. For too long, the study of sub-Roman urban continuity has been dominated by sites of a class that was always a minority in the Roman world – the large administrative city, with defensive walls in the late Roman period – just as they have dominated our study of Roman urbanism. The 'small towns', by contrast, would have been the most familiar urban form to most citizens of the diocese, and their sub-Roman history (or lack of it) holds the most promise for helping to model the nature of the fundamental changes that occurred between A.D. 400 and 600.

North Hertfordshire District Council Museums

Acknowledgements

Much of the detail of sites in Baldock derives from unpublished fieldwork carried out under the direction of Gil Burleigh in the 1980s for North Hertfordshire District Council Museums. His assistance in understanding the sites is gratefully acknowledged, but all errors of interpretation are my own.

Bibliography

Applebaum, E.S. 1932. Excavations at Baldock in 1932. *Transactions of the St Albans Architectural and Archaeological Society* (1932): 244–58.

Ashworth, H. 1990. *North Herts Museums pottery fabric series: Iron Age, Roman and sub-Roman.* Unpublished internal document. Letchworth: North Hertfordshire District Council Museums (Reference Series 2). Available at http://www.north-herts.gov.uk/fabric_series_1990.pdf.

Baker, E. & Hassall, J. 1979. The pottery. *Bedfordshire Archaeological Journal* 13: 147–240.

Baker, J.T. 2006. *Cultural transition in the Chilterns and Essex region, 350 AD to 650 AD*. Studies in Regional and Local History 4. Hatfield: University of Hertfordshire Press.

Burleigh, G.R. 1980. Excavations in Baldock, 1978. *Hertfordshire's Past* (Autumn 1980) 9: 35–37.

Burleigh, G.R. 1982. Excavations at Baldock 1980-81: an interim report. *Hertfordshire's Past* (Spring 1982) 12: 3–18.

Burleigh, G.R. 1993. Some aspects of burial types in the cemeteries of the Romano-British settlement at Baldock, Hertfordshire, England. In M. Struck (ed.) *Römerzeitliche Gräber als Quellen zu Religion, Bevölkerungsstrucktur und Sozialgeschichte: Internationale Fachkonferenz vom 18-20 Februar 1991 im Institut für Vor- und Frühgeschichte der Johannes Gutenberg-Universität Mainz*. Archäologische Schriften 3. Mainz: Institut für Vor- und Frühgeschichte der Johannes Gutenberg-Universität Mainz: 41–9.

Burleigh, G.R. 1995a. A Late Iron Age *oppidum* at Baldock, Hertfordshire. In R. Holgate (ed.) *Chiltern archaeology: recent work. A handbook for the new decade*. Dunstable: The Book Castle: 103–112.

Burleigh, G.R. 1995b. The plan of Romano-British Baldock, Hertfordshire. In A.E. Brown (ed.) *Roman small towns in eastern England and beyond.* Oxbow Monograph 52. Oxford: Oxbow: 177–82.

Burleigh, G.R. 2008 Temples, shrines and deities in Iron Age and Romano-British Baldock and its *territorium*, Hertfordshire, England, UK. In J. d'Encarnação (ed.) *Divinidades indígenas em análise: divinités pré-romaines – bilan et perspectives d'une recherche. Actas do VII Workshop FERCAN, Cascais, 25-27.05.2006*. Coimbre & Porto: Centro de Estudos Arqueológicos das Universidades de Coimbra e Porto: 189–219.

Burleigh, G.R. & Fitzpatrick-Matthews, K.J. 2010. *Excavations at Baldock, Hertfordshire, volume 1: an Iron Age and Romano-British cemetery at Wallington Road.* Letchworth Garden City: North Hertfordshire District Council Museums & North Hertfordshire Archaeological Society.

Burleigh, G.R. & Stevenson, M.D. 2000. *A decade of archaeological fieldwork in North Hertfordshire*. Archaeological Report 34. Letchworth: North Hertfordshire District Council Museums Service. Available at http://www.north-herts.gov.uk/a_decade_of_fieldwork.pdf.

Burnham, B.C. & Wacher, J. 1990. *The 'small towns' of Roman Britain*. London: B T Batsford.

Davis, S. 2005. Late and post-Roman burial to 19th-century brickmaking: excavations at the site of 40 Queen Street, Hitchin, SG4. *Hertfordshire Archaeology & History* 14: 57–74.

Duncan, H., Rackham, J., Guest, P., McKinley, J. & McPhail, R. 2009. Synthesis. In M. Phillips (ed.) *Four millennia of human activity along the A505 Baldock Bypass, Hertfordshire*. East Anglian Archaeology 128. Bedford: Albion Archaeology: 143–56.

Edgeworth, M. & Steadman, S. 2003. *Extensive urban survey for Bedfordshire: the Roman town of Sandy archaeological assessment*. Bedford: Albion Archaeology.

Faulkner, N. 2000. *The decline and fall of Roman Britain*. Stroud: Tempus.

Fenton, P. 1994. *An archaeological evaluation, A505 Baldock Bypass, Blackhorse Farm site*. Field Archaeology Report 23. Letchworth: North Hertfordshire District Council Museums.

Fenton, P., Winter, M. & Ashworth, H. 2003. *The former Health Centre, The Tene, Baldock, Herts*. Unpublished Assessment Report (Report 208). Baldock: The Heritage Network.

Fitzpatrick-Matthews, K.J. 2007. Subculture and small group identity in Iron Age and Roman Baldock. In B. Croxford, N. Ray, R. Roth & N. White (eds.) *TRAC 2006: proceedings of the sixteenth annual Theoretical Roman Archaeology Conference which took place at The University of Cambridge 24-25 March 2006*. Oxford: Oxbow: 150–174:

Fitzpatrick-Matthews, K.J. & Fitzpatrick-Matthews, T. 2008. *The archaeology of Hitchin from prehistory to the present*. The Archaeology of North Hertfordshire 2. Letchworth Garden City: North Hertfordshire District Council.

Fitzpatrick-Matthews, K.J. & Fitzpatrick-Matthews, T. 2009. *The archaeology of Letchworth Garden City*. The Archaeology of North Hertfordshire 3. Letchworth Garden City: North Hertfordshire District Council.

Frere, S. S., Hassall, M.W.C. & Tomlin, R.S.O. 1986. Roman Britain in 1985. *Britannia* 17: 363–454.

Frere, S. S., Hassall, M.W.C. & Tomlin, R.S.O. 1989. Roman Britain in 1988. *Britannia* 19: 257–345.

Goodwin, T. 1983. *Baldock 1983 – Wallington Rise Estate*. Unpublished typescript report for the North Hertfordshire Archaeological Service.

Griffiths, D. & Bangert, S. 2007. Ceramic: the St Menas ampulla. In D. Griffiths, R.A. Philpott & G. Egan (eds.) *Meols: the archaeology of the north Wirral coast. Discoveries and observations in the 19th and 20th centuries, with a catalogue of collections*. Monograph 68. Oxford: Oxford University School of Archaeology: 58–60.

Harris, A. 2003. *Byzantium, Britain and the West: the archaeology of cultural identity AD 400-650*. Stroud: Tempus.

Hillelson, D.J. 1986. *Baker's Close, Baldock: resistivity survey interim report*. Unpublished interim report. Letchworth: North Hertfordshire District Council Museums. Available at http://www.north-herts.gov.uk/bal-50_1985.pdf.

Jones, M.J. 1993 The latter days of Roman Lincoln. In A. Vince (ed.) *Pre-Viking Lindsey*. Lincoln: City of Lincoln Archaeological Unit: 14–28.

Koch, J.T. (ed.). 2006. *Celtic culture: a historical encyclopedia*. Santa Barbara: ABC-CLIO Ltd.

Matthews, K.J. 2003. Chester's amphitheatre after Rome: a centre of Christian worship? *Cheshire History* 43: 12–27.

Niblett, R. & Thompson, I. 2005. *Alban's buried towns: an assessment of St Albans' archaeology up to AD 1600*. Oxford: Oxbow with English Heritage.

Offer, C. 2002. *In search of Clofesho: the case for Hitchin*. Norwich: Tessa.

Pearce, S. 2004. *South-western Britain in the early middle ages*. Leicester: Leicester University Press.

Petts, D. 1998. Burial and gender in Late- and sub-Roman Britain. In C. Forcey, J. Hawthorne & R. Witcher (eds.) *TRAC 97: proceedings of the seventh annual Theoretical Roman Archaeology Conference, which formed part of the second International Roman Archaeology Conference, University of Nottingham, April 1997*. Oxford: Oxbow: 112–24.

Phillips, M. & Duncan, H. 2009. Blackhorse Farm, Baldock: summary of trial trenching. In M. Phillips (ed.) *Four millennia of human activity along the A505 Baldock Bypass, Hertfordshire*. East Anglian Archaeology 128. Bedford: Albion Archaeology: 157–60.

Rankov, N.B., Hassall, M.W.C. & Tomlin, R.S.O. 1982. Roman Britain in 1981. *Britannia* 13: 327–425.

Richmond, A.D.W., Burleigh, G.R. & Went, D. A. 1992. *An archaeological evaluation at The Engine Public House, Baldock, Hertfordshire*. Archaeological Report 17. Letchworth: North Hertfordshire District Council Museums.

Seebohm, F. 1883. *The English village community examined in its relation to the manorial and tribal systems and to the common or open field system of husbandry: an essay in economic history*. London: Longmans, Green & Co.

Selkirk, A. & Selkirk W. eds. 1983. Baldock. *Current Archaeology* 8 (3) (No. 86): 70–74.

Short, D. 1987. Braughing: a possible Saxon estate? *Herts Past* 23: 8–15.

Smith, A. 2008. The fate of pagan temples in south-east Britain during the late and post-Roman period. In D. Rudling (ed.) *Ritual landscapes of Roman south-east Britain*. Great Dunham & Oxford: Heritage Marketing & Oxbow: 171–190.

Stead, I.M. & Rigby, V. 1986. *Baldock: the excavation of a Roman and pre-Roman settlement, 1968–72*. Britannia Monograph 7. London: Society for the Promotion of Roman Studies.

Went, D.A. & Burleigh, G.R. 1990a. *Humberside to Buncefield pipeline: preconstruction archaeological survey report, Dane Field, Pirton, Hertfordshire*. Archaeological Report 3. Letchworth: North Hertfordshire District Council Museums. Available at http://www.north-herts.gov.uk/ pirton_ pipeline_preconstruction.pdf.

Went, D.A. & Burleigh, G.R. 1990b. *Humberside to Buncefield pipeline: archaeological investigation assessment report, Dane Field, Pirton, Hertfordshire*. Archaeological Report 6. Letchworth: North Hertfordshire District Council Museums. Available at http://www.north-herts.gov.uk/report_6.pdf.

Went, D.A. & Colley, C. 1990. *A catalogue of the archaeological finds from the garden of 'The Steppes', Springhead, Ashwell, Hertfordshire*. With contributions by F. Pewtress, A. Garwood and T. Offord. Archaeological Report 10. Letchworth: North Hertfordshire District Council Museums. Available at http://www.north-herts.gov.uk/report_10.pdf.

Wheeler, R.E.M. & Wheeler, T.V. 1936. *Verulamium: a Belgic and two Roman cities*. Society of Antiquaries of London Research Report 11. Oxford: Oxford University Press.
White, R. & Barker, P. 2002. *Wroxeter: life and death of a Roman city*. Stroud: Tempus.
Whitelock, D., Ker, N. & Rennell Rodd, F.J. 1968. *The will of Æthelgifu: a tenth century Anglo-Saxon manuscript*. Oxford: The Roxburghe Club.
Williamson, T. 2000. *The origins of Hertfordshire*. Manchester: Manchester University Press.